D1831625

HUMAN DEVELOPMENT

HUMAN DEVELOPMENT

Editors
RK Bhattacharya
Bharat Jhunjhunwala
VK Shrivastava

PUBLICATIONS
KALPAZ PUBLICATIONS
DELHI - 110052

HUMAN DEVELOPMENT

Rs. 790

ISBN: 81-7835-107-2

©Motilal Bhimraj Charity Trust

This book may be reproduced in any manner
without written permission.

Published with the cooperation of
Motilal Bhimraj Charity Trust
732, Modern Society, Sector-15, Rohini, Delhi-110085
Tel.: 2729-8589 / 2789-3673
and
Vivekanand Nidhi
149/1E, Rash Vihari Avenue, Kolkata, W.B. 700029
Tel.: 2337-5500 / 2464-2730

Published in 2003 in India by
Kalpaz Publications
C-30, Satyawati Nagar,
Delhi-110052
e-mail: kalpaz@hotmail.com

Laser Typeset at: Alphabet, Delhi
Printed at: Mehra Offset Press, Delhi

Contents

Preface 9

Acknowledgements 11

List of Contributors 13

Introduction 17

PART ONE
THE CONCEPT OF HAPPINESS

1. **Gita on Renunciation and Enjoyment** 31
Meena Shukla

2. **Consumption and Human Development** 35
Asok Barman

3. **Control of Senses** 41
Pradeep Kumar and M. Vandana

4. **Relevance of Material Comforts** 47
V.K. Hampiholi

5. **Self-Actualization: The Ultimate Goal of Human Development** 55
Reena Basu

6. **Happiness** 61
Dharmender Kumar Misra

7. **Materialism in the Rigveda and Charvaka** 65
Dharmender Kumar Misra

8. **Realization of the 'self-in-self' is the Key to Sustainable Development** 75
R.K. Bhattacharya

9. **The Rational and the Spiritual** 81
Surender Pratap

10. **Body and Soul in Human Development** 83
Om Prakash Dubey

11. **Food of the Mind** 87
Prasada Raju

12. **Indian Approach to Human Development** 93
V.K. Shrivastava and R.S. Dube

PART TWO
DHARMA AND HUMAN DEVELOPMENT

13. **Emerging View of Human Development — Where the East and the West Meet** 105
R.K. Bhattacharya

14. **Reconciliation of Consumerism and Sustainable Development** 115
Gautam Kumar Basu

15. **Global Equity and Human Development** 123
Sumita Sen

16. **Yoga in Sanatana Tradition and its Relation with Human Values** 127
Surender Nath Pal

17. **Expansion of Consciousness** 133
Kumar Mitra

18. **Role of the Market in the Health Sector** 139
Prajna Shrivastava

19. **Smart and Good Governnance — Our Cultural Heritage** 141
Neela Trivedi

PART THREE
HUMAN DEVELOPMENT INDEX

20. **Values and Character** 153
Onkar Nath Tiwari

21. **The Inner Self** 157
S.P. Das Gupta

22. **Role of Spiritual Education in Human Development** 173
Mukul Mukherjee

23. **Rabindranath Tagore and Amartya Sen on Human Development** 177
Ratan Lal Basu

24. **Moral and Spiritual Index of Human Development** 185
N.M. Lall

25. **Aesthetic Views of Swami Vivekananda** 187
Tapobrata Sanyal

26. **Oneness** 193
Lubna Marium

27. **Impact of Greek Philosophy and Christian Theology on Materialistic Concept of Human Development** 199
P.K. Patankar

28. **Economic growth versus Employment** 205
Raj Kumar Sen

29. **Social and Moral Role of Education** 215
Meenakshi Mishra

30. **Poverty Index** 217
Shekhar Mukherjee

31. **Human Development Index (HDI) in Madhya Pradesh: Reassessed** 235
A.S. Dey

PART FOUR
SOCIAL ORGANIZATION FOR HUMAN DEVELOPMENT

32. **Human Welfare in Hindu Scriptures** 249
S.K. Dixit

33. **Varna and Caste** 255
Dharmender Kumar Misra

34. **Importance of Varna System in the 21st Century** 265
Mala Pyasi

35. **Good and Bad in Varna System** 269
Mamchand Rewaria

36. **Impact of Casteism** 273
Raj Pal Singh 'Raj'

37. **Evolution and Function of Varna System** 277
Brij Bhushan Rajvanshi

38. **Caste Associations** 283
Ram Swarup

39. **Contradictions of 'Dalit' Literature** 285
Sharad Singh

PART FIVE
THE ROLE OF DEVELOPMENT WORKERS

40. **Sanatana Concept of Social Work** 291
Bhartendu Prakash

41. **Livelihood of the Social Worker** 295
Bharat Gandhi

42. **Social Worker and Society** 299
Satya Prakash 'Bharat'

43. **Social Worker and the State** 301
Roshan Lal

Index 305

Preface

This collection of articles is taken from a series of seminars organized by Motilal Bhimraj Charity Trust on Human Rights (Rishikesh, 1999), Human Development (Sagar, 2001), Eco-ethical Standards of Living (Kolkata 2001), Indian Values (Kanpur 2001 and Varanasi 2001), Indian Tradition of Social Work (Banda, 2001) and Inter-Caste marriages (Sagar 2001).

We thank the participants of these seminars for having helped bring out the issues in Huuman Development.

Author

Acknowledgments

This collection of articles is taken from a series of seminars organized by Motilal Bhimraj Charity Trust on Human Rights (Rishikesh, 1999), Human Development (Sagar, 2001), Eco-ethical Standards of Living (Kolkata 2001), Indian Values (Kanpur 2001 and Varanasi 2001), Indian Tradition of Social Work (Banda, 2001) and Inter-Caste marriages (Sagar 2001).

We thank Swami Shantidharmananda of Satya Darshan Ashram, Rishikesh who helped organize the first seminar of the series. The ideas that were unleashed during that seminar led to the organization of the subsequent ones.

We thank Shri R.S. Dube, Neelam Trivedi, B.N. Tiwari, Dharmender Misra, Bharatendu Prakash and R.D. Sharma who organized the various seminars.

We thank the participants of these seminars for having helped bring out the issues in Human Development.

List of Contributors

Gautam Kumar Basu, Department of International Relations, Jadavpur University, Kolkata.

Ratan Lal Basu, Reader and Head, Department of Economics, Bhairab Ganguly College, Belghoria, Kolkata 700056.

Reena Basu, Asst. Director, Population Research Centre, Department of Geography, Dr. H.S. Gour University, Sagar. Has undertaken doctoral research in psychology from University of Rajasthan.

Satya Prakash Bharat, Social activist associated with Yuva Parivar. Maitri Kendra, VPO Kurha, Tehsil Tiwsa, Dt. Amarawati, Maharashtra.

R.K. Bhattacharya, Formerly Senior Corporate Executive. Trustee-General Secretary, Vivekananda Nidhi, Koltata.

Ashok Burman, Head, Department of Economics, Scottish Church College, 1 & 3 Urquhart Square, Kolkata 700026.

A.S. Dey, Dy. Director, Population Research Centre, Department of Geography, Dr. H.S. Gour University, Sagar.

Pradeep Kumar Dixit, Reader and Head, Department of Sanskrit, Akbarpur Degree College, Akbarpur, Kanpur Dehat.

S K Dixit

Vanadana Dixit, Reader, Department of Sociology, JDVM P.G. College, Anand Bag, Kanpur.

R.S.Dube, Professor and Head, Department of Geography and Director, Population Research Centre, Dr. H.S.Gour University, Sagar. President, National Association of Geographers.

Om Prakash Dubey, Consultant on manpower development. Has written twelve books on education and Hindu dharma. 46/25-I Tagore Town, Allahabad 211002.

Bharat Gandhi, Social activist. 41 victoria Park, Meerut, UP 250001.

S.P. Das Gupta, Centre for Study of Man and Environment, Kolkata.

V.K.Hampiholi, Department of Sanskrit, Dr. A.V. Baliga College, Kumta, Karnataka.

Roshan Lal, Social activist. C-2/41 Ashok Vihar II, Hew Delhi 110052.

N.M. Lall, Visiting Professor, Jiwaji University, Scindia Chhaoni, Gwalior.

Lubna Mariam, Bangladeshi Research Scholar, Department of Sanskrit, Dr. H.S. Gour University, Sagar.

Meenakshi Mishra, Research Scholar, Department of AIHC and Archaeology, Benaras Hindu University, Varanasi. Undertaking research on Mahabarat mein dhatu *dhatu svam dhatu karm.*

Dharmender Kumar Misra, Research Scholar, Department of Philosophy, Benaras Hindu University, Varanasi. Editor, *Moolya Bodh.* Associated with Malviya Centre of Human Values, BHU.

Kumar Mitra, Head, Department of Philosophy and the Life-World, Vidyasagar University, Midnapore, West

Bengal. Shekhar Mukherjee, Professor and Head of Department of Migration and urban studies, International Institute for Popular Sciences, Mumbai.

Mukul Mukherjee, Director, Disha, Centre for Behavioural Studies and Vocational Training. Perceptor, Shri Ram Chandra Mission teaching meditation through Sahaj Marg method. Parijat Colony, Nehru Nagar, Bilaspur, Chhatisgarh.

Surendra Hath Pal has undertaken research on *Yoga* Darshana mein Sadhana Paddhati at Benaras Hindu University, Varanasi .

P.K. Patankar, Retired Teacher, Department of Economics, Dr. H.S. Gour University, Sagar.

Bharatendu Prakash, PhD in Physics. Social Activist.

Vihyan Siksha Kendra, Village Terahi Maufi, PO Tindwari, Dt. Banda, UP 210128.

Surendra Pratap, 773 DLC, 9 Mayo Road, Allahabad.

Mala Pyasi, Assistant Professor, Mahakosal (Sanskrit) Government Arts and Commerce College, Jabalpur.

Prasada Raju, Atheist and social activist. Shri Vasistha Sevashram, Dirusumarru, Bhimavaram Mandal, West Godavari, AP 534239.

B.B. Rajwanshi, Retired Company Executive, 422/3 Scheme 7, Shastri Nagar, Meerut 250004.

Mam Chand Rewaria, National Executive Member, BJP S/C S/T Morcha, A/C 23 Tagore Garden, New Delhi 110027.

Tapobrata Sanyal, FD473 Salt Lake, Kolkata 700064.

Raj Kumar Sen, Professor and Head, Department of Economics, Rabindra Bharati University, Kolkata and President, Bengal Economic Association.

Sumita Sen, House of Late Dr. A.K. Majumdar, 75 M C Ghosh Lane, Howrah, WB 711101.

Prajna Shrivastava, National Polio Surveillance, World Health Organization, Medical College, Gorakhpur.

V.K. Shrivatsava, Visiting Professor, Department of Geography, Dr. H.S. Gour University, Sagar. Former Professor and Head, Department of Geography, Deen Dayal Upadhyaya University, Gorakhpur.

Meena Shukla, Head, Department of Sanskrit, Ranchi College, Ranchi.

Raj Pal Singh 'Raj', Dalit activist and writer. A17/18 Bhagwat Gali No 1, Brahmapuri, Delhi 110053.

Sharad Singh, Dr. H.S. Gour University, Sagar.

Ram Swarup, Social activist associated with Arya Samaj. 12/343 Rajendrapuram, Hathi Bhata, Ajmer, Rajasthan.

Onkar Nath Tiwari, Senior Lecturer, Law, St. Andrews College, Gorakhpur.Consultant to UNICEF on Juvenile justice.

Introduction

Bharat Jhunjhunwala

It is undisputed that the purpose of life is 'happiness'. The difficulty arises in defining what exactly is happiness. The Western tradition defines happiness as material welfare. The Indian tradition defines it as realization of one's inner self. The two are not necessarily opposed to each other and indeed, are complementary. However, negation of either leads us into difficulties. The purpose of this book is to clarify how the two can be mutually supportive. V.K. Shrivastava and R.S. Dube, in their paper, have given an excellent overarching description of the two approaches.

The Concept of Happiness

In the Indian tradition a person is said to be born with certain 'inner desires' or vasana. These desires reside in the unconscious and push the person to act in order to fulfill them. As long as an individual acts in tune with these inherited desires he is 'happy'. But there are two difficulties. One, it is difficult to understand what exactly these unconscious desires are. Two, it is more difficult to comprehend the point at which these desires have been fulfilled. More often than not, one continues to persist in the old course when it is no longer necessary.

Say a person has the vasana to eat rosogullas. He eats rosogullas and is 'happy'. Now if he abstains from eating other sweets, it is indeed liberating. But if, in the process of eating rosogullas, he develops the desires of laddu and jalebi, then he gets into a circular trap. He creates more desires — of laddu and jalebi — and fulfils them. It then becomes like digging a pit and filling it up. Meena Shukla, in her exposition of the Gita, explains thus that happiness is secured by engaging in so much action as dictated by one's vasanas.

Ashok Burman explains that the way to limit consumption to levels necessary for the fulfilment of unconscious desires is to engage in action with a spirit of renunciation. By thinking that one is eating rosogullas as directed by god or by one's inner self, one is able to restrict consumption at the point where the unconscious desires are fulfilled. The level of consumption, therefore, is quite irrelevant for the securement of happiness. A person born with desires of jaggery would be 'happy' with eating jaggery while one born with the desires of sugar candy would be unhappy with eating even sugar. Jaggery can be happiness-creating while sugar may not be so. Human development, therefore, has to be reckoned in relation to one's inner desires, vasanas or unconscious desires.

This attitude of doing action while ascribing it to god is same as control of the senses. While engaging in consumption of rosogullas, one has to 'control one's senses' as explained by Pradeep Kumar. Controlling one's senses means that one does what is dictated by the heart or the inner-self rather than get swayed by the attractions that one sees in the outer world.

The problem can be understood through an analogy. Let us say we have to fill up a pot with water. A full pot signifies 'fulfilment' or happiness. One starts earning money and undertaking consumption of sweets, sex and the like. If, in this process, the pot remains of the fixed size then it gets filled up soon and the person is 'fulfilled'. But, if while undertaking such consumption, the pot become bigger then one gets into an endless trap. The more one fills up the pot the bigger it grows. The pot remains ever empty. By controlling one's senses, one prevents the pot from becoming bigger.

The Indian social structure has been designed to assist every person in reaching such fulfilment. V.K. Hampiholi explains that the life of a person has been divided into four ashrams or stages of brahmacharya (student), grihastha (householder), vanaprastha (social worker) and *sanyasi* (renunciator). The underlying idea, as

Reena Basu explains, is that one inherits not just one or two unconscious desires at birth but a bundle of them which are somewhat like peels of an onion. This life is very short for being able to fulfil all the unconscious desires even if one stayed dot on course. One may have inherited the unconscious desires of travelling around the globe, becoming a sportsman and playing the sitar. One life is scarcely sufficient for fulfiling these diverse desires.

The teaching, therefore, was for an individual to fulfil the most prominent of these unconscious desires in the stage of the householder. In this period, he can understand that happiness comes not from more consumption *per se* but from the inter-connection of the unconscious desires and the material world. If, therefore, the unconscious desires could be removed directly, then there would remain no need for action and consumption. Such a direct removal of unconscious desires is possible through meditation. That is the task of the stage of sanyasa. Vanaprastha is the intermediate step between grihastha and sanyasa. In sanyasa, the person meditates and sees the futility of fulfilling the myriad of inherited desires. He takes a short-cut and at one go removes a host of unconscious desires.

Dharmender Kumar Misra points out that true social work is that of teaching people to live according to their unconscious desires. This is the task of the vanaprastha. Having understood the role of inherited unconscious desires in his own life, and not yet developed the control of the senses required for sanyasa, he can spend this time teaching others. The ashrama system leads to both the development of the individual as well as the society.

The Indian approach combines materialism and spiritualism in a step-by-step manner. Materialism or consumption is considered to be necessary because it is the route to the fulfilment and removal of inherited desires. But it is not the end. Dharmender Kumar Misra makes this point in his critique of Charvaka's philosophy in his second paper. The positiveness of material consumption arises only as a stepping stone. R.K. Bhattacharya explains that material development alone is a inadequate. One needs to develop a sense of renunciation along with.

The Ashrama System

Stage	*Benefit for the individual*	*Benefit for the society*
Studentship	Inculcates the attitude of introspection; learns the techniques of his trade	Serves the sanyasis, teachers and elders
Householder	Fulfils his most prominent unconscious desires	Supports students, vanaprasthis and sanyasis
Vanaprastha	Begins the process of detachment to the senses	Works to create a society which is conducive to ashrama and varna systems
Sanyasa	Removes remaining desires by meditation	Teaches others to become introspective

It is important to note the negation of all material comforts — asceticism — is stipulated only for sanyasis. They have already passed through the material world and seen its limited contribution to their happiness. The Indian tradition does not in any way negate the material world. It only points out that it is but the beginning point from where one has to move many steps ahead.

Four types of efforts — purushartha — are advocated in the Indian tradition, namely, dharma, artha, kama and moksha (see Hampiholi's article on this). The ultimate objective is moksha or liberation from the stranglehold of the unconscious desires. The strategy is to fulfil one's dominant unconscious desire. This requires that one must earn both physical strength (kama), and money (artha) for without the two no desire can be fulfilled. But the two should be earned in a manner that is good for the society i.e., according to dharma.

Surendra Pratap thus makes the point that it is necessary to combine science and religion. Science here represents material fulfilment while religion represents the objective of removing all desires and becoming 'free'.

Om Prakash Dubey develops this same point from the angle of the progression from body to mind, intelligence and soul. The body is sustained by material dimension while to soul is liberated by renunciation.

Prasada Raju says that the beginning of this process has to be made with the control of one's food which has a decisive impact on one's mental orientation.

Dharma and Human Development

The earth's resources are limited. The use of resources by one person necessarily implies the loss of the same by another. The association of human development with income, therefore, implies that the high human development of one will necessarily come with low human development of another. In this context, R.K. Bhattacharya points out that the high-HDI countries are responsible for war and poverty in the developing countries. Gautam Kumar Basu brings out the inherent conflict between consumerism and sustainable development. Sumita Sen supports this view by pointing that 80 per cent of the world's resources are consumed by 20 per cent of the population.

Surendra Nath Pal explains that Indian thought holds that renunciation is the path to human development. Happiness comes from the removal or exhaustion of unconscious desires. This implies that their ever-increasing fulfilment is not necessary. The classical example is that the fire increases in intensity by the pouring of ghee. Western idea of human development is of the type of pouring of ghee. More material things can pull the person down in happiness by increasing his desires. The pot grows bigger and remains ever empty.

The Indian view says that it is better to attain happiness by reducing the desires or making the pot smaller rather than increasing the level of consumption or filling the pot. This making the pot smaller is equivalent to renunciation. It also eliminates the conflict between people. One who is more developed consumes less and leaves more resources for those who are less developed. This can lead to the establishment of genuine harmony. In fact, the higher varna were advised to control their senses, i.e., reduce their consumption.

This view also enables us to establish harmony with other living beings. The Christian dictum that God gave earth to man to rule implies an opposition between man and other living beings. This is the root of the problems of environment. The Indian view seeks to expand the concept of human development to 'development of all living beings'. Human development should be seen in conjunction with the development of other living beings. Kumar Mitra argues for such an expansion of human consciousness.

Prajna Shrivastava points out that the idea of economic development as an end in itself can be counterproductive. Money-making or income can hit at health, education and environment. She argues for reining the profit motive in the health sector. This idea of limiting individual freedom in public good is present in the Western culture also. But there it is presented as a second-best resolution of a necessary conflict. The Indian view, on the other hand, teaches each to abide by dharma. It places the onus of abstinence on the money-maker himself. Such abstinence simultaneously leads to (1) the abstainer's own development by strengthening of renunciation; and (2) the development of others by provision of better health, education and environment. Such synergy is not possible in the Western approach.

Human Development Index

We all seek happiness and it is for this that we are interested in human development. The final touchstone of human development would, therefore, be whether it leads to a happy society or not. Onkar Nath Tiwari explores this aspect of human development. The central issue is that income, health and education certainly enhance the capacity of human beings but they do not indicate the purposes or the ends for which these capacities would be used. Thus an educated, healthy and wealthy criminal would rank higher in the measure of human development in comparison to an illiterate, physically weak and poor monk. Tiwari points out that the absence of values and character as measures in the Human Development Index (HDI) is a major shortcoming. S.P. Das Gupta points out that the countries ranked high on the HDI also show a high level of personal distress.

The same nuclear technology can be beneficial if used for treatment of diseases and harmful if used to kill opponents. Similarly, the same education can be liberating if used to fulfil and quickly exhaust one's inner desires and it is entrapping if used to acquire newer desires. Basu specifically criticizes Amartya Sen for ignoring morality and ethics.

Mukul Mukherjee, Ratan Lal Basu and N.M. Lall develop this theme further to say that spiritual education is true education. Tapobrata Sanyal explains the importance of art in human development. 'Spiritual' in the Indian view is not a negation of the material, rather it builds on it. A person who does business as his dharma and makes money is simultaneously materialist as well as spiritual. His objective is not accumulation of wealth or consumption of luxuries. His objective is to do his dharma, i.e., to work according to his unconscious desires. This introversion is spiritualism while his moneymaking is materialism. The same moneymaking would be spiritually fallen if it was engaged in with a sense of egoism and attachment.

Lubna Mariam points out that epics and folklore have a great value in inculcating these values. Formal education or the skills of reading and writing are certainly beneficial if they come *after* the epics.

This criticism should not be taken as an opposition to the furthering of health, education and income. It only points out that these are not end in themselves. As Tagore once said that the purpose of the cooking is in the eating. There is no value to cooking food if it is not eaten. Similarly, these attainments are entirely desirable but first it has to be seen whether the purposes for which they will be used are in place. Only afterwards these attainments assume a positive value.

P.K. Patankar and V.K. Shrivatsava and R.S. Dube explore the possibilities of developing alternatives of human development indices which incorporate these values.

A more specific objection to the conventional HDI is made by Raj Kumar Sen. He raises the question of the importance of work as a value in itself. Working enables a person to fulfil his desires and also develop capacities for future growth. The milkman not only makes money for his evening meal, he also develops his skills at doing business. These skills help him to move on to the fulfilment of higher desires. Let us say a person has the unconscious desire of eating roti. This can be provided to him directly by redistribution or by giving him work which enables him to buy the flour from the market. The desire of roti is fulfilled in both cases. But fulfilment through work is better. Work leads to the development of his skills which make it possible for him to go on to the fulfilment of the next layer of desires. Redistribution brings this process to a halt. Work is essential for the fulfilment and removal of unconscious desires.

Meenakshi argues that even work is not central. Education has today become a mere tool for getting a job. It does not help a person to develop according to his unconscious desires and tendencies. Raj Kumar Sen's case in a favour of employment should not be taken, therefore, to mean that work is the final panacea. The final objective is only removal of unconscious desires. Sen is arguing that work is a better route than redistribution. Meenakshi is saying that even work has to be oriented to one's inner self.

This view is endorsed by Shekhar Mukherjee who points out that human development is highly influenced by unemployment. He and A.S. Dey show that alternative parameters of human development lead to entirely different results. These papers indicate the narrow nature of the present HDI.

This is important because the concept of human development as income, health and education, in absence of an overarching stipulation of introspective values, actually leads to a model of consumption-as-development and becomes opposed to human development itself. It takes human consciousness away from his unconscious desires. It leads to lower human development because the unconscious is implicitly negated.

Social Organization for Human Development

The basic problem of the society is that individuals pursue their own desires. The desire of one to eat sweets can make him steal the same and hit at the desires of the sweet seller. The desire of the king for acquisition of power through taxation and military campaigns can hit at the desire of the businessman of paying less taxes. Some rules are required so that all can fulfil their own desires while assisting, rather than obstructing, others in fulfilling theirs. This is dharma. The individual cannot himself understand how his actions may hurt others and this can lead to conflicts in the society. Dharma is the social consensus that regulates these conflicts. The individual is himself 'shortsighted' and can often think of only his own good. Dharma is codification of such rules that harmonize the desires of different individuals. This point is explained by S.K. Dixit.

Varna and jati are the social system for securing human development. The unconscious inclinations determine a person's varna. Birth, parents, pre-natal and childhood experiences — or caste or jati — may contribute to the determination of these desires, but they are not the final determinant. Dharmendra Misra makes this distinction between varna and jati.

Mala Pyasi, Mam Chand Rewaria and Raj Pal Singh 'Raj' make the point that varna is not determined by birth. The latter two of the above authors are dalits. Their understanding of varna is of great significance. The implication of these views is that a person may be born of dalit parents but can yet be a brahmin if his tendencies are such.

It is here that technology and economic development enters as a great liberator. The Manu Smriti says that it takes seven generations for one to change one's varna. But the high level of economic development makes it possible to fulfil desires and transcend them at an pace unprecedented in the past. Indeed, at the time of the writing of Manu Smriti, it may not have been possible for a person to fulfill his unconscious desires of consumption and move on progressively to the fulfilment of the desires of money, power and self-knowledge within this life. But today this is possible. Therefore, criteria of income, health and education, as used in the Human Development Index all do contribute to human development. The difficulty arises when they become end-in-themselves.

The desires have been classified in four categories — physical pleasures, wealth, power and self-knowledge — corresponding to the four varna of sudra, vaisya, kshatriya and brahmin. Statistically, it may be true that those who do business would generally harbour the desires of wealth. But this is not necessary for an individual. It is possible for a teacher, for example, to teach with the objective of (1) getting a salary for securing physical comforts; (2) making money in tutorials or private colleges; (3) indulging in politics of teachers, universities, etc.; or (4) for a pursuit of philosophy and self-knowledge. The same occupation — or *jati* — can be consistent with all the four varna.

B.B. Rajwanshi points out that the four varna system was not 'created' in one go as implied by a superficial reading of the Purusha Sukta of the *Rigveda*. Rather, it evolved gradually. This strengthens the case for a dispassionate study of the varna system and making modifications in the same if found necessary.

The word 'caste' has played great havoc on the understanding of Indian society. It is used for (1) varna, or unconscious desires or tendencies; (2) the present occupation or jati such as that of a chamar or mochi; and (3) of one's parental or family occupation or historical jati or 'community' such as yadav or kayastha. In the past, mobility between professions may have been less both due to low level of economic development as well as rigid social rules. But now freedom in selection of one's occupation is both necessary and desirable. The pitfall is that the jati was also a social system of support in times of crisis. The task is to retrieve the benefit of the social support of the jati system while providing inter-occupational mobility so that individuals can choose such occupation which is most conducive to the fulfilment of their unconscious desires. Ram Swarup suggests that occupation-based associations— or a new type of flexible and mobile jati — should be re-established so that human beings can pursue their unconscious desires in a supportive environment.

Sharad Singh brings out an interesting contradiction in the existing mainstream dalit position. Dalit literary figures, she points out, often claim that one who is born a dalit alone can write dalit literature. This is an affirmation of the principle of birth-based determination of tendencies. Only he is a dalit who is born a dalit. In the same breath they argue that there should be no birth-based discrimination. This is negation of the principle of birth-based determination of tendencies. A dalit cannot claim equality with the non-dalit if he claims his birth as the basis of dalithood.

The central point made by these authors is that human development should be understood as expression of one's tendencies or 'personality'. This leads to a fourfold classification of unconscious desires and the establishment of the varna system.

But people of different occupations will have similar tendencies. The teacher, astrologer and journalist can all be pursuing self-knowledge. Therefore, we also need associations of teachers and astrologers. We have to create a jati system of occupational associations and a varna consciousness which guides the individual as to the objectives he may pursue within that occupation.

The Role of Human Development Workers

Who is to secure 'human development', and why? All human beings seek their own happiness. Why should they work for human development of others? Bharatendu Prakash deals with this question in his report of a seminar on social work organized at Banda.

The primary task of the householder is to fulfil his desires. The restriction is that he should do so in a way that promotes the welfare of others. A shopkeeper should, for example, not sell adulterated foodstuffs. If he did, the king would punish him. His objective in selling unadulterated things would not have been the securement of welfare of society per se, but his own welfare. Such beneficial effect is like Adam Smith's invisible hand. It was not the objective of the shopkeeper to promote the health of the purchaser.

In a similar manner, householders earning their livelihood in the social sector seek the fulfilment of their own desires. The impact of their work on the society is not their primary concern. They have a tendency, therefore, to define social needs in a manner which serves their own self-interest. A social worker will, for example, provide such education which will get him a promotion or money and pass it off as a social need. The problem of NGOs is that they are mere agents of the donors or employers. The real key to their work remains in the hands of the latter. And the donors would themselves define social work in a manner to serve their self-interest. Foreign donor agencies, for example, will promote school education which produces comprador clerks rather than nationalist politicians. Yet, this will be passed off both by the donor as well as the NGO-social worker as social betterment.

The solution to this problem is to give the responsibility of social work to those who have transcended their desires of material advancement and seek spiritual advancement. They will be able to define social work dispassionately because there will be no conflict between their own material interests and those of the beneficiaries. This leads to the conclusion that social work should be the sole preserve of vanaprasthis. These persons would be doing social work with their own self-earned wealth. They would be giving in the material plane and receiving at the spiritual plane. There would be no conflict of interest at the material plane.

In this background, Bharat Gandhi and Satya Prakash Bharat hold that the livelihood of the social worker should come from the society for whom he works. That would make him accountable to those for whom he is allegedly working. It should not come from the state or other 'external' donors who may be pursuing their own agendas. These authors plead for the society to support social workers or vanaprasthis. This is equivalent to the Indian dictum that the householder must support the other three asramas. This reinforces the view that the householder should earn his livelihood and support social work by others instead of making social work his own means of livelihood.

Roshan Lal more specifically points out that the social workers should be free of the state for his livelihood. The central issue of governance is how to keep the state on the right track. This cannot be done by those who are themselves dependent on the state.

This leads the conclusion that 'professional' social work is a self-contradiction. 'Profession' denotes own material self-interest while social work denotes other's material self-interest. It follows that no householder should engage in social work. In doing social work he may do more damage by doing things which are motivated by his personal self-interest and not truly in interests of the beneficiary. He should concentrate, instead, on the fulfilment of his desires while following dharma.

Part One

The Concept of Happiness

One

Gita on Renunciation and Enjoyment

Mina Shukla

At the ordinary plane one must engage in action which leads to social good. On the higher plane he may abstain from all action.
—Editor

The very first incantation of *Isavasyopnishada,* profusely pregnant with deep meaning, directs man to enjoy the world and not be enjoyed by it. After having got the best of it, throw it away as nothing in it permanently belongs to you. So find enjoyment in renunciation. Do not covet, whose is the wealth? God is cause of movement. Enjoyment is out of His grace. So enjoy in renunciation as it is out of His bounty that you enjoy. Nothing belongs to you. So have things and do not have them. Can enjoyment and renunciation go hand in hand? These appear to be contradictory. But the statement is true. *Gita* propounds:

"*Sanyasa* (renunciation) according to sages, consists in abstinence from the performance of actions (duties) which are apt to fulfil desires. *Tyaga* (relinquishment) is abandonment of the desire for the fruit of all actions."

Actions should be done leaving aside attachment and fruit. Action will bear fruit. It is inevitable but do not aspire for that fruit because that is not in one's hands. Fruits should not become the motive for an action. This reasoning leads us to contentment. Hindi poet Raheem says that one should not have more than what he needs.

Duty is properly done if it is performed for its own sake. Its performance should be free from attachment and uninfluenced by the idea of the result that might accrue from it. In the first few verses of 18th chapter of *Gita* renunciation and relinquishment are illustrated. But it is not proper to renounce obligatory duties. Perform obligatory duties without any attachment to its consequences. So relinquishment does not deny enjoyment. Without the notion of enjoyment, relinquishment cannot be imagined. The fifth chapter of the *Gita* says,

"The self-controlled person renounces all actions through his mind, rests at ease in the body without himself acting or causing anyone else to act." (5/13)

In the 12th chapter it is said:

"Be self-controlled and renounce the fruits of all actions."

On one hand, renunciation of action is stressed upon and on the other hand, renunciation of the fruits is emphasized. One may find it difficult, if not impossible, to fulfil this twofold condition of the performance of duties. It may lead to non-performance of duties. But in another verse it is said.:

"Man wins not freedom from action by abstaining from activity, nor by mere renunciation he rises to perfection" (3/4).

It is also in verse, Chapter 3

"No man can remain inactive even for a moment, for helplessly is everyone driven to action by the qualities born of nature."

Abstinence from duty is possible in the case of those persons who have reached spiritual heights only. So performance of duty is obligatory.

Actions are of three types

1. Routine, indispensable.
2. Casual or fortuitous.
3. Desirable or wishable.

Desirable actions entangle man in mundane existence. Relinquishment of these actions is indispensable to achieve bliss. For example *'Putrakamo Yajet'* and *'Swargkamo Yajet'* denote desirable actions. These actions obstruct the realisation of bliss. It is also said not to have any desire for the fruits of actions. Gita says,

"Thy business is with the action only never with the fruits." (2/47)

It is clear that inaction is not at all advocated. At another place it is said:

"A man attains perfection as a result of his devotion to his own duty." (18/45)

Man cannot live without enjoyment so long as he is living in this world. But this enjoyment should not cause harm to anybody else. It is logical to ask, "What harm does a man cause to another man if he enjoys the fruit of his own action?" Achievement of fruits does not eliminate desire and it leads to passion for yet more possession. This possessiveness creates conflict in the society.

Finding it impossible to fulfil the condition of the performance of duties without expecting results, man may think that it would be best not to perform any duty in order that the difficulty in question may be averted. No actions would lead to no fruits. This view is tantamount to the doctrine of actionlessness. One cannot attain perfection by mere renunciation of actions. The *Gita* says:

"No one can remain inactive even for a moment" (3/5)

"Acts of sacrifice, gift and austerity should not be relinquished but should be performed" (18/5)

Renunciation of obligatory (*niyata*) duties due to delusion is *tamasika*. Sometimes infatuation makes man relinquish even obligatory actions. Performance of such actions (duties) not only purifies man's conduct but it benefits other people also.

Further it is said in *Gita*:

"A person is said to perform an act of *Rajasika* relinquishment if he relinquishes an action from fear of physical pain or irksome, thus performing a passionate relinquishment he does not obtain the fruit of relinquishment" (18/8). This act of Rajasika depicts passion for body.

About Sattvika, the *Gita* says:

"Relinquishment is Sattvika when obligatory work is performed on the understanding that it ought to be performed and without any attachment to it or its consequence. This relinquishment is pure" (18/9). In the 2nd sloka of chapter 18 of Gita it is said that relinquishment is in reality an act of Rajasika. "Relinquishment is abandonment of the desire for the fruit of all actions."

Thus an act of Rajasika relinquishment does not deny

performance of action but desire for any fruit is absent. Such action is the best. The doctrine of unattached enjoyment is justified. A performer of the act of Rajasika relinquishment undergoes pangs which result into happiness. Moreover, he does not have desire of such happiness which puts him in the cycle of this mundane world. "No embodied being can completely relinquish action. So he who relinquishes the idea of the fruit of action is called a relinquisher in the real sense of the word." (18/11)

So there should be no desire for fruits. *Gita* also says:

"He who sees inaction in action and action in inaction is wise among men. Such a person remains poised despite his preoccupation with multifarious activities." (4/18)

Above gist of *Gita* endorses the verse of *Isavasyopanishada*—Have it and do not have it. Enjoy unattached the gained object. Thus relinquishment of fruits of the action and enjoyment with renunciation are the two facets of the same coin. Vedas are the primary source of this view point inherent in Indian culture. This part of the mantra culled from *Isavasyopanishada* is in the form of an aphorism, a short precept. Its extensive and comprehensive description is proclaimed through utterances of God which is Smriti. It can be called Vivriti also. So, there is no question of anomaly. Their sermonic souls are different but mystery inherent in them is the same. Both are intimately connected.

Two

Consumption and Human Development

Asok Barman

Maximum increase in consumption does not lead to happiness. It also leads to ecological destruction.

—Editor

According to Micheal Argyle, "Any relation that does exist between happiness and income is relative rather than absolute. The happiness people derive from consumption is based on whether they consume more than their neighbours and more than they did in the past."

The first lesson of Economics is that resources at the disposal of man are limited but he wants to fulfil unlimited needs. The gospel has an underlying assumption that man knows what is required for him and he does not want something that would bring him anxiety and tension. Gandhi had once said: "There is enough on earth for everybody's need, but not for everyone's greed." Then why are people so much obsessed with the lust for having more? Why do they believe that the quality of life is so much dependent on their acquisition of costly items that would bring them more physical comfort and improve their social status? The answer to this question is to be sought in the words of wise men of India, quoted by Swami Vivekanand from the *Vishnu Purana*:

> *Na jatu kamas kamanam upabhogena samyati*
> *Habisa krsnavartameba bhuyay ebhavibhardhate*

Swamiji interpreted this as "Desire is never satisfied by the enjoyment of desire, it only increases the more , as fire when butter is poured upon it." He adds "This is true of all intellectual enjoyments of which the human mind is capable."

Let us look at the scenario in the Western countries first. The Western countries have been experiencing unprecedented and unimaginable progress of science and technology. This has resulted in a metamorphosis of consumers' psychology due to the introduction of new goods and gadgets and vigorous and careless campaigning and advertisements by corporate sectors. The acquisition-oriented society relentlessly tells us that the way to more happiness is more consumption. This is being termed as consumerism which encourages us to desire more and newer items. It is indeed a crazy pursuit leading the Western world to an unknown destination. At least five important things draw our attention immediately. Has growth made people better off? Can people accommodate such stupendous expenditure? Can society continue on this path of endless economic growth? How the fabric of human relationship woven over centuries is going to be affected? What will be the implications for the nature and ecology?

Before making an attempt to answer the questions we want to find what has led to such a state of affairs. We cannot deny the fact that man has weakness for material well being and falls prey to new and costlier goods unless he has a moral backbone. Here lies the role of spiritual lessons to which he must be exposed. There has been a degradation in this respect due to the constant devaluation of institutions that preached healthy values. There is a lack of movement to create awareness among the people about the danger of consumerism. On the other hand, we find vigorous and extremely powerful advertisements by the corporate sectors. People are exposed to well organised, psychologically fabricated advertisements everyday through television, magazines, films and internet. The sole purpose is to create addiction to satisfying wants by possessing more, newer and costlier goods. Media goads us to associate happiness and success with new and expensive items. Simple life is ridiculed and frustration is created among those who cannot have new things with their limited earning.

Swami Vivekananda says that the root cause is a false sense

of happiness. He says that we easily love objects of sensuous pleasure since they appear to be most realistic.

We can now try to answer the questions we have raised earlier. Do more products mean more happiness? We have noted that fulfilment of desire need not make us happy. What matters is contentment. Thus, happiness requires a mind that can properly feel that the need is satisfied and he should now look inside taking care of his spiritual urge.

Rabindranath Tagore says that he who thinks the world is the ultimate, cannot lead a peaceful life. He quoted from *Ishponishad:*

"Tena tyaktena bhunjitha ma gridhaya kasyasbiddhanang."

The theme is that when you consume you should have a mind that you can renunciate it. This is indeed not easy. This requires a mind that forbids us not to cause sufferings to others by our greed.

Regarding sustaining economic growth that draws its nourishment from consumerism, let us first look at some evidence. The rate of economic growth has been falling for quite sometime. The recession in the United States has become a major cause of concern. People are becoming disillusioned with the frustrating performance of several key sectors. The selfish policies being pursued by Western countries have not enabled the poor countries get a fair share and they cannot buy more from America and other rich Western countries. The prediction about the rich countries is also not optimistic. Once people realize the hollowness of the consumerism the scenario will be further disappointing.

A major casualty of consumerism is the fabric of the society based on mutual cooperation, respect and trust. In this age of fast food, cold drinks and machine made lunches and dinners, the touch of sympathy and love are disappearing very fast. There is little time to think of friendship, fellow-feeling and sympathy. Man has very little time to think of others and advise and help them in their hour of need. He also does not expect the same from others.

We now come to a very important aspect: man and nature in the context of consumerism. This is an issue that sends an alarming signal to everybody. The environment is at stake now. It seems that many of us have forgotten that man himself belongs to nature. Like all other creatures, man is also nourished by nature. He breathes in nature, gets food from nature and his mind is soothed by nature. Like other living beings man damages nature to some extent, but nature takes care of itself and the damages are healed. But when man pollutes and destroys, such self-healing is not possible. This affects the ecological balance endangering flora and fauna of which man is a part. The so-called modern living style means a high level of pollution. There are thousands of tons of throwaway goods related to production, packaging and transporting. Land water and air are being filled with harmful chemicals and wastes.

Consumerism is a pattern of behaviour that ruthlessly damages and even destroys the environment, personal and financial health, human relationships and age-old time tested values and institutions. This pushes the society further in the direction of unhealthy competition, isolation and loss of peace of mind.

We now briefly look at the impact of such lifestyle on the third world. At the very outset we should note that globalisation is something which we cannot ignore whether we like it or not. The world is more integrated now and we are constantly exposed to everything in the rich world. On the one hand a handful of our countrymen emulate the consumerist lifestyle presenting a contrast to billions of poverty-stricken people. On the other hand, the multinationals are pouring in costly, mostly unnecessary, often harmful commodities and spending huge amount of money in attractive advertisements. Domestic companies are preaching same thing. The combined effect is disastrous for the society. I would dwell on one aspect only. Such production pattern has distracted our attention from more urgent programmes.

This situation calls for popularising what our wise men have said time and again. A broad-based social consensus is called for. Amartya Sen has warned us against the blind imitation of the policies of Western countries and indiscriminate globalisation which cannot solve our problems of the squalor, disease, poverty, unemployment and gender discrimination. Since state sponsored resistance is no longer possible, a powerful campaign in favour of a morally upright and healthy lifestyle is urgently required.

We must remember what Rabindranath Tagore said: the

innate goodness of a man is so powerful that a man with poor resource but having clear mind, good purpose and resolution is sure to get help from different quarters; even providence would help him.

I shall end with a rather long quotation from my favourite book, *Three Men in a Boat* by Jerome K. Jerome.

"George said: 'You know we're on the wrong track altogether. We must not think of the things we could do with, but only of the things that we can't do without.

'I call that downright wisdom, not merely as regards the present case, but with reference to our trip up the river of life generally. How many people, on that voyage, load up the boat till it is ever in danger of swamping with a store of foolish things which they think essential to the pleasure and comfort of the trip, but which are only really useless lumber.

'How they piled the poor little craft most high with fine clothes and big houses...; with expensive entertainments that nobody enjoys, with formalities and fashions, with pretence and ostentation, and with - oh, heaviest, maddest lumber of all—the dread of what will my neighbour think, with luxuries that only cloy, with pleasures that bore...

'It is lumber, man - all lumber! throw it overboard. It makes the boat so heavy to pull, you nearly faint at the oars.. . You never know a moment's freedom from anxiety or care, never gain a moment's rest for dreamy laziness... throw the lumber over, man!'"

Three

Control of Senses

Pradeep Kumar and M. Vandana

The central Sanatana value is control of senses. The purpose of life is to realize one's inner self. All social values are designed to lead the individual towards such introversion

—Editor

The word 'Veda' is in the root of the word Vedic. Veda is synonymous with knowledge. All the truths beneficial and useful for human life which our sages have gathered on the strength of their worldly and otherworldly knowledge through their penance come under the umbrella of the word, Vedic, which is all-pervasive and comprehensive. It is a box containing the combined knowledge of the universe—material and spiritual.

Sanatana means immortal. The whole world is mortal and subject to destruction. But some immortal element is inherent in this mortal world whose presence helps us to visualise, realize and experience the existence of the mortal world. That immortal element is God, spiritually speaking. It can also be recognised as the values of human life which are permanent. Our sages and seers have pondered over these values of human life and testing them on the basis of usage and conduct, have laid them down for welfare of all humans. Seen externally, they may exhibit some differences because of the influences exerted by place, time, culture and atmosphere. So, the word Sanatana denotes that universally accepted immortal existence, consciousness and inspiration of human life which does not end though human beings do. 'Vedic Sanatana values' means those human values found in the ancient

Vedic literature of the sages and traditional literature from time immemorial which, defying the commands of place, dharma, time, culture, atmosphere, circumstances, community, traditions, dogma, custom, faith and sect, have remained intact. Man adopts such Vedic Sanatana values, their exalted and reasonable circumstantial forms and nature according to his personal capacity and natural belief and reverence. Reverence is an indispensable quality. It is that universally accepted sensation, perception or knowledge whereby man accepts a universal element out of the differences apparent in the entire world.

Sri Madbhagvata Mahapurana (7/11/8-12) propounds 30 characteristics of religion—truth, compassion, penance, purity, control of senses, non-violence, Brahmacharya, renunciation, regular study of scriptures, humility, contentment, dispassionate service of great sages, gradual abandoning of worldly indulgence, discriminating power to distinguish between proper and improper, endurance, mental control, the thought that efforts made with pride result into something contrary, silence, introspection, division of eatables as per capacity, sensation of soul and one's own identity in human beings, worship and human singing in praise of Lord Krishna, recitation in praise of God, service of sages, worship and obeisance, surrender, servitude and close familiarity.

Truth is the most significant pillar in Vedic values. Truth invokes reverence and veneration. Characteristics of dharma have been eulogized in our scriptures and *granthas* and they are our invaluable possession. Many verses of Vedas eulogize *brahmacharya* in a moving way.

"The Brahmachari, shining and bright, holds in him the divine knowledge. Thus all the divine qualities concentrate in him. Let him generate in us the force of *pran*, *apam* and *vyan* (force of anabolic process, of catabolic process and metabolic process). In the Brahmachari, all these processes are in equilibrium. (*Atharvaveda*. 11/5/24)

"By the hard life of endurance and self control, the life of Brahmacharya only, the ruler can protect the state. The teacher also can aspire to have the respect of his students by the observance of Brahmacharya" (*Atharvaveda*. 11/5/17)

According to Vedic culture, *brahmacharya* is the key to

successful material as well as spiritual life. A *brahmachari* is one who has planned his life as a movement towards greatness. So, his life can provide guidance to the students so that they achieve success in different fields.

Purity is also a significant value. "O Omniscient purify my mind. Let my mind be of noble resolve. Mind that drives men, as the good charioteer drives the fast running horses holding them by the reigns, let that mind of mine, situated in the heart, immune from old age, of immense speed be of good resolve. (*Yajurveda*. 34/6).

Vedic mantras urge us to guide our mind in the right direction. For this blessings of the Omniscient are invoked. "O Almighty purify my mind. It be of noble resolve so that I may be an instrument of noble deeds, not of evil deeds." Being possessed of constructive and destructive forces, mind can do good as well as evil, hence prayer to God to fill the mind with noble resolve.

Control of senses is basic to Sanatana values. Self-control makes man treat other women as mothers. Self-reliance is a cardinal virtue. Only through it body and mind can be conquered. Its absence makes man fall into the pit of indulgences. Lust will not dry up then. Human creation is nobler than satisfaction of animal wants. "For them who cling to pleasure and lordship, whose minds are captivated by such teaching cannot attain single-minded determination which is alone competent to bring about the concentration on the Lord" (*Gita* 2/44)

Uncontrolled senses accelerate the march towards downfall. He who has conquered the senses can conquer anything worldly or otherworldly.

Vedic Sanatana values sprout feelings of universal brotherhood. The entire world is a family. Verses denoting this lofty ideal abound in our sacred books.

"God is being, Becoming, Bliss. We meditate upon the adorable and worship God and pray the Lord to direct our intelligence on the right path (*Yajurveda* 3/35)

The worshipper does not invoke blessings for himself but for all the creatures. He wants universal welfare. For men who are engrossed in selfish interests and are in pursuit of materialistic gains this prayer of *Yajur Veda* would provide a guiding light. It is postulated:

Sarve bhavantu sukhinah,
Sarve santu niramayh,
Sarve bhadrani pasyantu,
Ma kaschid dukh bhagbhvet.

This incantation seeks happiness for all and nothing for one's own self. Thus we see loftier than the loftiest ideas in our great *granthas*.

Abnegation and tolerance are integral parts of Sanatana values. Vedic dharma does not prohibit indulgence but it must be with the feeling of detachment. To remain attached to sensuous objects is to remain in the whirl. One who does not possess anything as his own is a sage who has seen the right path. Feelings of detachment and tolerance lift us up from the slush of materialism, narrow-mindedness and turmoil. Materialistic advancement has became the be all and the end all of our life. Feelings of abnegation and endurance can supply us with effective checks on this. Lofty lines like *Satyam vad, Dharman char, Matri devo bhav, Pitri devo bhav, Acharya devo bhav, Atithi devo bhav, Par dravyesu losthavat, Na hinsyat sarvbhutani* depict many Sanatana values which can give rise to a world free of tensions and full of prosperity and all-round tranquility.

It is a matter of regret and sorrow, however, that the values which entailed glory and greatness in our national character and which infused undying vigour and indestructible life in us are losing their grandeur and splendour. These values were our guide, philosopher and teacher at one time. But these values are not seen to be of importance anymore and that has caused all-round chaos.

Selfish interests and their fulfilment have made man blind to noble traits of human life. He is engaged in finding new ways of dispossessing others of their possessions, mating with other women, keeping parents away, and abhoring teacher and guest. By abandoning hard work, abnegation and truth and putting on the robes of falsehood and false pride he has been fooling himself.

The need of the hour is benevolence and rational sacraments.

These should be inculcated in the very childhood. If done, socialization, nationalism and universalization would develop along with the development of personality.

The follower of old values brings relief to others and he himself takes no pride in it. He is respectful to all. He is self-controlled in speech, in action and in thought. He holds all in equal regard. He is loyal to one woman and is ever truthful. He believes in renunciation and so is free from all desires. He covets nothing and is free from guile. If we want to make the world worth living we must adopt these eternal values. Without this, our seminars, discussions and arguings, scholarly meetings and workshops would be a sheer wastage of time, money and energy. Let us inculcate Sanatana values in us and give practical shape to the lofty ideal of *'vasudheiv kutumbkam'* — the entire world is one family.

Four

Relevance of Material Comforts

V.K. Hampiholi

Material comforts and physical pleasures have a positive place in the Indian thinking. They are stepping stones to happiness. But they are not the ultimate end.

—Editor

Man is an organism of biological, psychological and social elements. He is forced to fulfil his biological needs. He is compelled to satisfy his emotions even while he has to conform to the norms of his society. According to Abraham Maslow, the famous psychologist of the school of humanism, hunger, thirst, sex, sleep and so on are the basic needs of the body; protection, stability, fearlessness and so on are the needs of the mind; love, compassion, affection, self-respect and fame are the needs from the social world. Every man tries his level best to fulfil his physical, psychological and social needs. Men who succeed in the gratification of their needs will lead a happy life and they will help the other members of the society. The generosity of such people will form the basis of healthy society. But most people in the society are selfish and self-centred. They are not ready to share the comforts which they have secured. They always think about self- welfare and not the welfare of others. Such behaviour of selfish people gives birth to conflict in the society. This conflict gradually leads the society on the path of disorganisation and debauchery. Hence, the society should train its members in such a way that everyone enjoys the comforts within a limit and shares them with others. Such harmony will ensure welfare in the society. Such a society was possible in ancient India where the laws of *dharma* prevailed.

Ancient Indians recognised four human goals for the development of the individual as well as the society viz. *dharma, artha, kama* and *moksha*. Among these, the first three are related to worldly life and the last one relates to another world. *Moksha* is the supreme goal of man and other goals help an individual to attain it. *Dharma, artha* and *kama* are recognised as "*trivarga*". These three are concerned with man's moral, material and physical needs respectively. Our ancestors were aware that man is basically an animal. His behaviour when taking food, sleeping, expressing fear and indulging in sex is similar to that of animals. आहारनिद्राभयमैथुनं च समानमेतत्पशुभिर्नराणाम्। Hence, they gave importance to physical and psychological needs at the first step and moral needs in the second step. Indians knew the importance and the necessity of sensual and material pleasures in life. So, they considered them as *purusartha* and allowed practice of *kama* and *artha*, with separate treatises on *kama* and *artha* helping a man to systematically enjoy the sensual and material pleasures in life.

The Sanskrit term *kama* bears wider meaning. It refers to all the desires. The term *artha* denotes the whole range of tangible objects that can be possessed and enjoyed. It refers to all the means necessary for acquiring worldly prosperity. Kautilya states that *artha* means people's living, maintenance, income, wealth and well-being. It also denotes the land wherein people live and prosper.

मनुष्याणां वृत्तिरर्थः। मनुष्यवती भूमिरित्यर्थः।

Kautilya felt that one should not lead an unhappy life (न निःसुखं स्यात्). Hence, everybody needs *artha* to live happily. According to Vatsyayana, the term *artha* denotes the acquisition, protection and increase of arts, land, gold, cattle, wealth and friends.

विद्या भूमि हिरण्य पशुधान्य भाण्डोपस्कर मित्रादी नां अर्जनं अर्जितस्य विवर्धनमर्थः।

The desire of more comforts urges man to acquire more *artha*. But the texts on *dharma* frame rules and regulations about the ways and the means of acquiring *artha*. They direct a man to procure *artha* in the right way i.e. as prescribed by *dharma*. *Dharma* describes the means by which *artha* can be acquired so as not to hamper the interests of the society.

The word *'kama'* denotes love as well as lust. Prominently the word refers to sex. The scope of *kama* is wide. It includes good food, good drink, pleasant and charming company, fine clothes, perfumes, ornaments, garlands, decorated room or bed and the like. A man is the source of *kama* for a woman and a woman is the source of *kama* for a man. Both man and woman should understand the merits and demerits of their respective partners. In this connection, the texts on erotica help them understand each other. The correct practice of *kama* will make man and woman happy. Indians knew that sex is an instinct and it is not possible to suppress it. Therefore, they gave practice of sex for pleasure its due importance. Moreover, they wrote a number of treatises on *kama* and narrated the various ways and means of deriving maximum pleasure from sex. The authors of these treatises are revered as *munis* and *rishis*. They insist that man and woman should enjoy sensual pleasure but they direct that they should enjoy this pleasure with the consent of *dharma*. Vatsyayana, the author of the *Kamasutra,* begins his book by saluting *Dharma, Artha and Kama.* धर्मार्थ कामेभ्योनमः। In the end he writes that the man who studies *Kamasastra* will act according to *dharma, artha, kama,* self confidence and custom. Thus, the authors of the texts on erotica have depicted *kama* with the intention that it should be practised within the periphery of *dharma*.

धर्ममर्थं च कामं च प्रत्ययं लोकमेव च। वश्यत्येतस्य तत्त्वज्ञो न च रागात्प्रवर्तते।।

Artha is another *purusartha* and it is necessary for a man to enjoy the *kama*. Man cannot fulfil his desires without money. Vatsyayana also says that a man whose lifespan is of hundred years should practise *dharma, artha* and *kama* at different times and in such a manner that they may harmonise and not clash with one another in any way.

शतायुर्वै पुरुषो विभज्य कालमन्योन्यानुबद्धं
परस्परस्यानुपघातकं त्रिवर्गं सेवेत्। (1.2.1)

Vatsyayana prohibits those activities that conflict with any one of the *trivargas*.

त्रिवर्गसाधकं यत् स्याददयोरेकस्य वा पुनः।
कार्यं तदपि कुर्वीत न त्वेकार्थं द्विबाधकम्।। (1.2.40)

In the *Mahabharata* it is said that a man should equally attend to *dharma, artha and kama*. The man who devotes himself to only one of them is certainly an inferior man. He is said to be a middling who devotes himself to only two of them. He is the best of his species who attends to all the three.

धर्मार्थ कामाः सममेव सेव्या
यो ह्येक भक्तः स नरो जघन्यः।
तयोस्तु दाक्ष्यं प्रवदन्ति मध्यं
उत्तमो योभिरतस्त्रिवर्गे।। शान्तिपर्व (167.20)

Thus *kama* and *artha* were not treated as an obstacle to *dharma*. They were considered as supplementary to *dharma*. They were neither superior nor inferior to *dharma*. They gained a status equal to that of *dharma* in ancient India.

Our ancient sages studied keenly the nature of the *trivarga* and understood that the pleasure derived from *dharma* is superior to the material pleasure. The happiness given by the material comforts is temporal. The desire for that happiness is unquenchable. Manu says that the desire of man or woman cannot be totally quenched by the enjoyment of objects.

प्रभवार्थं च भूतानां धर्मप्रवचनं कृतम्। कर्णपर्व (69.57)
प्रभवार्थाय भूतानां धर्मप्रवचनं कृतम्। शान्तिपर्व (109.10)

Dharma is created with the object of keeping all creation free from any harm.

अहिंसासार्थाय भूतानां धर्मप्रवचनं कृतम्।
यः स्यादहिंसा सम्पृक्तः स धर्म इति निश्चयः।।

Krishna further adds that dharma is so called because it protects all; dharma preserves all that is created.

धारणाद् धर्ममित्याहु धर्मेण विधृताः प्रजाः। (109.11)

Thus all that is free from doing harm to any created being is certainly *dharma*. The scope of *dharma* is wide. The concept of *dharma* may change from place to place, time to time, and man to man. But it should be noted that *dharma* always gives importance to the welfare of the society without neglecting the welfare of the individual.

Dharma holds that material pleasures are necessary for a human being for his all round development. Therefore it has provided ample scope for enjoyment of material pleasures i.e. *kama* and *artha*, in the *grhasthasrama*. *Dharma* instructs a man to be in *brahmacaryasrama* to qualify himself to become a house-holder. A man during *brahmacaryasrama* undergoes training which makes him fit physically and psychologically to enjoy *kama* and *artha* successfully after marriage. At this stage, a man learns the nature of the material pleasures and the role of *dharma* in their enjoyment. Our ancestors have given equal importance to each component of the *trivarga*. Manu says that the good of the humanity lies in a harmonious management of the *trivarga*.

श्रेयस्त्रिवर्ग इति तु स्थितिः। (11.224)

It grows stronger like fire fed with ghee.

न जातु कामः कामानामुपभोगेन शाम्यति।
हविषा कृष्णवत्मेव भूय एवाभिवर्धते।। (11.94)

The man who is after the material pleasures will lose his physical and mental health and will become unhappy. The unhappy person needs more comforts for his happiness. He may snatch the comforts belonging to others. Further, he may indulge in anti-social activities.

Artha is necessary to lead a comfortable life. But *artha* alone is not able to provide the happiness. Man needs other things besides *artha* for his happiness. Unfortunately, many people are not happy with the *artha* they possess. They want more and more money to procure more comforts. The *Kathopanishad* declares that no man is satisfied with the money he has.

नं वित्तेन तर्पणीयो मनुस्यः।

The covetous man may snatch other's property, cheat others, threaten others, rob others or kill others for wealth. He gathers more and more wealth and makes others poor. The poor, having little money, lead a miserable life and express their hatred towards rich people. This makes the society disorganised.

The authors of *dharmasastra*, knowing the nature of material comforts and man, response to them, therefore gave importance to the restraint of mind and sense organs i.e.

मनोणिग्रह इन्द्रियनिग्रह

Manu, Yajnavalkya, Narada and other authors framed various injunctions and prohibitions for an individual keeping in view the welfare of the society. Therefore, every man belonging to any *varna* or any *asrama* should act according to *dharma* for the good of the society. A celibate is instructed to lead a disciplined life in the *brahmacaryasrama*. He should live with his teacher in the hermitage and control his sense organs for the development of austerity.

सेवेतेमांस्तु नियमात् ब्रह्मचारी गुरौ वसन्।
सन्नियम्येन्द्रियग्रामं तपोवृद्ध्यर्थमात्मनः।।

Dharma ordains a householder to enjoy material comforts during *grhasthasrama*. It permits husband and wife to sleep together for pleasure. But at the same time, it frames some rules regarding the time and the place for coition.

ऋतुका लाभिगामी स्यात् स्वदारनिरतः सदा।
पर्ववजं तदतो रति काम्यया।। (III.45 मनु)

The rules and the regulations framed by *dharma* denote the quality and the quantity of the material pleasures. By helping a man to control his mind and sense organs, they ensure morality in the society. *Dharma* prohibits adultery in strong terms as it destroys the happiness of the family and peace of the society. *Dharma* advises that one should seek satisfaction with one's married partner only as this makes the family sound and safe.

संतुष्टो भार्यया भर्ता भार्या थर्तृा तथैव च।
यस्मिन्नेव कुले नित्यं कल्याणं तत्र वै ध्रुवम्।। (III.60 मनु)

Thus *Dharma* controls enjoyment of *kama* even while it allows its enjoyment without disturbing the customs, traditions and social norms. Therefore Krishna in the *Gita* states, "I am the *Kama* not opposed to *dharma* in the creatures."

धर्माविरूद्धो भूतेषु कामोऽस्मि भरतर्षभ। (VII.11)

Kautilya also opines that one should practiase *kama* without opposing *dharma* and *artha*.

धर्मार्थाविरोधेन कामं सेवेत्।

In this way, *dharma* depicts the correct meaning of *kama*.

Artha, which is necessary for enjoying material comforts, should be acquired in the right way. Manu says, "One should opt for such a profession which is not harmful or which is less harmful to other creatures."

अद्रोहेणैव भूतानां अल्पद्रोहेणव वा पुनः।
या वृत्ति तां समास्थाय विप्रो जिवेदाजापदि।। (IV.2)

A man should earn money for his livelihood; he should

select a blameless profession (कर्मभिरगर्हितैः) for that; he should not punish his body too much to gather money (अक्लेशेण शरीरस्य कुर्वीत धनसंचयम्). Manu opines that contentment is the source of happiness and discontentment is the source of unhappiness.

सन्तोषमूलं हि सुखं दुःखमूलं विपर्ययः। (IV.12)

Hence one should be content with the available comforts. Man should not run after material pleasures because they appear like a mirage. They attract the mind of the fickle man and make him a slave for enjoyments. Therefore one should not attach too much importance to pleasures.

अतिप्रसक्तिं चैतेषां मनसा सन्निवर्तयेत्। (IV.16 मनु)

Dharma played a major role in restricing sense organs of the individual and promoting welfare of the society. Manu says that non-violence, truthfulness, non-stealing, cleanliness and restraint of sense organs are the constituents of *dharma*.

अहिंन्सासत्यमस्तेयं शौचमिन्द्रियनिग्रहः।
एतं यामासिकं धर्मं चातुर्वण्येऽब्रवीन्मनुः।।

Yajnavalkya adds charity (दान), kindness (दया) and forbearance (क्षान्ति) as constituents of *dharma*.

अहिंसासत्यमस्तेयं शौचमिन्द्रियनिग्रहः।
दानं दमो दया क्षान्तिः सर्वेषां धर्मसाधनम्।।

All these qualities make man use material comforts within a limit. The concept of *ahimsa* prevents a man from harming his fellow creatures. Man may utter a lie to acquire temporal pleasure. But the vow of truthfulness bars him from uttering a lie. The concept of *asteya* teaches a man not to wish for other's property. The concept of cleanliness directs a man to lead a pure life. Manu says that 'Among all the modes of purification, purity in wealth is the best.'

सर्वेषामेव शौचानामर्थशौचं परंस्मृतम्।

The concept of *jnanendranigrah* helps a man acquire satisfaction within available material comforts. The concept of *dana* induces a man to donate his earnings to others who are unable to get the basic needs. The concept of *daya* creates compassion for the poor, the distressed and weaker sections of the society. The concept of forbearness helps a man to forgive others' mistakes and offences. Thus, all these constituents of *dharma* help man directly and indirectly to enjoy the material comforts in a limited way and to allow others also to enjoy the pleasures.

Today, the concepts and rules of *dharma* are not accorded any importance in society. Acquiring money for more comforts is the goal of life. Deception between husband and wife hankering after sensual pleasures and material benefits is ruining the stability and peace of family life. As a result, unrest and chaos reign over society. Only when every member of the society acts according to *dharma* can a peaceful society be established. This society will then be an ideal one.

न राज्यं न च राजासीत् न दण्डो न च दाण्डिकः।
धर्मेणैव प्रजा सर्वा रक्षन्ति स्म परस्परम्।।

Five

Self-Actualization: The Ultimate Goal of Human Development

Reena Basu

The author builds on Maslow's Hierarchy of needs to show that education should train the human being to seek self actualization and not get trapped in the lower physiological needs.
—Editor

The present study is intended to understand human development in the context of self-actualization. Material development and self-actualization are two dimensions of human development. The first is the physical and the other is the spiritual. In the modern times, more emphasis has been laid upon the physical aspect of human development. Throughout the world, nations are striving to improve the physical quality of life for its people. However, conflicts, crimes and violence nullify the concept of human development in present times. Efforts have been made to explain human development at the individual level. Here, the Indian and the Western viewpoint of self-actualization and also how the individual can achieve that state have been discussed at length. It is concluded that rigorous training of the mind is essential for the spiritual growth of man, which in turn will help balance material development for the benefit of humanity at large. Parents, teachers and spiritual leaders will have to play a leading role in this process of individual development.

The definition of human development will remain incomplete without understanding its meaning at the micro level i.e. at the level of the individual. Conflict that is visible in the modern world arises from the conflict within the individual.

For psychologists, development is a process of growth of the individual in different stages from birth to death. This includes biological and cognitive growth and also development of social behaviour and world view. The Western model of human development as propounded by eminent psychologist Maslow (1987) is based on need fulfilment approach. The model can be conceptualized as a pyramid in which the more basic needs are at the bottom and the higher level needs are at the top (Fig.1). For Maslow, self-actualization means becoming all one is capable of becoming. It is a state of constant striving for the organism to realize his inherent potentialities, to grow as a human being and thereby identify with his real self. In this process the individual is oriented towards self-consistency and there is no duality between his self-concept and actions of behaviour. Roger (1961) has further discussed the four steps involved in this growth process. These are (i) increased differentiation, (ii) expansion (iii) socialization and (iv) autonomy. Differentiation helps the individual to make more subjective value choices, to understand the difference between constructive and destructive forces so as to overcome the destructive tendencies within. The person's self expands in the sense that he becomes capable of self evaluation. He learns to accept himself and from self-acceptance he moves towards accepting others. Further, in this process of socialization he outgrows self-centredness and moves towards other-centredness. Ultimately, he becomes an independent/autonomous being capable of taking complete responsibility for his actions in congruence with his self.

Fig. 1: Maslow's (1987) hierarchy illustrates how our motivation progresses up the pyramid from basic needs to higher order ones.

The Indian perspective on total development of any human being is based on the four *purusharthas* or the guiding principles of life from birth to death. They are (i) *artha* (ii) *kama* (iii) *dharma* and (iv) *moksha*. Like Maslow's need hierarchy, '*artha*' and '*kama*' operate at the physical and biological levels of human existence. Dharma is the norm which sustains the universe and postulates the basic values of truthfulness, forgiveness, non-injury, non-accumulation and goodwill towards all. They are necessary requirements to regulate society and ensure that each member of the society can live and grow fully so as to sustain the social order and physical environment. *Dharma* regulates *artha* and *kama* and acts as a bridge between them and *moksha*.

Moksha is the final value in the Indian hierarchy of values. The ultimate aim as elaborated in the *purusharthas* is to reach a state of spiritual perfection and put an end to all longing in the human heart. It is a state of self-fulfilment. The state of *moksha* is comparable to Maslow's need for self-actualization. Once having reached this state people realize their highest potential. It also reduces the yearning and striving for greater material fulfilment and provides a sense of satisfaction with the existing situation.

As lay persons, we identify material abundance with development and poverty with backwardness. However, both Indian philosophical thinking and the Western psychological viewpoint lay emphasis on maximizing the spiritual quality of life along with other forms of development. Then the fundamental question arises, what is the ultimate goal of human development? And what is the aim of human life?

The aim of life is to develop and maximize the positive potentials which are inherent. Individuals can be initiated to grow and become constructive if they are given adequate training in body and mind in their formative stages, and if they are provided with an optimum environment for realizing their potentials. Rigorous training is essential to cut out negativity and conflicts which culminate into violent actions both individually and collectively. Once this conflict within the person is contained each living being will be a self-actualized and self-realized entity always determined to achieve the goal of self-improvement and betterment of his fellow beings. To create a conducive, balanced and harmonious environment certain guiding principles revolving round basic human values must be a part of the individual's personality development and curriculum. It should include the following principles as suggested by Swami Yuktananda (1989):

1. Emphasise on the quality of means because it determines the quality of end.
2. Clarify values because values motivate and regulate human action.
3. Respect others seeking development so that there is identification with life in totality.
4. Blend moral values with material values.

How to translate these principles into action? The need is to identify role models from the society. Parents and teachers are the earliest role models and ideal for the children with whom they easily identify. They have to constantly ensure that basic human values are inculcated in their children. For this they might themselves have to undergo empathy training.

Further, moral education must be made a part of the syllabi of schools and colleges. Education must prepare the individuals for their duties and responsibilities in nation building. School programmes can sensitize and reinforce spiritual values time and again with the help of spiritual leaders. Education aimed towards a culture of peace and reinforced with spirituality will yield good and responsible citizens with a sense of duty.

Then human development will mean spiritual growth of the human being. In this self-actualized condition, he will behave in consonance with his positive self-image and positive regard for others. This will foster and develop peace all round. To quote Dr. Radhakrishnan, "The transition that we have to effect today, if we are to survive, is a moral and a spiritual revolution which should embrace the whole world."

Let us, therefore improve our minds, while improving physical quality of life, because it is ultimately the mind which governs matter. Then alone we shall achieve our goal of optimum human development.

References

1. Feldman Robert S. (1993), *Motivation and Emotion*, McGraw Hill, pp. 340-373.
2. Maslow, A.H. (1987), *Motivation and Personality*, (3rd ed.) Harper & Row, New York.
3. Radhakrishnan, S. (1947), *Religion and Society*, George Allen & Unwin Ltd., p. 102.
4. Rogers, C.R. (1961), *On becoming a person*, Houghton Miffin, Boston, Mass.
5. Swami Yuktananda (1989), *Values and Ourselves: Value Systems and Human Relationship. Values from the East, Vivekananda Nidhi*, The Institute of Value Orientation and Environmental Education, p. 37.

Six

Happiness

Dharmender Kumar Misra

True social worker is one who guides people to work according to their inclination and thereby become happy.

—Editor

We speak of Indian religion, philosophy and culture as being *Sanatana* in nature. *Sanatana* is associated with the word *dharma* which brings under its purview religion, philosophy and culture. But what do we understand by the terms *sanatana* and *dharma*? *Sanatana* permeates and pervades every activity of man in every branch and department of life. It is kneaded into the entire universe and takes in its fold all creatures and is beneficial to all. *Sanatana* means eternal. It remains unchanged in all times, places and circumstances.

Dharma is a comprehensive term. In brief we can say, what is held is *dharma*. But *dharma* is not something of an intensely narrow, cramped and circumscribed character. The Supreme Being permeates *dharma* and thus it is *sanatana*, eternal. *Sanatana Dharma* prevents us from going down, ruining ourselves in any manner or respect whatsoever and allows our all-round welfare, progress and upliftment. It is all-comprehending. *Sanatana* means eternal and *dharma* means religion (for practical purposes) and the compound word carries with it four splendid meanings:

1. *Sanatana Dharma* means the religion of the Eternal One namely God himself.
2. It is eternal.
3. It makes and keeps eternal those who believe in it and act according to it.

4. He who follows the path laid down by *Sanatana Dharma* becomes *sanatana* and becomes one with God.

Sanatana Dharma is beneficial to the whole humanity.

In ancient times, on the basis of Vedic decrees, man created four *varnas* and four *ashramas* for a peaceful and progressive society. Each *varna* had its allotted work and thus a specific significance in society. The four *varnas* were equated to different parts of the human body. The description visualises the scientific order of the society which holds good for all times and countries. When the social set-up based on qualities and actions transformed into a caste-based system, it resulted in disintegration of society.

This universe is the creation of the Virat Purusha. Vedic tradition speaks of God as incarnate in the world or the world as God incarnate. God is in all things. With the passage of time man started believing in the material world and lost touch with the existence of Virat Purusha, who is all pervasive and omnipresent. This world and human body, which were instruments to realise and visualise the Virat Swarupa of the Virat Purusha, became grounds for indulgence and enjoyment.

Social Work

The purpose of social work is to bring about a social change by nurturing the innate abilities in people and encouraging them to strive for a peaceful and prosperous society. Some thinkers are of the view that social work means protection of the people. Lokamanya Tilak opines that it is to collect people, nurture them and bend them in such a way as to inculcate in them abilities through their mutual concord and make them steadfast and engage them in the work to achieve prosperity and good fortune. It requires showing the right path to the people going astray. The *Gita* propounds— "It is through action that Janaka and others realized perfection. Considering that your performance of deeds may serve as an incentive to other people to act, you should perform deeds." (*Gita* 3/20)

The gist of the philosophy of the *Gita* is that man is to shoulder the responsibility to nurture and protect all creatures. It is his sacred duty. So man's performance of his duties in a disinterested manner as per the decrees and dictates of the four *varnas*, in order to save people from vices and misconduct and to engage them in virtues and in good conduct, is social service. This is the highest type of social work. Even God descends on this earth to uproot evil and to establish the rule of *Dharma*. *Gita* says, "For the elimination and destruction of evil, unrighteousness and the wicked and to instal righteousness which is a form of social work God brings himself into being" (4/7).

The meaning of social work which surfaces in the context of *Sanatana* conception and as described in the *Sastras* is protection of the people. Such a protector of the people is he who performs his duties as per the dictates of *varna dharma*. He may be any member from any *varna*. Followers of all the four *varnas* can perform the role of a social worker.

Inspiration for Social Work

Why should man work for society? By serving society man in reality serves himself because his fate is linked with the fate of the society. Glory, grandeur and splendour of society and man are interlinked. Vivekananda says, "To serve man is to serve God." Tulsidasa thinks that the supreme religion is to serve others. "They too realise Me who with their senses under control, with their minds functioning uniformly everywhere and with devotion of the welfare of all creatures worship Me" (*Gita* 12/4).

All religions preach not to inflict pain on others and to remove sufferings of others. Desire for the happiness of others grows in the heart of man only when they are ready to do away with the comforts which involve exploitation of other creatures. The concept of *dharma* provides such an inspiration.

Norms of behaviour and conduct for individual are established and dictated by *dharma*. Man is controlled by *dharma* at every step. But this control does not obstruct progress of man. *Dharma* imparts discipline and discipline checks the baser instincts of man. Discipline is not blind submission to authority and it does not negate our liberty. It is the means by which man can elevate his personality and attain glory by living a good and prosperous life.

Role of Society in Social Change

There should be a basic change in the society. There should be all-round structural change in the social organisations along with change in their work culture. For this task, selfless workers who can inspire the masses are needed. This task is enjoined on all who have firm faith in social change. The task of social change is possible only by living in society, by being intimate with society, and by making people understand the ground reality and awakening and inspiring them for social change. The laws enacted can by themselves never bring about social change. This is possible only through people's strength.

Seven

Materialism in the Rigveda and Charvaka

Dharmender Kumar Misra

Vedic materialism is a stepping stone to higher objectives while Charvaka's materialism is an end in itself and not acceptable.
— Editor

Vedas are the prime *granthas* of *Sanatana Dharma*. There are four Vedas—*Rigveda, Samveda, Yajurveda* and *Atharvaveda*. *Rigveda* is the oldest.

In the different hymns of *Rigveda* right from its first *mandala* to 10th *mandala,* the blessings of the gods have been invoked to bestow on the worshippers the gifts of health, wealth, long life, sons and grandsons, wife and property. Desire of materialistic happiness pervades the *Rigveda*. *Artha* and *kama* are not ignored. Their realisation is circumscribed by the dictates of *dharma*. But Vedic materialism is theistic because it accepts existence of soul, gods and goddesses, the other world and other worldly objects, rebirth, cycle of birth and death along with the *karma* theory in toto.

The Charvaka philosophy, on the other hand, is materialistic. It accepts the existence of material objects—earth, water, fire and air—and does not accept any conscious existence named soul. The philosophy views the body as soul. Out of the four labours of life it accepts only two labours—*artha* and *kama*. It denies the existence of *dharma* and salvation. Pure materialism is its forte. It is very much atheistic in nature favouring indulgences and enjoyments. *Sanatanis* have given it the name of philosophy because it is reasonable and because it is desirable to start thinking right from the lowest level to the higher levels of awakening. Thorough knowledge of animal instincts is a must to march from manliness to godliness. As the thoughts of Charvaka enlighten on this aspect they are considered to be a philosophy.

On the basis of *Gyanmimansa*, *Tatvamimansa* and *Acharmimansa*, a comparative study is attempted here to bring out the differences between the materialism of *Rigveda* and *Charvaka* to delve deeper into these views.

Difference on the Basis of Gyanmimansa

The Vedas impart knowledge of the inconceivable design through tangible proofs and of the transcendental design through conjectures. But the very foundation of the Charvaka doctrine is that what is tangible is the only proof. All human knowledge originates from this. Human knowledge is limited to it. Tangible here means that which can be felt by the senses alone is to be accepted. Estimation and guesswork find no place in this philosophy. Devotees of *Sanatana Dharma* have recognised the Vedas which are not created by man as absolutely unblemished and indisputable wordy proofs whereas Charvaka does not give any credence to such a point of view.

Difference on the Basis of Tatvamimansa

The *Rigveda* accepts the existence of five prime elements – sky, air, fire, water and earth. Their combination has created this multifarious world. Different gods are considered to be creation of this world. Polytheistic approach holds that with the power generated through *yajnas* gods created this universe. These gods symbolise the five prime elements. All this world is the manifestation of the *Purusha*. The past and the future, whatever the world has been and whatever will be, is His manifestation. The fundamental life force, God so to say, created this universe. Nothing was manifest but everything was present in the seed form in the primordial nature, that is '*Prakriti*'. With the grace of *Purusha*, the universe came into being.

Charvaka philosophy does not recognise the entity sky because its knowledge is not attained through the tangible but through estimation. Inanimate and animate world is said to be born out of the four elements—water, air, fire and earth. They are the primary sources of this perceptible world. Existence of God, soul and sentient powers is denied. It is held that to link gods, goddesses and demons with natural phenomena and happenings is idiotic. Nature works by herself. God, gods goddesses and demons do not interfere. The multifariousness of the world is self-originated. The *Rigveda* propounds that body is perishable but the soul is imperishable. But in Charvaka philosophy body and soul are considered to be one and the same thing. When body perishes, the soul also perishes.

Difference on the Basis of Acharmimansa

The *Rigveda* gives due credence to four labours of life and advocates moderate indulgence in *artha* and *kama* too within the parameters prescribed by *dharma*. *Moksha* i.e., salvation also falls in the category of the four labours. Charvaka philosophy recognises only two labours — *arth* and *kama*. *Dharma* and *moksha* do not find any place in it. *Kama* is considered to be the supreme labour. *Artha* is accomplisher of *kama*.

Physical happiness and spiritual happiness go hand-in-hand in the *Rigveda*. Happiness acquired through unethical and immoral means is denied and is prohibited. According to Charvaka philosophy, whatever happiness is derived is propitious. Bodily and sensual happiness is in no way inferior to spiritual happiness. All happiness is auspicious. An action giving happiness is auspicious and action giving unhappiness is unauspicious. Action which results more happiness is *Dharma*.

Some *suktas* of the first *mandala* and the tenth *mandala* of the *Rigveda* clearly express views pertaining to the other world and heaven. Conceptions of rebirth and salvation are clearly described. According to *karma* theory all the creatures have to undergo the consequences (reactions) of their actions. As you sow, so you shall reap. This dictum forms the cardinal characteristic of *Rigvedic* philosophy. As Charvaka philosophy considers tangible and perceptible means the only means of knowledge, it refutes the doctrine of *karma* and rebirth. It believes in empirical consciousness. It regards birth through combination of elements as a peculiar phenomenon only. This consciousness has no pre-natal history nor has it any existence after death. There is no immortal soul because there is no direct or visible proof of it. Body is soul. Death of the body finishes everything. Charvaka philosophy considers rebirth and salvation as false on the basis of imperceptibility of soul. It considers religious rites and rituals, *yajna* and prayer as meaningless and superfluous and based on superstitions.

Performance of *yajna* is harbinger of worldly happiness according to the *Rigveda*. This doctrine of happiness is linked with ethics, morals and common will of the people. Charvaka negates ethics and morals. It strikes at the roots of human values.

Thus we see that the Rigvedic approach does not disregard materialism but firmly believes that there is something worthwhile beyond materialism. Materialistic, sensuous and sensual happiness cannot be considered the supreme aim of man. Material gratification is transitory. It is invariably mixed with pain, sorrow, and agony. The supreme aim of man is *moksha* and its realisation ends all sorrows, all agonies and brings bliss, *parmananda*.

Materialism in Rigveda

Most of the Western and some Indian scholars are of the view that the essentially materialistic attitude necessary for man to prosper in the worldly life was lacking in the ancient Indians. This explains why India is materialistically and economically backward. Let us understand the term materialism in all its ramifications.

The doctrine of materialism considers material elements, the primary elements and the cause of all animate life. So, description of the world is only possible through materialistic interpretations. Followers of materialism are of the firm view that human development is only possible through materialistic means because being free and self-productive, they can progress in the desired manner. Materialistic attitude is feeling-oriented. Whatever senses apprehend directly comes under the cover of materialism. Materialism is directly related to visible, conceivable and known things. It is an outlook intimately related to material knowledge, technique and intellect.

Two types of materialism can be traced in the ancient Indian tradition: Deranged materialism which can be seen in the Vedas and Upanishads and Arranged materialism which is found in Charvaka philosophy. Vedas and Upanishads do not propound materialism directly but there are undercurrents of this philosophy. A mantra (ऋ. 3.113) depicts materialistic prosperity and in its latter part, spiritual ripeness and maturity. Nature is depicted as an accumulation of power in the *Rigveda*. Vedic gods symbolise natural or physical powers. This explains the significance and priority given to nature worship. Dr. Radhakrishnan in his book *Indian Philosophy* opines that in the hymns of the *Rigveda* seeds and germs of materialism are clearly visible.

Nature worship started with the very creation of this world. Blessings of God were invoked for good health, wealth and beauty and it appears from some hymns of the *Rigveda* that desire of worldly prosperity was considered more appropriate. Craving for wealth and materialistic happiness is found in the hymns of the *Rigveda* and there is emphasis is on performance of *yajnas*. Sages of *satyayuga* are seen praying to nature gods for materialistic gains, health, longevity, children, spouse, property and so on. God Agni (fire) is worshipped for material, psychological and spiritual gains.

Mantra nos. 14 and 15 of the fifth chapter of first *'Astak'* in the first *mandala* depict a unique prayer for acquiring children having expertise in all works, unconquerable in battle, who are lustrous annihilators of enemies, rich, praiseworthy, all wise and who will have a long life of 100 years.

Another prayer depicts: "Bless us with the wealth of virility, wealth of unconquerable power and wealth of steadfastness." The third and fourth mantras of third chapter in the first *mandala* describe a desire for wholesome food thrice a day and night. *Avidya* or materialism is said to be helpful in crossing the river of death; overcoming of death means overcoming of diseases by drugs invented by science. So, prayer is performed to the god Soma for life-saving drugs to overcome diseases. Another mantra describes the Moon God as a giver of prosperity, destroyer of diseases and giver of wealth. Different *suktas* provide man with the knowledge of weaponry, war strategy, agriculture and administration. Rigvedic sages were well accomplished scientifically and technically. Wheeler Villacus, an American woman, in her book, *Sublimity of the Vedas* (page 83), writes that Vedic sages were well aware of electricity, radio, electricity and other material advances.

From a book titled, *Yantra Sarvasva*, written by a sage named Bharadwaja, it appears that the ancient Indians had deep knowledge of aeronautics as well.

Followers of *Sanatana Dharma* progressed a lot materially. In the mantra no. 14 of 15th *sukta* of seventh *mandala* in the *Rigveda*, we read about many things and implements made of iron. The 88th *sukta* of this very *mandala* describes that Aryans disliked houses made of mud and they had different types of instruments with which to dig earth.

Sanatanis used to smear their bodies with the paste made of medicinal herbs to beautify their bodies (7.25.3). Dancing girls danced (1.92.4) and musicians played on the musical instruments.

Goldsmith, carpenters, weavers, nurse and physicians have been mentioned in the *Rigveda*. Traders and moneylenders were in plenty. Thieves and gamblers were also there. Wine was prevalent and it was offered to the gods in *yajnas*. Agricultural produce was in plenty. Rearing of cattle was well-managed and milk from them came in plenty. This description displays a form of materialism which shows that people were indifferent to spiritualism. Use of wine and beauties and harlots performing dance reveal a materialistic mentality of the people.

Labour is the fundamental doctrine of Hindu ethics. All round rise and development of human life is completely based on labour and work. Four labours are enjoined by the Vedas on man. They include those rites, rituals and activities under worldly labour which are indispensable to meet the worldly responsibilities. *Artha* and *kama* are the prominent labours. *Artha* means all those material things which are essential to run a smooth domestic life, to establish family and to fulfil religious activities. Rigvedic Aryans were eager and jealous to have all these material things. Next comes *kama* under worldly labour. *Kama* means all those desires and their fulfilment which are related to the senses. They encourage man to sit in the lap of luxuries and enjoy life. In the baser sense they are satisfaction of juvenile tendencies. In many *suktas* of the *Rigveda* we come across many hints about *kama* labour in the sense of something baser. They abound in topics related to heart, mistress and prostrate woman, husband by selection, transformation of the old tattered Chayavana sage into a youth by the twin sons of the sun, adultress and unbashful women, gender change, exploits of the lewds, a command to woman to remain faithful to and cling to her husband, ordering the recently married woman to remain faithful to her in-laws, sister-in-law and brother-in-law, pubs, abortion by wanton women in private, illegal physical relations between brother and sister and extra-marital sexual relations. So much so, partners completely engrossed in sexual intercourse are also mentioned in the *Rigveda*.

Through Sanatanis assimilated materialistic tendencies as is the case in the present society, fortunately, enough of spiritualism was circumscribed by *dharma* to balance the thinking. Morality-based immaterialism cannot be irrelevant. Religious and spiritual values got as much importance as material advancement.

Rigveda and Soul

In spite of all the materialism in the *Rigveda*, it nevertheless justifies the existence of soul. According to the Vedic sages, even after death the body remains for a while though without any movement. Who stops the movement of the body? Something must have left the body and rendered it dust? It means there must be something imperceptible that leaves the body. It is the soul.

Soul and oversoul live together in the body. The soul undergoes the reactions of the actions done while the oversoul simply views the reactions and is not at all connected with them in any way. Soul is immortal. It is covered and surrounded by *maya*, illusion. There is always a war between soul and body. Soul aspires to immerse in oversoul. The embodied soul casts away old bodies and puts on new ones. This process goes on till the soul mingles with the supreme spirit.

Comparative Study of Charvaka Philosophy and Rigvedic Materialism

Charvaka philosophy depicts a systematic materialism in Indian philosophy. Body is the combination of the four elements. Body is soul. None of the four elements has consciousness. So how can there be consciousness in the body which is a combination of these elements. In the revolving forms of inert matter, consciousness is present as mixture of catechu, lime, betel leaf and betel nut. So mobility is inherent in these elements. Death of the body means *moksha* because body and soul are one and the same thing. Strangely enough we have no proof of the existence of soul because, unlike the body, it is not visible and tangible.

Enjoyment, indulgence and licentious activities are end of life in Charvaka philosophy. Virtuous actions are a fallacy and delusion. Only enjoyment is real and solid. Life ends with death. So this materialism believes in indulgence of the senses. Fulfilment of the body desires is the ultimate aim. There is no need to check or control natural and animal instincts because instincts are inborn and are bestowed on us by nature as our inheritance.

Morals and ethics are man made. Out of fear of pain we need not ignore the pleasures which we are capable of experiencing and which nature has bestowed on us. This philosophy vehemently contradicts the Vedic thoughts. Rites and rituals are considered as merely means of livelihood for those who perform them and so they are considered fraudulent. Man must live happily and enjoy life fully till death as death ends all and nothing remains. Life is for enjoyment and so, if provisions of enjoyment are not there, do create them on borrowed money. Body reduced to ashes after death will not come back.

In the *Rigveda,* God himself has created the elements and the material world permeates in them. Material identities described in the *Rigveda* are gods because they bestow on man their blessings in the shape of food, water, light and so on. Vedic sages worshipped them for such blessings. So, the description of material identities of the universe was religiously, materialistically and spiritually coated in the Vedas whereas Charvaka accepts them in the materialistic form only. The aim of the Rigvedic sages was to lead a moral life based on *dharma,* to perform *yajna* and penance for worldly and materialistic gains and to establish a social order for the welfare of the masses. But Charvaka philosophy believes only in *artha* and *kama* and opposes *dharma* and *moksha* vehemently as ostentatious concepts intending to provide the Brahmanas a means of livelihood by fooling innocent people.

The materialist attitude to life prevalent today is similar to what was advocated by Charvaka philosophy. The Vedic conception is sound and reasonable. The Vedic concept is a synthesis of materialism and spiritualism as both are real. Real in the sense that the world does exist and the soul and God also exist. A happy blend of both dispels darkness of *avidya* and utter darkness of *vidya*. The materialist is fortunate in that he at least enjoys the world; the spiritualist is unfortunate because he neither enjoys the world nor spiritualism leads him to utterly negate the existence of matter. So spiritually-oriented materialism, as found in the Vedas, is the need of the hour.

Eight

Realization of the 'Self-in-Self' is the Key to Sustainable Development

R.K. Bhattacharya

According to Swami Vivekananda material development is instrumental for securing spiritual expansion.

— Editor

The second half of the last century experienced exponential economic growth nearly six fold. Global output of goods and services grew from just under $ 5 trillion in 1950 to more than $ 29 trillion in 1997. The economists were happy but the ecologists noted that the growth was taking place at the cost of the earth's natural resources. Ecologists found the key environmental indicators to be increasingly negative. The economy had been in continuous expansion but the ecosystem had not benefited.

An analysis of the situation revealed that a certain kind of perception was responsible for this state of affairs.

1. The universe was viewed as a mechanical system composed of basic building blocks.
2. Humans were taken as the source of all values and were kept above or outside the non-human sphere i.e. nature.
3. Values behind all actions were anthropocentric. Man exploited nature beyond all limits.
4. The emphasis was on unlimited material progress to be achieved through economic and technical growth.
5. Faith in a 'denominator' system like patriarchy. Females were given only 'instrumental' or 'use' value, similar to the treatment meted out to nature. This had a negative

effect on social ecology, leading to the emergence of the concept of 'Ecofeminism'.

World thinkers were in search of a different type of development which would not impair the potential of the environment to provide sustenance and life support for the people of the world in future.

In 1981, Lester Brown of the World Watch Institute defined a sustainable society as one "that satisfies its needs without diminishing the prospects of future generations."

The UN World Commission on Environment and Development (WCED, 1987) observed, "What is needed now is a new era of economic growth — growth that is forceful and at the same time socially and environmentally sustainable ... Sustainable development requires a change in the content of growth, to make it less material and energy intensive and more equitable in its impact."

Gro Harlem Brundtland, Prime Minister of Norway and Chairman for the formulation of 'a Global Agenda for Change' which emerged as 'Our Common Future' advocated 'new norms of behaviour at all levels and in the interests of all'. The report urges changes in attitudes, social values, and aspirations. Here arises the question of ethics in our physical and social environments. The Brundtland Commission gave a thrust to the concept of 'Sustainable Development' for debate.

In the Earth Summit of June 1992, Agenda 21 emerged. It was a hands-on instrument to guide the development of the earth in a sustainable manner. Principle 3 of the agreement stated, "The right to development must be fulfilled so as to equitably meet developmental and environmental needs of present and future generations."

Agenda 21 had six core themes:

1. The quality of life on earth.
2. Efficient use of earth's natural resources.
3. Protection of our global commons.
4. Management of human settlements.
5. Management of waste.
6. Sustainable economic growth.

It was observed that:

(a) The overall level and pattern of human consumption and production must be compatible with finite capacities of the earth.

(b) The quality of human life depends largely on the physical, social and economic conditions of the settlements where people live.

(c) If industrial production continues to increase across the globe and excessive consumption patterns remain in place, economic development may well be overwhelmed by the amount of waste and pollution that it produces.

(d) A world has to be created in which suffering is not taken for granted, a world in which nature is revered and not exploited, a world which is just, secure and prosperous.

In the preamble to Agenda 21, it has been stated that no nation can achieve what is required on its own, that is, fulfilment of basic needs, improved living standard for all, better protected and managed ecosystems and a safer, more prosperous future. But together we can — in a global partnership for sustainable development.

These cannot be achieved by imposing laws. The law can only punish the guilty for committing a crime but cannot stop him from committing it. Agenda 21 was formulated as a counter-drive to development which was designed by man, driven by his senses, to satisfy his selfish ends.

F. Douglas Muschett says: "Sustainable development is not strictly a problem of science or engineering or economics or proper management. The roots are found in values, ethics and culture of both developed countries and developing countries."

This calls for a total change in outlook. Swami Vivekananda remarked about a century before WCED in 1987: "We may convert every house in the country into a charity asylum, we may fill the land with hospitals, but the misery of man will still continue to exist until man's character changes."

Swami Vivekananda had deep respect for Indian wisdom and was fully aware that if the concept of *nishreyas* (renunciation) was not coupled with that of *abhyudaya* (material development), mankind would have to suffer. The human goal is *nishreyas*. It is the terminal value. But *abhyudaya* is instrumental. Without *abhyudaya* man cannot look beyond his animal state of being. A hungry man cannot be an unselfish, noble man. Being a religious preacher he said, "... There [runs] an economic struggle through every religious struggle. This animal called man has some religious influence, but he is guided by economy. Individuals are guided by something else, but the mass of mankind never made a move unless economy was [involved]. You may [preach a religion that may not be perfect in every detail], but if there is an economic background [to it], and you have the most [ardent champions] to preach it, you can convince a whole country.... Whenever any religion succeeds, it must have economic value. [For] man is guided by the stomach."

To reconstruct India and improve the condition of the masses he wanted ... technical education and the development of industries so that men may earn enough to provide for themselves, and save something for a rainy day.

Swami Vivekananda was in favour of consumerism to the extent of its requirement for economic development : "We talk foolishly against material civilization. ... Material civilization, nay, even luxury, is necessary to create work for the poor. "But at the same time, he could also see the non-ethical side of industrial development.

While Vivekananda welcomed material development he wanted it to be of a different kind. He had a clear conception about the right dynamics of development. He said: "No nation can be said to have become civilized only because it has succeeded in increasing the comforts of material life by bringing into use lots of machinery and things of that sort. The present-day civilization of the West is multiplying the wants and distress of men." P. A. Sorokin, a sociologist of great repute, seems to echo his thoughts when he says, "The principal outcome of this self-indulgent worldly civilization is science and technology. But this civilization has been detrimental to mankind. As a price of his greed and illusion, the incontinent man has used science to create poisonous gases. Spiritual civilization develops humaneness in man, merges with his divine nature and brings out the real man. This civilization based on spirituality is therefore of the utmost necessity today."

According to Swami Vivekananda, "... What we want are Western science coupled with Vedanta, Brahmacharya as the guiding motto, and also '*shraddha*' and faith in one's own self." A 'brahmachari' has to follow some 'yoga' fundamentals, '*aparigrahata*' or contentment is one of the steps. In the language of Lester R. Brown of the World Watch Institute, "One alternative to materialism is what is often described as voluntary simplicity. ... Put simply, to practise voluntary simplicity is to acquire goods only to satisfy basic needs and to seek a high satisfaction in personal development, in human relationships, in intellectual and spiritual growth." Over-consumption or the desire for unlimited growth reflects *rajas*, the attitude of enjoying everything. This attitude brought about the crisis in physical and social ecology. Vivekananda was vocal about transforming *rajas* to *sattwa* which comes from Indian wisdom. He wanted human development first, development of a complete man. Everything else would follow automatically.

Swami Vivekananda thought that Vedanta infolds the real man as against the biological man and helps him think and act beyond the sensory level. He said, "... Tremendous power is being acquired by the manufacturer of machines and other appliances... That is why the Vedanta wants to preach against it, to break down the tyrannizing over the souls of men. ... Excess of knowledge and power, without holiness, makes human beings devils." Vedanta does not separate man from his environment, proximate and distant, or man from man, but makes him realize the interrelatedness, interdependence and interconnection between things, events and consciousness. There is no separatist attitude in the concept of Vedanta. It views the world as an organic whole, where human life is a component in the web of life — a part of natural and social environment, not apart from it.

This oneness is the Vedantic view of the world. When man's actions are conditioned by this concept we have a different type of development. The attitude and behaviour of man is changed. In the words of Arne Naess, the Norwegian philosopher, "Care flows naturally if the 'self' is widened and deepened so that protection of free Nature is felt and, conceived as protection of ourselves... . Just as we need no morals to make us breathe ... [so] if your 'self' in the wide sense embraces another being, you need no moral exhortation to show care ... .You care for yourself without feeling any moral pressure to do it..... If reality is like it is experienced by the ecological self, our behaviour naturally and beautifully follows norms of strict environmental ethics."

This is the ecological world-view in the modern language of the last century and it is nothing but the spiritual or Vedantic world-view which reflects an Indian wisdom of thousands of years. It was this that was thrust upon the world community by Swami Vivekananda in 1893, more than a hundred years ago. This ecological view which, in contrast to the anthropological view, sees the world as a network of phenomena interconnected and interdependent and as a collection of isolated objects. Fritzof Capra observes, "It is, therefore, not surprising that the emerging new vision of reality based on deep ecological awareness is consistent with so-called 'perennial philosophy' of spiritual traditions, where we talk about the spirituality of Christian mystics, that of Buddhists, or the philosophy and cosmology underlying the native American traditions."

The Vedantic world-view can bring a change in human character by changing attitudes and aspirations and fulfil the developmental needs of the present and future generations.

Bibliography

1. Brown, Lester R., *The Future of Growth*
2. Brown, Lester R., *Building a Sustainable Society*
3. World Commission on Environment and Development, *Our Common Future*
4. Sitarz, Daniel, *Agenda 21*
5. Muschett, F. Douglas, *Principles of Sustainable Development*
6. Fritzof Capra, *The Web of Life*
7. Swami Vivekananda, *Complete Works*
8. P.A. Sorokin, *Social and Cultural Dynamics.*

Nine

The Rational and the Spiritual

Surender Pratap

Science and religion should be blended with each other so that science becomes an aid in helping man to realize God.

—Editor

Our ancient sages experienced God through their thinking power. They could unravel the mysteries of this universe. To reach the stage of experiencing the Supreme Being our wise men concentrated all their energy on one point. Concentrating it on one point increased it further and ultimately created a reservoir of energy.

Supple mind is powerless and is incapable of taking any decision. Concentration provides peace of mind and a mind at rest becomes a reservoir of thoughts. Good thoughts are the key to worldly and spiritual success. A mind at rest bestows discerning intellect and only a discerning intellect would enable us to understand the basic causes of our problems.

Modern educational system is based on science. But this zeal for scientific system is one-sided. Dharma, morals and ethics have no place in our present educational system. Religious education is absent. But religion binds us together whereas science is based on the culture of division and disintegration. So the traditional rivalry between religion and science is still there. Science deals with the material world whereas the realms of activity of religion are spiritual and metaphysical. Religion and science must go hand in hand. Spiritually-oriented scientific progress will certainly usher in an era of prosperity and peace. Here religion does not mean a particular religion but religion of humanity where the discerning intellect reduces disparity between man and man.

Scientific methods must be adopted in religious fields as, for instance, the Hypothetico-deductive methods of arriving at knowledge. Observation and experimental verification should be introduced in spiritual matters also. Intuition and faith, however, are not to be discarded. We should remember that the goal of science is achievement but that of religion is realisation. Formula plays a vital role in scientific study and investigation for further progress. This should be introduced in spiritual study also.

Science and religion present two dimensions of the human being, the rational and the spiritual. They cannot be divorced from each other. They must be coordinated, integrated and correlated. True religious sense is indispensable for using the great instruments bestowed by science.

Ten

Body and Soul in Human Development

Om Prakash Dubey

A human being is an entity made up of the body, mind, intelligence and soul. Emphasis on the body alone cannot do justice to the completeness of the human being.

—Editor

Historic Indian tradition goes back to the middle of the first millennium B.C. when political theories and institutions for the development of human being were well-advanced. The Brahmans were extremely influential royal advisers and teachers at this time and kingship was in most cases hereditary. Trade, commerce and industry had expanded and large cities were coming into existence. Music, drama and other arts together with a popular literature were growing vigorously. The early concepts of human development were evolving and a profound tradition was being created.

The ideas of human development in India are to be found in a rich variety of sources ranging from the early Vedas to the writings of Gandhi and Tagore. The theories for the progress of mankind were expressed by writings of the sacred law books of Gautam and Manu, the historical tales of the Puranas and the administrative manuals of Kautilya and his school.

Indian thought regarding the human development cannot be isolated from the main body of Hindu philosophy. In the West, we have accepted a tradition, partly Machiavellian, of a science which rests upon its own empirical basis. But the great works of human development in Indian tradition are part of a vast and integrated system of reasoning which poses and interprets the very problem of human existence. Gandhi speaks in the Indian tradition when he says, "I claim that human mind or human society is not divided into watertight compartments called social, political and religious. All act and react upon one another." Even Kautilya advises the king, "Restraint of the organs of sense on which success in study and discipline depends, can be enforced by abandoning lust, anger, greed, vanity ... whosoever is of reverse character ... will soon perish, though possessed of the whole earth bounded by the four quarters."

Body, mind, intelligence and the soul—these make up an individual. But they cannot be separated from each other. We cannot think of each part separately. The confusion that has arisen at present is due to the fact that each of the above aspects of human being is treated separately without any relation to the rest. It is important to think of the integrated human being. In the Indian tradition this matter has been thoroughly considered. Often it has been said that Indian tradition thinks only of salvation of the soul. It does not bother about the rest. This is not true. Upanishads declare in unambiguous words that a weakling cannot realise the self. Again, body is truly the primary instrument to discharge the responsibilities that *dharma* enjoins. The fundamental difference between Indian position and that of the West is that the whereas the West has regarded body and satisfaction of its desires as the aim, Indians regard the body as an instrument for achieving the aim of highly civilized society. In the Indian tradition, human development holds the ideal of the fourfold responsibilities of catering for the needs of the body, mind, intellect and soul with a view to achieving the integrated progress of man. *Dharma, artha, kama* and *moksha* are the four kinds of human efforts. The longing for *dharma, artha, kama* and *moksha* are inborn in man and satisfaction of these give him joy. Even though *moksha* has been considered the highest of these *purusharthas*, efforts for *moksha* alone are not considered to give benefit to the soul. On the other hand, a person who engages in action, while remaining unattached to its fruits, is said to achieve *moksha* inevitably.

Artha includes political and economic policies. It used to include justice and punishment also. *Kama* relates to the satisfaction of various natural desires. *Dharma* defines a set of rules to regulate the social activity — *artha* and *kama,* so that an individual can progress in an integral and harmonious way and attain not only *kama* and *artha* but also *moksha* eventually.

Though *dharma* regulates *artha* and *kama,* the three are interrelated and mutually complementary. *Dharma* helps to achieve *artha*. Even in business, one requires honesty, restraint, truthfulness, etc. which are the attributes of *dharma*. Without these qualities one cannot earn money. One may acquire fortunes by *adharma* but these bear other evils whereby the true satisfaction of *artha* and *kama* is not attained. It must be admitted that *dharma* is instrumental in attaining *artha* and *kama*. But *dharma* is not just an instrument in acquiring *artha*. It is a fundamental principle of civilized life.

Eleven

Food of the Mind

Prasada Raju

The material world is only one input to the mind. There are other mental inputs that required attention. Ignoring these mental dimensions leads to unhappiness and ecological imbalance.

— Editor

Principle of Universe

Says, Swami Vivekananda, "We can see that what exists in a small part, must also be in the whole universe. .... "every part of the universe must have been built on the same plan as the whole. So naturally, we think that behind the gross material form which we call this universe of ours, there must be a universe of finer matter which we call thought and behind that there must be a Soul which makes all this thought possible, which commands, which is the enthroned king of the universe. Soul behind each mind and each body is called *pratyagatman*, the individual *atman*, and that Soul which is behind the Universe as its guide, ruler, and governor, is God." (*The Complete Works of Swami Vivekananda, Soul, Nature and God,* Vol. II, p. 425)

Supremacy of man lies in his thought and his execution of it. Man as head of the ecosystem has to think about all other partners in it, i.e., the entire living system. As such, man is a strand in the web of universe. He is the first partner influencing the entire system.

Law of Human Being

Says Swami Vivekananda, "Good and bad deeds are not the direct causes in the transformation of nature, but they act as breakers of obstacles to the evolution of nature, as a farmer breaks the obstacles to the course of water, which then runs down by its own nature. As soon as the barrier is broken. In rushes the water out of its own power and force. This mass of power and purity and perfection is in the Soul already. The only difference is the "Avarana" — this veil that has been cast over it. Once the veil is removed the Soul attains to purity and its power become manifest. (Vivekananda, Speech Delivered in Calcutta, Vol. III, p. 335)

It means the eco-ethical standard of living. The Indian tradition is based on the principle that in every creature resides the same omnipresent, omniscient soul. It is the real nature of humans. It is governed by various factors — external environment, internal environment, pre-acquired traits, genetic factors, existing perceptions, feelings and impressions, thoughts and ideas, and various stimuli of our daily life.

Vivekananda identified Patanjali's *Rajayoga* particularly *Astanga Yoga* as the best method to inculcate values in men to bring out originality in them and to help them develop an integrated personality. Vivekananda considered two factors in particular — one is the process, the second is the processers. The process is the *Astanga Yoga*. The processers are based on the construction of body and mind, energy dimensions and conditions of the mind. These processers are:

(A) Three Constituents (Bio elemental Reactions):
   1. *Sattva*
   2. *Rajas*
   3. *Tamas*

(B) Three Levels (Bio-electrical Reactions):
   1. Consciousness
   2. Sub-consciousness
   3. Super consciousness

(C) Four stages (Bio-chemical Reactions):
   1. Mind (informative nature)
   2. *Buddi* (determinative nature)
   3. *Chitta* : Will (consolidative nature)
   4. *Ahankara* : Ego (exit outcome)

(D) Five conditions (Three Combined Reactions):
   1. Scattered condition

2. Darkening condition
3. Gathered condition
4. One-pointed condition
5. Concerned Condition

The above factors determine the internal process that occurs between incoming and exit behaviour. The body requires proteins (body building factors), vitamins and minerals (protective factors), carbohydrates and fats (energy yielding factors). Let us call it as body foods. Likewise mind is also in need of variety of 'foods' i.e. perceptions as building factors, impressions and feelings as protective factors and thought and ideas as energy yielding factors. All these 'mind foods' will be processed through the above mentioned processors ultimately resulting in the exit behaviour. It indicates that the mind also requires a continuous balanced nutritional food (rich mind foods).

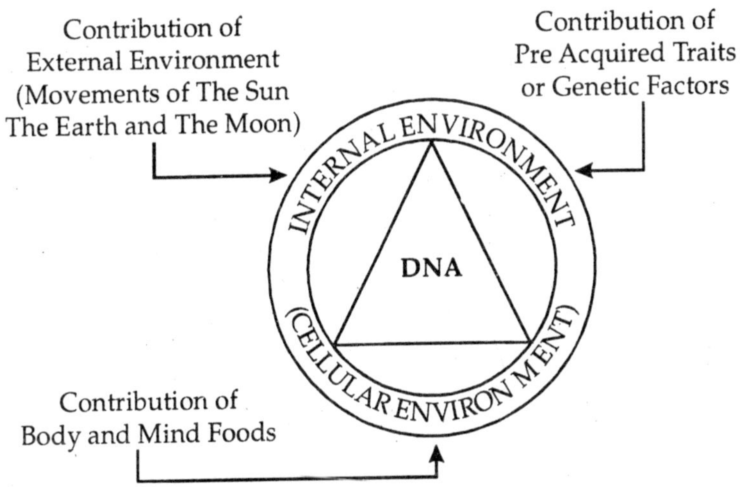

Method or process: Eight stages of *Astanga Yoga*. For each and every stage Patanjali designed an input with a specific purpose based on the processers.

Stage: I Yama

a. *Ahimsa* (Harmlessness): Abstaining from killing any living being or abstaining from hurting anybody by thought, word or deed.

b. *Satyam* (Truthfulness): To liberate oneself from the human tendency to conceal things by untruth and dishonesty by sticking to *satyam* or truth.
c. *Asteyamu* (Non-stealing): Away from the nature of stealing.
d. *Brahmacharya* (Self-restraint, continence): To liberate oneself from the gross carnal instinct, the brute passion and lust by practice of *brahmacharya*.
e. *Aparigraha* : not accepting gifts from anybody under any circumstances.

The intention of this stage is to free one from the *tamasa* (low direction of mind) bondage. These factors will purify the mind and neutralize the effect of unwanted influences or pre-acquired characters or genetic factors. It means that these will stop the flow of the mind in the negative direction or control the negative personality traits.

Stage II: Niyama

a. *Soucha* or purity (Transforming human nature into divine nature): It implies both outer cleanliness and inner purity. Patanjali described this in three ways: (i) Personal Cleanliness: Body, clothes, environment and everything around oneself should be clean. (ii) External Behaviour Cleanliness : speech, action and behavioural factors should be clean (iii) Internal Cleanliness: imagination, thoughts, feelings and motivations should be clean. Various regulations devised by our ancestors are only to make a person conscious that he must keep himself pure.
b. *Santosh* or contentment: It is a weapon to destroy the domination of senses and their appetite.
c. *Tapasya :* It is a direct confrontation with sense behaviour and mortification of organs through a specific food schedule.
d. *Svadhyaya:* A regular daily intake of mind by transforming, illumining and awakening new ideas through constant daily study or the right type of literature.
e. Self-surrender to God: A great devotion towards teacher or knowledge or God.

These five objects will give strength to the mind and also act as a step in the positive upward direction.

Ultimately these two stages or ten objects will provide a balanced nutritional food for mind.

Stage III: Asana:

It is the right sitting posture for meditation. The chief object of the science of yoga is to prepare a person to meditate physically and mentally. So a comfortable posture is very important. It indicates the importance of the preparation of the body.

State IV : Pranayama

It is the science of breath. Here the five vital energies (five airs) connect the body with the mind. These five airs form the base for psychosomatic factors. The condition of *prana* (air) thus influences the condition of mind. It means *prana* is the vital key to control of mind and all thoughts. Continuous *sadhana* will yield stability and steadiness, which improve the efficiency of all sensory organs.

Stage V : Pratyahara

This is a scientific process as well as a philosophical outlook concerned with the introspective nature of mind. The vision of world before the internal eye is related to *pratyahara* which initiates the concentration on all internal and external objects. This is the foundation stage which establishes all moral values. At this stage, mind possesses control of all the sensory organs. At the same time the effective consolidation of knowledge is attained.

Stage VI : Dharana

It means concentration i.e., holding the mind fixed at one point and at one place, for a sufficient length of time. It gives a specific exercise to the mind. This is the beginning stage of introspective intelligence.

Stage VII : Dhyana (Meditation):

This is the most important method designed by Patanjali to safeguard all the above stages based on the last five conditions of mind. It provides the extra energy and strength to the mind. This stage provides all the values that come into action spontaneously without any special effort in thoughts, words and deeds.

Stage VIII : Samadhi

This is the super-conscious stage of mind.

Law of Nature - Consumerism

Swami Vivekananda says, "Whatever we do, we expect a return. We are all traders. We are traders in life. Give and take is the Law of Nature. Give what you have to give. It will come back to you but do not think of that now. It will come back a thousand fold. Learn that the whole of life is giving, that nature will force you to give. So give willingly."

"The sun is taking up water from the ocean to return it in showers. You are a machine of taking and giving. You take in order to give, ask therefore, nothing in return but the more you give, the more will come to you. And the more one struggles against this law, the miserable one feels." (*The Complete Works of Swami Vivekananda*, Vol. II, pp. 4, 8)

Ahara suddi or pure food means acquiring the requirements within the limits governed by the law of nature or within the framework of eco-ethical standard of living. The emphasis of Indian economic theories is on rightful earning and spending. In the spirit of this, commuters are only trustees managing the process. As long as this ethos is inoperative there will always be a sound social life, leading to continuous material progress through economic and technological growth.

For creating a sustainable community most individuals must be empowered with the scientific process of *Astanga Yoga* designed by Patanjali. It holds good at all times. It is the truth of nature. This is the quintessence of the doctrine of Vivekananda.

Twelve

Indian Approach to Human Development

V.K. Shrivastava and R.S. Dube

This paper is an overview of the issues in Human Development.

—Editor

The issue of Human Development has been a very debatable issue. In a world where we are faced with a number of problems of survival of mankind such a debate is but natural. After seeking development for more than three hundred years, the future of man is on the brink of disaster. Man has sought the acquisition of highest quality of life. The cost at which high quality of life is achieved threatens the very existence of human beings. It is therefore necessary to re-think the meaning of human development.

Contemporary modern life is urbanised, industrialised, differentiated, professionalised, bureaucratized, mobile and globalized. Are these the signs of human development? If yes, then why do tension, crime, conflict, suicide, divorce etc. prevail? These are certainly not signs of human development. All men want peace. The development which cannot give peace is not desirable. The issue then is whether modernization is conducive to human development.

Human Development and Modernity

The theory of modernization is often divided into two schools. The Marxist school claims that economic development conditions the political and cultural characteristics of a society.

On the other hand, the Weberian school claims that culture shapes economic and political life. Both the schools, however, agree that key political, social and economic characteristics are closely linked. At a stage in the phase of modernization, economic growth becomes less central. But cultural and institutional changes occur which are related to quality of life. The quality of life may be viewed in material terms, i.e. in terms of physical gains resulting in eating, drinking and being merry or in spiritual terms, i.e. the perception of the supreme being or the attainment of *'nirvana'* or *'moksha'*. The perception of human development may differ but there cannot be two definitions of human development. It, therefore, demands that the two principles on human development be discussed in detail.

In general human development is defined as the satisfaction level of wants of human beings. Man has endless wants and he goes on multiplying them. Consequently, the quantum of consumption of goods also increases. The higher consumption levels need multifarious means for satisfying the needs. For satisfying the needs one must have purchasing power, i.e. income. In addition one must remain in good health. Sound health, therefore, becomes a criterion of human development. This approach of human development thus yields three criteria to measure the level of human development—

1. Consumption
2. Income
3. Health

It may be noted that the inherent tendencies of human beings, i.e. *kamana* (desire), *vasana* (intense longing) and *trishna* (greed), dominate over human actions. Thus the satisfaction of human desires becomes the goal of human development. It leads to increased consumption of goods which in turn require more income. For the satisfaction of requirements one must be in good health and for good health one must eat well. But *kamana, vasana and trishna* are unending hence all the effort does not lead to satisfaction. This is now the vicious circle of development works in modern times.

Conflict, Tension and Human Development

The level of Human Development is not necessarily related to the full satisfaction of wants alone. Even poor persons may be able to achieve the objective of life, i.e. self-actualization.

Despite the higher levels of development, socio-economic and political conflicts, discrimination, prejudice, poverty, disease and hunger prevail in those very areas which we term developed. Higher development of man must result in tensionless life.

Development Profile

In the modern age the focus of human development has been on the economic well being of the population. If the income standards are high the population is able to satisfy its wants and is also able to lead a healthy life. Development or well-being must be of the masses, not of the few. Throughout the history of human endeavours, the disparity between persons and nations has increased. Development also means ensuring better social relations among the communities, regions and nations. The modern scenario smudged with apartheid, casteism, conflicts, crime, ethnic nationalism, political instability, weakening of democracy, terrorism etc.

Human development also discloses a concern towards the quality of the environment. The degeneration of environment has threatened the existence of future generations. Air, water and land have become polluted. Livable space is decreasing rapidly. Potable water is in short supply. The lifestyles of human beings are not sustainable. Energy fuels, minerals, forests and soils are irreplaceable resources. They have been overexploited and this is leading to their exhaustion.

Western Viewpoint

The Western concept of human development is based on the concept of eat, drink and be merry. According to this concept God has sent man on the earth to enjoy the resources. This has resulted in action-oriented scientific view of unraveling nature's laws with a view to overpower nature and to satisfy human wants to the maximum. This model is hardly 300 years old.

The Western model of human development has proven

erroneous. Man cannot make unlimited use of nature's resources, as resources are limited. Overexploitation of resources ultimately jeopardizes human existence. Man is an integral part of nature. But this concept has not been incorporated in Western model of human development. The Western philosophy encourages playing games with the human mind by increasing human desires. This leads to exploitation of limited resources for unlimited wants, which leads to unsustainable future.

This mechanistic worldview has alienated man from man and man from nature. It considers the material world as multitude of different objects assembled in huge machine. This view ignites the exploiting nature in man. The balance between nature and man is lost. Crisis develops leading to anti-thesis of development. In this system economic growth takes place but the actors develop a spirit of competition, rivalry, anger, etc. that leads to dissatisfaction.

Money is the pivot of human development in the Western philosophy. It leads to the concept of 'haves' and 'have nots'. This leads to two overpowering phenomena i.e. exploding population and exploding knowledge. Exploding population is the result of scientific advances made in the field of controlling diseases, preventing child deaths, enhancing longevity and slashing mortality rates. The explosion of knowledge has also added new uses of resources. Both are being exploited to the maximum leading to scarcity of resources.

The Western model of human development has collapsed. There is so much violence, crime, conflict, suicides, divorce, poverty, hunger, war, terrorism, environmental degradation, pollution etc. The Western model does not reflect upon the integral concept of nature professed in ancient Indian philosophy. It is meant to take hold of all resources of the world under a single umbrella to serve the needs of the powerful.

The Indian Viewpoint of Human Development

Human Development is the ultimate goal of human endeavour. The soul tries to reach perfection while living in its body form. The human soul has the potential to become supreme. The concept of human development incorporates the development of body, mind (mana), intellect and soul. The role of religion and spirituality is important in human development. Spirituality caters to the needs of the soul.

For realizing the higher level of human development the environs must be peaceful. Peace should not be gauged in political sense alone. It is the state of wantlessness. Those keen on the physical quality of life as a measure of human development believe that peace is the negation of activity, and the negation of activity may make man a coward. But really, peace is not the negation of activity.

The basic weave of Indian thought of human development is achieving transcendental truth. This value is defined as 'simple living and high thinking'. Simple living does not imply poverty or lack of income. The homilies of sages have filtered into the hearts of people through the social faculty of 'mimesis' via the pics and *Puranas*, which have influenced generations. Men are not born with goals. They are guided, influenced and shown the goal by the sages.

Time and Development

The ancient Indian approach of human development rests on the role of *Kal*—Time. It has been pictured as the ultimate and supreme principle of the universe out of which both gross and subtle elements of life have evolved. Ancient sources conceive Time as the main creative and destructive force. It moves the process of evolution by activating both material and non-material elements. It has been established as a derivative of Brahma or God, which ultimately decides the course of change through which the whole universe moves.

Everything is predestined and moves through a pre-decided course and pattern shaped by the force of *Kal*. Modern scientific ideas also envisage change in a cyclic fashion that proceeds along a set course. Examples may be those of population cycle, land use cycle, cycle of erosion etc.

The *Atharvaveda* gives a developed concept of *Kal*. According to it no activity, no transformation is possible without *Kal*. Change has been viewed as series of movements of a given phenomenon in infinite time span (*Atharvaveda* XIX-53-54). *Kal* is conceived as the prime creator and sustainer.

The *Ahirbodhanya Samhita* narrates the process of creation tracing presence of *guna* and *Kal* in the foetus-like energy of God. This energy has been termed as *Kal-Shakti*. Time is associated with the operation of *gunas*, both contained in the womb of *Shakti*. At one stage, the universe is shown to exist only as Time *(Kal)*. Thus *Kal* is considered as the chief transformer of all the things and by implication, it may be conceived as the prime force into which everything revolves.

Sustainability

The Indian system of development leads to sustainable social growth and entails continuous production of wealth along with preservation and conservation of natural and human resources.

The ancient system of human development was holistic. It was based on the doctrine of *abhyudaya-nihsreyasa*. The stress was laid on the overall improvement of the intellectual makeup of the mind and on value-addition and value re-orientation. The basic concepts are as follows:

Loksamgraha: Generation of mass awareness for sustenance of the world order based on dissemination of fundamental knowledge, wisdom and harmony.

Abhyuday or Abhivridhi: Growth of wealth, prosperity and exaltation of human individuals based on value orientation and intellectual development.

Nihshreyas (Human liberation): Attainment of knowledge, which brings about the highest liberation in human spirit.

Hit prapti and santi: Development of a sense of overall physical and ethical well-being and mental peace for all members of the habitat and ecosystem.

Man and Nature

The ancient Indian philosophy of human development is deeply rooted in the laws of nature. If the balance between man and nature is maintained, a state of peace can be achieved. Laws of the universe cannot be manufactured in laboratories nor they can be modified. These laws are contained in Vedic literature. Incorporating the directive principles of the Vedas in one's lifestyle may lead to real human development. Vedic contribution incorporates geographic principle of activity and change. World is one. Development would mean the development of the whole world. This is the geographic principle of unity.

Sanatan View

The basic parameters of Sanatan perspective of human development are value consciousness, culture orientedness, faithfulness towards society and the motto of *'service above self'*. In this way it incorporates both the ancient and the modern streams of thought. The sanatan tradition is realized on community based efforts. It is a reflection of decentralized development. It stresses upon revitalized community management structure which is intrinsic in Indian rural scenario.

Indian philosophy of human development is based on religion or *dharma*. It is better known as *Sanatan Dharma*, meaning thereby that religion is perpetual. Sanatan view lays stress on the intrinsic parameters of development such as advancement of *'mana'* (inner-self), *'buddhi'* (wisdom) and *'atma'* (soul). The watchwords of sanatan approach of human development are *'appa deepo bahva'*, *'aham brahmasmi'*, and *'tatwam asi'*. The inner enlightened self and its perpetuation is the hallmark of the development in sanatan view.

Income and Expenditure

The Indian concept of income involves only that earning which is obtained through rightful means. Income through violence, adulteration, theft, blackmailing etc. is not accepted. The expenditure too should be guided by principles laid down in *dharma*. It is *dharma* which leads to the knowledge of the ultimate, which is the goal of human development. Part of the income is supposed to be spent on religion and in satisfying the needs of those who are poor and weak. The income should be distributed in five ways, i.e. for *dharma*, *yasha* enhancement of wealth, consumption and for close relatives. If these rules of expenditure are followed by man then he can attain real happiness. Such an income and expenditure plan will promote self-actualization.

The Sanatan view is based on *care and share*. Human warmth, *tyag* and *daan* are its pillars. It leads to the concept of *vasudhaiva kutumbkam*. It is reflected in the quality of togetherness. It is based on self-help and mutual aid. *Tyag* and *daan* are reflections of self-sufficiency and abundance, which is an indicator of physical development of man.

Mahatma Gandhi

Mahatma Gandhi's perception of human development involves the concept of *sarvodaya*, which means the development of all human beings. It also explicitly includes the poorest of the poor. Developing them is called 'Antyodaya'. They are at the bottom of the development ladder. The minimum need theory is best exemplified in Gandhian thought. According to Gandhian thought, a poor man may be economically poor but at the same time a rich man may be ethically poor too. Thus, economic poverty does not necessarily reflect lower human development. *'Sarvodaya'* is concerned with the development of the whole society and not of individuals. According to this concept the soul of a man is pious. Freedom, equality, justice and universal brotherhood are human values which lead to human development. A man should develop control over himself for only then he can follow the path of real human development. The sages and *rishis* were poor economically but they were rich in knowledge, virtues, philosophy and ethics. Their life styles were examples of developed human beings.

Gandhi has given the concept of 'Trusteeship'. The rich persons should act like trustees of the society and spend their wealth for the development of the society as a whole. Similarly Gandhi said that the poor *(Daridranarayan)* must be worshipped like God. The aim of human development should be to wipe out both economic and ethical poverty. Gandhi said that the resources belong to God, not to nations or people. All people have an equal right over resources.

The Human Development Index

The evaluation of development should not be made on scales of modernity. It is based only on material gains of humanity, i.e. income, education and health. Income is required for ever increasing consumption. Education is aimed at increasing man's capacity to exploit nature. The concept of good health is instrumental in unlimited expansion of human needs and desires. This development brings the world to the brink of disaster.

This necessitates the identification of correct variables of human development. The following indices may proposed for constructing a new index of human development:

1. Health – health of the child and mother and the aged.
2. Culture – Job satisfaction, regularity, devotion etc.
3. Equality – Equality in all aspects of physical life.
4. Level of corruption.
5. Charity – Participation in social and natural disasters, contributing to social well being of man, social service, social organization etc.
6. Moral and spiritual development.
7. Duty consciousness.
8. Environment – Level of pollution, degradation, destruction of resources etc.
9. Social security – Security against diseases, crimes, service, entertainment etc.
10. Socio-economic tensions and conflict resolution.

Part Two

Dharma and Human Development

Thirteen

Emerging View of Human Development—Where the East and the West Meet

R.K. Bhattacharya

Indian view of human development, in contrast to the Western view, recognizes the importance of broadening the perspective from biologically limited to one embracing the total existence. Central to this Indian philosophy are the values of *yam*, *niyam* and *aparigraha*. The paradigm shift in the Western view from mechanistic to ecological betrays a convergence with the ancient Eastern perspective.

—Editor

We have to take the Western concept of human development by the horns. We have to go deep into the real meaning of the term and attempt to decipher an alternative Indian pattern and philosophy for human development in its real sense.

This discussion is set against the background of UNDP indices for human development.

The world of today displays a crisis of human development mostly brought on by the 'advanced' Western countries that boast of a high Human Development Index (HDI). They have created situations that threaten the peace and security in Third world situations.

There are invisible hands to trigger off ethnic problems in the Third World countries, which provide the markets for military equipment by buying arms from the developed countries. Mankind as a whole has failed to measure up to the great scientific and technological miracles which have been its own creation. The hollowness of man's inner environment is evident in the restless, self-centred and tension-ridden lives of the people of the countries with high HDI. They are not capable of managing themselves and reflect a dismal state of the human mind.

The actions taken by these people — by minds without an ideal or a clear view of an acceptable purpose, minds with no sense of noble tradition to live up to, minds which are indisciplined — are threatening the well-being and survival of life on earth. The operation of the nuclear reactors, for instance, threatens the health of living creatures and future life on earth by endangering the ecosystem.

Man has excelled in education, life expectancy and income — to be precise, in biological growth. But, to Bertrand Russell, "Unless men increase in wisdom as much as in knowledge, increase of knowledge will be increase of sorrow."

When we talk of social evils like crime, personal distress, pollution, imbalance of the eco-system, the dynamics underlying the problems are the same. It lies in the crisis of perception. We are not able to identify the value behind our action, and shift or share it when required for the good of the society. The purpose of this paper is to clarify how values condition our actions.

The Importance of Values

Any evil or good in society is the outcome of man's action. Action is initiated by decision and decision is based on the values of an individual or a group. Value-attitude-behaviour is a complex. Value initiates attitude which is reflected in behaviour. Thus value is the driving force behind every action. Fig. 1 displays the process of development of an individual from the micro-biological state. It is the process of the biological evolution of man. An individual matters when he/she starts interacting with others as a member of society. Now his/her values come into play as his/her actions are driven by his/her personal values. Fig. 2 shows the process of value formation. Here we find that education, economic condition of society, religion, culture and belief of the society one lives in, are major influences in forming values, over and above those that one has inherited genetically.

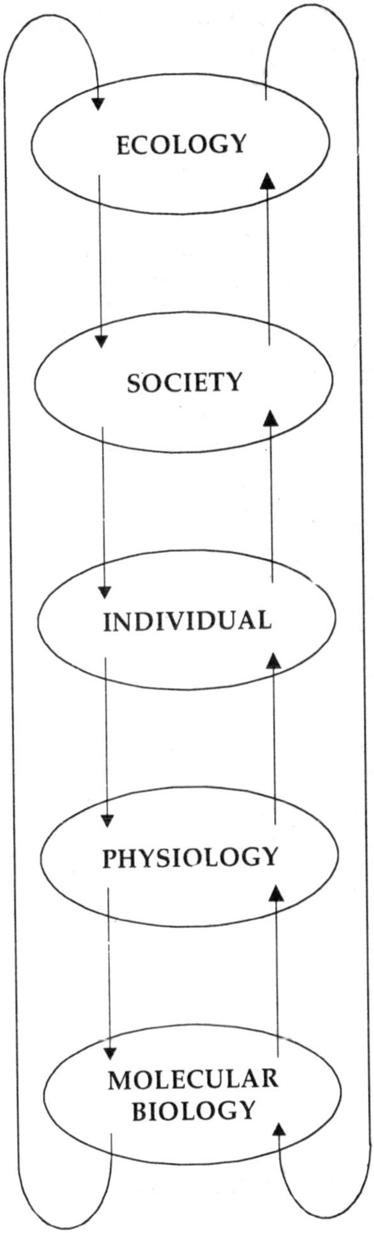

THERE IS A NEED FOR CONSIDERATION OF DETAILS IN THE CONTINUUM FROM THE MOLECULAR LEVEL TO THE ECOLOGICAL. AN APPROACH TO HUMAN PROBLEMS NOW REQUIRES ATTENTION AND UNDERSTANDING OF NOT JUST ONE BUT ALL LEVELS, AND SOLUTIONS WILL REQUIRE KNOWLEDGE IN ALL REALMS.

Fig. 1.

COMPREHENSIVE VIEW OF THE COMPLEX FACTORS INVOLVED IN HUMAN LIFE

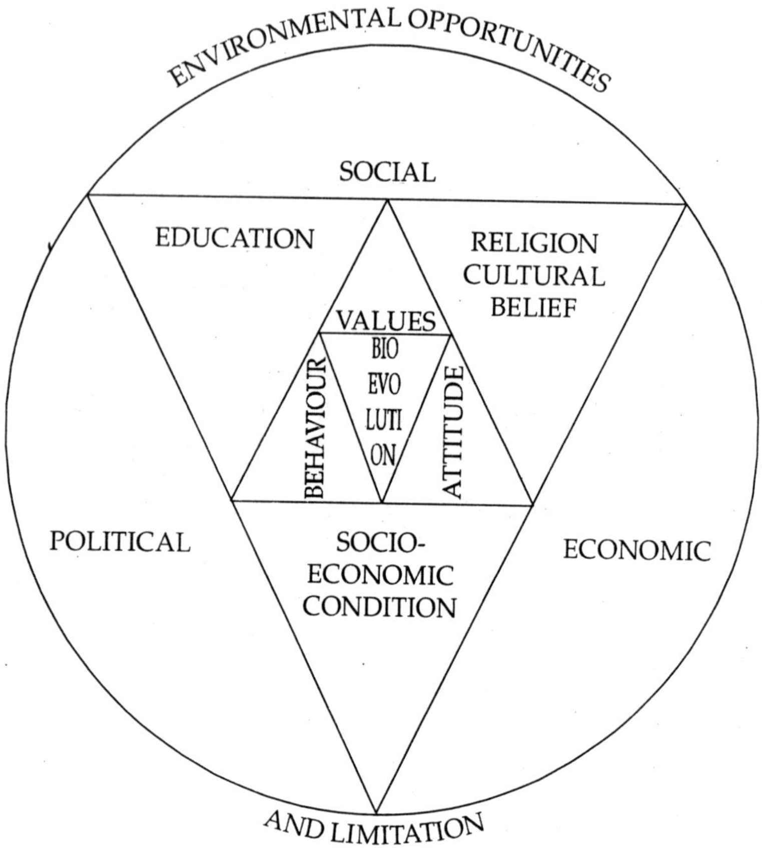

PART OF SOCIAL ENVIRONMENT THAT IS BOTH SHAPED BY AND, IN TURN, SHAPES INDIVIDUAL

Fig. 2.

The Western World-View

Western culture is influenced by the ideas of Maslow, Freud, McGregor, Mintsberg and others. The need hierarchy of Maslow has had a major impact. The highest level in this hierarchy is self-actualization which means personal growth. These hypotheses advocate that material need motivates and shapes human behaviour. They speak for material prosperity, higher standard of living, consumerism and competition, following the concept of 'Survival of the Fittest'. This concept shapes an individual's mind, resulting in his mindset. The quality of a society or a nation depends largely on the quality of the decision-makers, the people wielding power — power of administration, power of influencing the intellect of the masses, power of controlling the economics, and so on. It is the mindset of these people which determines the condition of the society. The scenario takes a certain shape when they are static individuals. It changes when they become dynamic persons or citizens.

The crisis of perception is the root cause of the difference in the mindset of a static and a dynamic person. The hypotheses mentioned above has sprung from the mechanistic worldview of Descartes and Newton. This view looks at the universe as a mechanical system composed of elementary building blocks. It looks upon the human body as a machine and life in society as nothing but a competitive struggle for existence. This view advocates unlimited material progress through economic and technological growth. It fails to unfold or nourish the true nature of man. As such the purpose of human life is ignored.

According to late Sir Julian Huxley, man's evolution is not only biological, but it is also psycho-social. Man in his true nature wants to enter into, and be entered into by, other human beings. In order to achieve human fulfilment, man breaks open the narrow genetic circle and establishes relationships of affection with others, even if he is not genetically related to them. This is expansion of the inner environment or spiritual growth of the static individual into the citizen. The feeling of human concern breaks down all genetic barriers. Such spiritual growth from the genetically limited ego of individuality to the spiritually expansive personality is the fountainhead of all human concern, i.e., all ethical awareness and social feeling. Huxley defined the term 'persons' as individuals who transcend their merely organic individuality in conscious participation."

This expansion hints at another layer in the hierarchy of the process of human development. In modern terminology this layer is called Ecology. (Fig. 3)

The Eastern World-View

Indian wisdom recognized the urgency of expanding one's view from the biologically limited to the unlimited expanse of the total existence — *bhumaiba sukham, nalpe sukhamasti.* When an individual identifies himself as a part in the web of life, he is one with others. He is not isolated and the separatist attitude is dissolved in the vastness of oneness. This experience changes the selfish nature of the animal called man. Then demand is transformed to obligation, exploitation to service, sensory pleasure to the blissful happiness of *tyaga*. This is the Indian worldview. Eastern philosophies like Buddhism, Taoism and others show a similar concern.

The Emerging World-View

There has been a paradigm shift in the worldview from the mechanistic to an ecological one. According to the emerging view in the West, the world is organic — an integrated whole — not a dissociated collection of different building blocks or different parts. It identifies the fundamental interdependence of all phenomenon and reveals that we are all embedded in the cyclical process of nature. One is indebted to Quantum Physics for such a world-view. It shows that there are no parts at all. A part is merely a pattern in an inseparable web of relationships.

We have talked about spiritual expansion of the genetically limited ego. Spiritual Deep Ecological experience says that nature and self are one. Arne Naess, the Norwegian philosopher, is of the view that "care flows naturally if the self is widened and deepened so that protection of free Nature is felt and conceived as protection of ourselves... . Just as we need no morals to make us breathe ... [So] if your self in the wide sense embraces another being, you need no moral exhortation to show care ... You care for yourself

A Hierarchy of Work Motivation

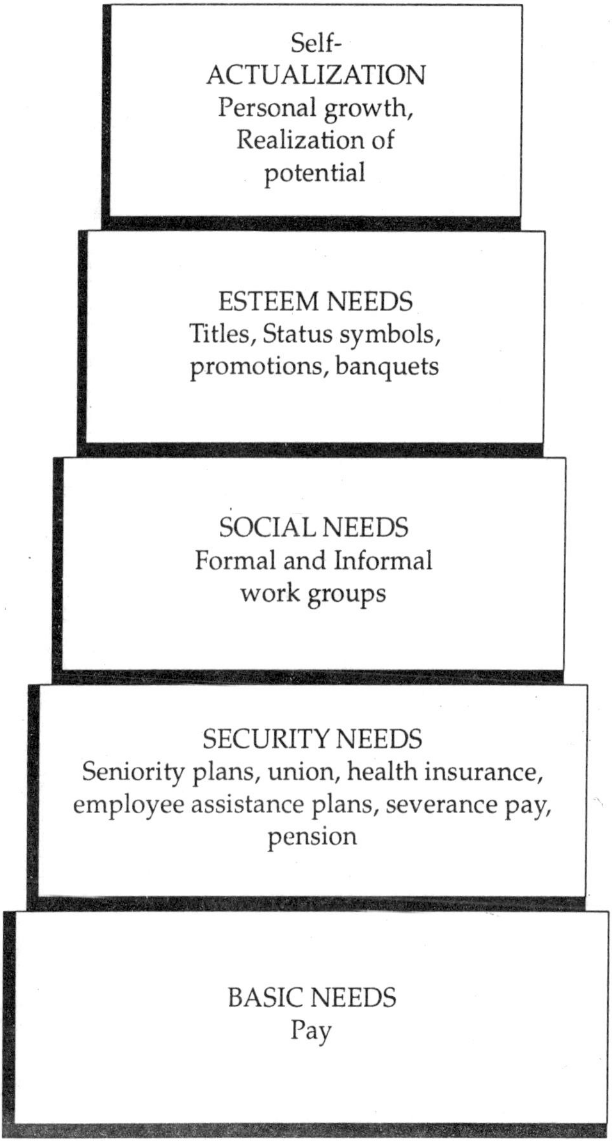

Fig. 3.

Panchakosavivek

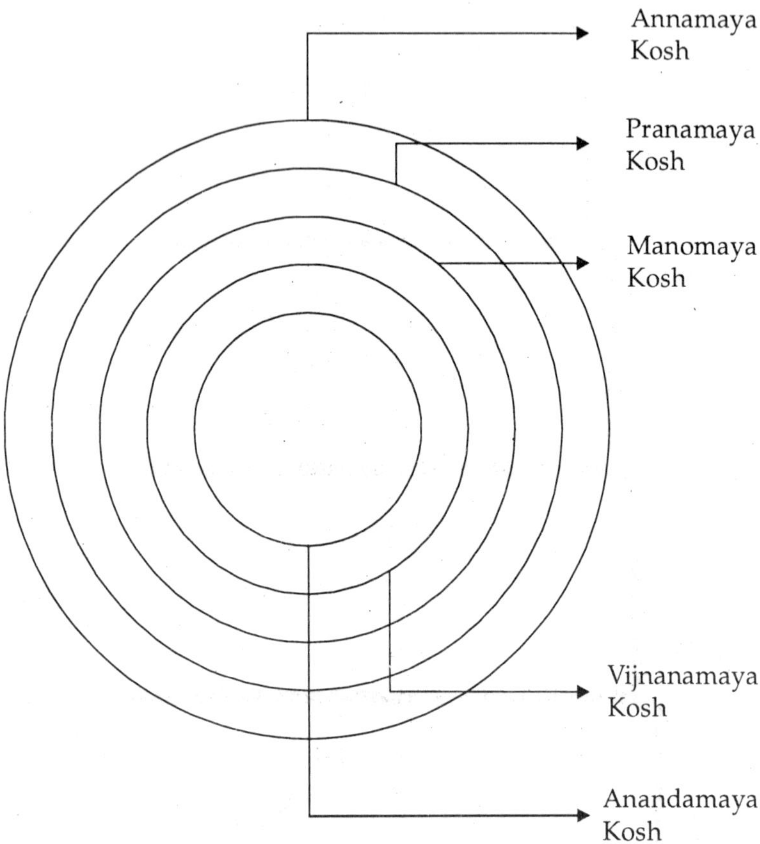

Annamaya Kosh	→ Physical body → Sustained by basic needs
Pranamaya Kosh	→ Lifeforce sustaining the existence of an individual.
Manomaya Kosh	→ Mental identity of an individual who thinks, acts, resolves, loves and hates.
Vijnanamaya Kosh	→ Intellectual awareness that is capable of discriminating/making judgements.
Anandamaya Kosh	→ A perception of being in bliss, but not of being bliss itself.

Fig. 4.

without feeling any moral pressure to do it... If reality is like it is experienced by the ecological self, our behaviour naturally and beautifully follows norms of strict environmental ethics."

India has experienced the truth of this statement — 'because I exist my world of experience exists'. Proceeding a step further, the experience is rewarding — I am the creator of my world of experience, or I am extended everywhere' which is termed 'selfhood' or '*atmabodha*' in Indian philosophy. Deep Ecology contributes to this worldview.

Indian scriptures have also identified the state of the mind as the root cause of a worldview — mechanistic or spiritual. One has to elevate the state of mind from the bottom level to the top one, from *annamaya kosha* (sheath) to *anandamaya kosha* through *pranamaya, monomaya* and *vijyanmaya koshas* (Fig. 4) — from the mechanistic worldview to the spiritual one. We are in the mode of *tamas* when the mind or energy or *shakti* is at the *annamaya kosha*. A little elevation lifts the mind or *shakti* to *monomaya kosha*. We become dynamic, which means the *rajas shakti* is dominant in us. Further elevation pulls up the mind or *shakti* to *anandamaya kosha*. One attains the *sattva* mode when one gains the spiritual or ecological world-view. The solution for a correct perception lies in the dynamics of these three *gunas* in a human being — *tamas* to *rajas* and then to *sattva*. What is required most is *sattva* with the spirit of *rajas*.

Values Condition our Actions

Indian philosophy has never ignored the material prospect, termed as '*abhyudaya*', in the *Mahabharata*. But it is not recognized as the terminal value of human existence. *Abhyudaya* is instrumental in achieving *nihshreyasha* or liberation, which is the ultimate. Indian wisdom believes that either knowingly or unknowingly, man is proceeding towards it. But this achievement requires a disciplined life-style. One has to follow the steps of *yam, niyam, aparigraha* and the like. The Western world has lately been vocal about *aparigraha* or simple sufficiency. This attitude keeps one content with the minimum or bare requirements in life and helps control world entropy which is otherwise rapidly increasing. The steps of *yam, niyam, aparigraha, pratyahara* build character and increase will power, the two vital requirements for a quality human life.

Swami Vivekananda has provided us with a formula for Human Quality Improvement when he says: "These conceptions of the Vedanta must come out, must remain not only in the forest, not only in the cave, but they must come out to work at the bar and the bench, in the pulpit, and in the cottage of the poor man, with the fisherman that are catching fish, and with the students that are studying. ...How can the fisherman and all these carry out the ideals of the Upanisads? The way has been shown. It is infinite; religion is infinite, none can go beyond it; and whatever you do sincerely is good for you. ...If the fisherman thinks that he is Spirit, he will be a better fisherman; If the student thinks that he is the Spirit, he will be a better student. If the lawyer thinks that he is the Spirit, he will be a better lawyer, and so on,..."

Bibliography

Capra, Fritzof, *Tao of Physics, Turning Point, The Web of Life*
Ranganathanand, Swami, *Eternal Values* and *Values in a Changing Society*
Rifkin, Jeremy, *Entropy*
Salk, Jonas and Jonathan, *World Population and Human Values*
Yuktananda, Swami (Vivekananda Nidhi), *Values and Ourselves*
Human Development, *UNDP Report 1999 & 2000*
Srimadbhagavat Gita

Fourteen

Reconciliation of Consumerism and Sustainable Development

Gautam Kumar Basu

Consumerism and sustainable development are in conflict with each other.

— Editor

Environmental change is a social process. It is both 'constituted' and 'reconstituted' by human activities. Despite its scientific and technological bias, such change involves 'political exercise' (Ronnie D. Lipschutz 1996). Broadly speaking, on the one hand, environmental politics deals with the processes through which "humanity organises itself to relate to the nature that sustains it", and as such "encompasses matters of how people deal with the planet and its life, and how they relate to each other through the medium of environment." (John Dryzek and David Scholsberg 1998) Consumerism, on the other hand, tends to project the image of a society based on conflicting self-interests of individuals. Thus, while environmental security aims at achieving a decent way of life for individuals consumerism tends to emphasize self-interest creates side walls which prevent him from coming into contact with his fellow individuals. One can easily identify one contradiction between these two concepts — one emphasizes community welfare through reciprocity, the other concentrates on egoistic behaviour or concern for private interests. Consumerism tends to project the vision of a man and the model of a society which may not be consistent with the requirements of environmental security. The main purpose of this paper is to examine the problems that have arisen from the development of such consumerism and its impact on environmental security.

The problematic arises from twin developments of the late-twentieth century: on the one hand, in an increasing placeless, distanceless, borderless and virtual world order, market appears to be the dominant discourse; on the other hand, the limit of the 'carrying capacity' of the ecosystem and the limitations of the 'environmental space' compel the humanity to aim at achieving sustainable development through what has been described as 'glocalism'. We intend to raise two questions. First, is it possible to replace hedonistic utilitarianism by a much more revised form of utilitarianism known as 'welfare utilitarianism'? The concepts of privatization, marketization and globalization project the image of man as an egoist, utility-maximizing entity and look at society as a collection of individuals with competing and conflicting interests. But we tend to adopt a different assumption — i.e., individuals may also derive 'pleasure' or 'happiness' through 'society-related activities'. Secondly, is it possible to ensure rights of individuals to a healthy and ecologically sound environment based on reciprocity in the face of marketization and globalization? The assumption is that environmental security seeks to inject 'moral life' by developing human relation on a consensual basis. This paper does not aim at providing any final answer to these questions, but it will try to offer the following argument in a modest way: reconciliation of private interests with ethical preferences requires an understanding of what we can describe as the 'politics of sustainable development'.

Consumerism aims at achieving material affluence. To be rich means to have inherited or earned the fruits obtained from domination of nature. Consumerism encourages environmental destruction through over-consumption and through a lack of concern for depletion of natural resources (Hempel 1995). At the same time, it tends to project the image of a civil society based on conflicting self-interests of individuals. Environmental politics goes beyond the struggle for hegemony and seeks to prescribe a normative order which will bring about a balance between individual and nature.

To study the interrelationship between consumerism and environmentalism, one must look into the historical context in which the problematic of such an interrelationship has emerged. The purpose is to see whether and to what extent 'objective reality' produces certain rituals and manufactures knowledge. Theoretically speaking, a consumer society is an economic system based on private ownership of goods, within which individuals work, acquire goods, exchange them and intend to satisfy their own requirements. This is a system based on fulfilment as well as satisfaction of personal needs. Still, it can help one attain individuality in two different ways. On the one hand, it helps an individual to fulfil his personal desires and needs, although such satisfaction does not necessarily constitute an important means of personality development; on the other hand, through possession as well as exchange of goods, an individual transforms himself as an economic agent in a given society, and thereby secures recognition from the society. In this sense, consumerism may be viewed as justification for private property. But such a system can be truly effective where law is enforced and administered impartially and uniformly. Beyond this, such consumerism may lead to the following consequences. First, because of its possessive character, it may compel an individual to distance himself from other members of the community and its welfare. Secondly, because of its inherent competitive nature, an individual may try to impose his domination over others through extra-legal means as well as by manoeuvring existing legal mechanisms, and thereby deprive other members of the community of their own dues. Finally, since each member seeks to advance his claims over others and gives priority only to his own interests over others, social life may assume a Hobbesian anarchical character and each individual may, in turn, feel oneself alienated from the community. The point is: consumerism may generate a tension between the 'self ' of an individual and the individual as a member of the community in which he lives.

Historically, such tension has been reinforced by the emergence of a 'New Right Movement' since the mid-1970s. Such movements have initially gathered momentum in the Western developed countries and ultimately engulfed developing countries as well. The nature of such movements were almost the same: reduction of public welfare, adoption of fiscal austerity measures, low wages, employer-friendly labour laws and disinvestment of public sector units. If the welfare system has been rejected on the ground that it has produced a parasite class, very little effort has been made to regenerate the economy and ensure employment. What is very interesting is that each and every state has been trying to formulate policies which would be acceptable to the bankers, industrialists and the wealthy section of the society.

The result is that: the state is no longer an entrepreneurial state. It does not participate in the welfare-oriented activities of the people. The civil society too is guided by the laws of classical political economy. It does not participate in the community oriented activities nor does it care for community interests; and as such, it neither decides in which direction the state will move nor does it assess the extent to which the state has been working in community interests. Thus, the ethical components which characterized the liberal political thinking since John Stuart Mill through Green, Hobhouse, MacIver and Dewey have been done away with by today's neoliberal regimes in the third world. This, however, does not mean that the wheels have been turned back, but only that it has another grand design. The individuals in a 'privatized' society live in isolated cells and, as such, can hardly merge with other individuals with the consequence that no political party can be formed along class lines (Basu 1992).

Is it possible and feasible to evolve a normative order through which environmental security can be ensured? One may prescribe certain measures such as adoption of a communitarian philosophy as prescribed by Amitai Etzioni or emergence of a cosmopolitan democracy as developed by David Held towards achieving such goals. These prescriptions are, however, all-comprehensive and require a structural transformation at a global level. One may, however, look at the concept of sustainable development which has come to stay as a solution towards contradictions between material needs of human beings and security of the environment. Sustainability may be studied at two different levels: on the one hand, sustainability requires a managerial perspective as it involves identification of priorities and formulation of strategies; on the other hand, since sustainable development involves a radical transformation in developmental priorities, it becomes crucial whether and how such transformation will face historical-structural constraints.

The managerial perspective tends to highlight the following features. In the North, emphasis should be more on the linkage between economic development and the environment, rather than on resolving food security and extreme hunger. Secondly, despite controversy whether the state should be the major agent in the processes of sustainable development or emphasis should be given on economic instruments which decentralize decisions to market place, it has been agreed that a shift to sustainable development should ensure increasing involvement of sub-national levels of government in environmental management. Thirdly, sustainable development involves promoting sustainable consumption and sustainable production. Sustainable consumption means meeting needs, improving quality of life, improving resource efficiency, increasing use of renewable energy resources, minimizing waste and emphasizing equity, while sustainable production refers to cleaner production and thereby ensuring what is called ecological modernization among firms. Fourthly, the scholars are of the view that the policy of sustainable development should be integrated into other sectors, such as tourism, industry, energy, transport and agriculture. Finally, it has been agreed that incorporation of environmental groups within the decision-making process should be considered as a pre-requisite for successful implementation of sustainable development policies.

The historical-structural perspective, on the other hand, lays stress on the following features. Firstly, it sees a continuity in the politico-economic processes of resource extraction and explotation of resources from colonial days to post-colonial days. Only the actors have changed. Techniques remain the same. Secondly, political and economic elites are closely intertinked as far as the processes of resource exploitation and resource extraction are concerned. Thirdly, the role of civil society is not straightforward. Its role is constrained by local political conditions as well as the tolerance of the state vis-a-vis the popular protests and movements. Non-governmental organizations can play a significant role in environmental management but it seems that these groups will continue to confront extremely limited political space to raise the issue of basic needs of present and future generations. Fourthly, the role of the state appears to be highly doubtful, as it may simultaneously encourage indiscriminate exploitation of resource base and project its image as protector of environment. We do not intend to go into the relative strengths and weaknesses of these two approaches but one can say that environmental degradation can be attributed to the emergence of a global market economy and as a consequence of unlimited, uncontrolled consumerism.

Where do all these lead to? One can conclude that there exists an inherent contradiction between consumerism and environmental security. Ours is an era of hypocricy: on the one hand, we clamour for a social order where individual freedom and choice will be ensured without compromising or impairing the right of both contemporary and future generations to meet their equitable needs; on the other hand, we tend to idealize market as panacea for all evils in a given society and project it as a force which will produce an 'all winners and no losers' situation. Our point is: once we accept such hypocrisies as 'normal', we do nothing except institutionalize anarchy as major determinant of social relations. This, in turn, compels us to justify power as a dominant discourse shaping such relationship and identify the state exclusively as a regulatory mechanism by taking away its welfare functions but keeping its repressive teeth intact. Contrarily, sustainable development injects ethical dimension by emphasizing the need for conducting social relations on a consensual basis, rejecting rationalization of power relations and invoking the principle of moral-practical rationalization. After all, human beings, as principle 1 of Rio Declaration States, "are at the centre of concerns for sustainable development" and "are entitled to a healthy and productive life in harmony with nature". The problem lies in the fact that if it is very difficult to reverse the wave of consumerism, it is also equally evident that the necessities of sustainable development cannot be ignored. How can we reconcile these two contradictory, but inevitable, tendencies — i.e. the demands of consumerism, on the one hand, and the urgency of sustainable development on the other?

Bibliography

Alker, Hayward and Nazli Choucai (eds.), *Global Accord : Environmental Challenges and International Responses*, Cambridge, MIT Press, 1993.

Basu, Gautam Kumar, *Global Environmental Politics: Towards New Territorial Challenges in International Relations*, Asian Studies, Vol. XVI No. 2,1998.

'The Question of State Autonomy and Regime Transformation in the Third World', *Asian Studies*, Vol. V, 1992.

Dryzek John and David Schlosberg (eds.), *Debating the Earth : The Environment Politics Reader*, Oxford University Press, Oxford,1998.

Etzioni, Amitai, *The Spirit of Community*, Fro Press, New York, 1993.

Hempel, Lamont, *Environmental Governance : The Global Challenge*, Affiliated East West Press, New Delhi, 1995.

Lipschutz, Ronnie D., *Global Civil Society and Global Environmental Governance : The Politics of Nature from Palace to Planet*, Albany, SUNY Press, 1996.

Low, Nicholas (ed.), *Global Ethics and Environment*, Routledge, London, 1999.

Pepper, David, *Modern Environmentalism : An Introduction*, Routledge, London.

Sachs, Wolfang (ed.), *Global Ecology : A New Arena of Political Conflict*, Zed Books, London, 1995.

Fifteen

Global Equity and Human Development

Sumita Sen

Excessive consumption of earth's resources by industrial countries is destabilizing global ecology as well as society.

—Editor

Theories and practices of sustainable development have come to face challenges of environment, economy and society. At the root of issues is a shift in values which is yet to be understood. The gaps between the advanced industrial countries and the backward countries is ever widening, making it difficult for the latter to cope with their socio-economic problems of poverty, malnutrition, illiteracy, etc. These poor countries also lack scientific and technological capabilities to make better use of technology for realising their goal of improving the 'quality of life' index. This clearly indicates that neither the economic practices as dictated by the powerful global actors nor the pure ecological measures provide an answer to the dilemma of development of human society. A balanced relationship between human development and the earth's ecosystem is yet to be achieved.

Anthropojenic interventions have always put pressure on the natural support system for their survival. The extent of destruction of this system during the second half of the twentieth century has been unprecedented. However, the improved economic achievement of the industrially powerful nations continued to direct the global trend towards economic development. While the world output of goods and services quadrupled, little attention was devoted to analysing its impact on the earth's ecosystem. Failure to balance the priorities have threatened every country and every society, since development cannot subsist upon a deteriorating environmental resource base.

The growth and higher income levels influenced the consumption of resources. For instance, the developed countries with 26% of the world's population became the most important consumer of products that were highly resource intensive. In fact, the accepted economic growth pattern with the interplay of market forces led to severe environmental degradation, putting the future of the resources and the people at risk.

The ecological crisis brought new considerations before the international community. The 1972 Stockholm Conference on Human Environment indicated environmental problems faced by mankind as a whole on the one hand and the backlash of nature on the other. Moreover, the kind of development experienced by the industrial countries proved to be a cause for environmental destruction. The conference highlighted the related social concerns of the developing nations.

The decade of the eighties witnessed severe environmental problems like global warming, ozone depletion, desertification, etc. The very survival of human beings was at stake. The famine in Africa, nuclear disaster in the USSR and Bhopal gas tragedy in India occurred in the 1980s. Once again, questions on the limits to growth, patterns of growth, and their dimensions of approach were raised. The need, therefore, was for introspection into the underlying ethical issues for the overall progress of mankind. The concept of sustainable development continued to be stressed in the 1990s. During this decade, the consumption demand led to overexploitation of the earth's resources which led to global warming, deforestation and pollution. The UNCED in 1992 again identified linkages between environment-economy-capital for the sustainable use of world's resources. The Earth Summit of 1992 also highlighted the consumption and production patterns of the richer nations, pointing out that 20 per cent of the population was consuming 80 per cent of the world's resources and thus significantly contributing to the current environmental crisis. Thus the debate continued on conceptual and practical issues of environment and economy.

The Indian thinkers and philosophers at different points of time have emphasised the significance of nature and conservation requirements in the greater interest of human development. Such a relationship between sustainable development and upliftment of the classes cannot be overemphasised.

India with its rich biodiversity and resources is currently facing an ecological crisis. An analysis of India's traditional and administrative practices and policies during the ancient and colonial period, would indicate some measures for balancing the environment and economy. Post-independent India has witnessed both change and continuity in this regard.

The 1990s witnessed a spurt in economic and scientific activities that had a direct impact on India's environmental condition. The adoption of an approach to environmental issues with the focus on the ecosystems people as well as the traditional ethos, is one of the pressing issues before India. Exercising eco-ethical conduct has become a contingent option for the stratified society in India. While the ever-growing consumerist world tends to iconise conspicuous consumption and pecuniary canons of taste with a total disregard to the rational exploitation of the resources, the indigenous stock struggling for life support often is rendered ecologically weak. No doubt, the practice of eco-ethical values is at a crucial juncture. For a holistic, pragmatic and people-oriented world view, the eco-ethical standard should find an acceptance in the realms of both theory and practice of eco-ethics that are applied in everyday life of the human beings.

Sixteen

Yoga in Sanatana Tradition and its Relation with Human Values

Surender Nath Pal

Yoga helps a person in the control of his senses. This leads to a spirit of renunciation and social harmony

— Editor

The word 'yoga' is derived from the Sanskrit root *'yuj'* meaning to unite or integrate. The science of yoga appears to have been a part of the culture of India before the advent of the Aryans in the country. By the Upanisadic period, it gained eminence in their culture as well. *Yoga Sutra,* a work of Patanjali of the second century B.C., makes it clear that the Yoga tradition was part of the Indian cultural lore of the time.

The science of yoga is a branch of the Sanatana Hindu *Dharma*. Hindu *dharma* is timeless and ageless. It will not be wrong to say that the ancient and eternal culture of India is nothing else but *Sanatana Dharma*. Thus, our Yoga tradition is also eternal. It survives despite untold changes that have imperceptibly crept into our glorious culture.

The seals and coins of the Indus Valley Civilisation depict postures of *yogis* sitting with legs crossed, sitting on hams and sitting on legs rolled round. The posture of the *yogi* sitting on legs rolled round symbolises Pashupatinatha. Later on, this posture got the name of *Padmasana*. In *Rig Samhita,* Yoga is explained thus: "No Yajna act is accomplished without Yoga. This Yoga is nothing but restrictions on mental faculties. It permeates Karmas" (1/18/7).

"Yoga is the state of cessation of all fluctuations in mind and its related faculties. All ripples in the mental faculties are subdued and subsided."

The learned person having impenetrable and impregnable faith in God and wholly devoted to yoga grasps the imperishable through the practice of yoga. This spiritual knowledge imparts bliss and integrated growth and fulfilment of the human being at all possible levels — physical, emotional, intellectual and transcendental or spiritual. Then the yogi is established in the fundamental nature and he rejoices in the cosmic self; intellectual cognition bears the truth.

In *Kathopnishada* Yoga is defined thus : "This, they consider to be the state of yoga, this firm holding back of the senses, when one is completely undistracted."

Talking about Yoga, the *Gita* propounds that man should not be attached to inaction and expectation of result brings misery.

"Have recourse to Yoga which is none other than skill in the field of activity" (2/5).

"To remain established in the state of Yoga, give up attachment and be unmindful of success or failure concerning all your actions. It signifies the state of equanimity called Yoga" (2/48).

"One is said to attain the state of Yoga when one's mind is well controlled, one remains steadfast in the self alone and is free from craving for all kinds of enjoyments" (6/18).

Yogi is like a lamp having no flicker. "Yoga is disconnection from the union with pain. Yogi is not shaken even by heavy sorrow. One well-established in yoga is not mentally disturbed even by great pain" (6/23).

Patanjali, who established yoga as a scientific process in the 2nd century B.C., defines yoga as:

"Yoga is the state of cessation of all fluctuations in the mental being" (*Yogasutra* 1).

Then the *yogi* experiences bliss that can be grasped by the pure intellect.

We find elaborate mention of yoga in Buddhism and Jainism. Their granthas elaborately deal with meditation *asanas*, ways of meditation and other restraints governing yoga.

Around sixth century A.D., Guru Gorakhnath established *hatha yoga*. Later on, in the medieval period, Sufi saints and devout poets maintained this tradition and modern thinkers like Vivekananda, Maharishi Arvind, M.K Gandhi and many others have contributed much towards yoga's popularity.

The yoga tradition is extremely relevant in the present time of turmoil and tribulations, chaos and anarchy. In the international arena, science of yoga has envoked enthusiasm. The present crisis confronting humanity can be resolved only through a transformation in consciousness and the yoga tradition can play a vital role in bringing about such a transformation.

The Yogic tradition embraces ideas, concepts, theories, techniques, practices, laws, rules and regulations. Patanjali's Yogasutra is a *grantha* par excellence. It deals with eight constituents of Yoga practice. These are eight steps of '*Yoga Sadhana*'. They are as follows:

A. *Yama* — It denotes
   (a) Non-injury; non-violence; non-falsehood
   (b) Truth
   (c) Non-stealing - *Asteya*.
   (d) Non-possession of things more than needed, renunciation, control over senses.
   (e) *Brahmacharya*.

   They promote external ecology.

B. *Niyama* — Niyama denotes cultivation of purity (within and without), positive attitudes, self-study, contentment and *tapa*. They promote internal ecology.

C. *Asanas* — They are different kinds of body postures. They help to keep the body in ease and comfort.

D. *Pranayam* — It is control of the energy cycle particularly breathing.

E. *Pratyahara* — It is practice of relaxation through withdrawl of the senses from without.

F. *Dharana* — It is concentration of thought force on an object.

G. *Dhyana* — It is unidirectional flow of thought force towards the object concentrated upon.

H. *Samadhi* — It denotes unitive experience devoid of subject and object duality. Here the votary of yoga experiences *sadhya* or the desired one.

Adherence to *Astanga Yoga* makes a yogi experience the transcendental. Then he gains different kinds of wisdom and he serves humanity through them.

Has it got any link with human values? Has this science of yoga any importance for the youth?

For a devotee the aim of *yoga sadhana* is not only self-elevation but also well-being of the entire humanity. All the '*angas*' of yoga are directly linked to human values because these very values have germinated the '*angas*'. *Yama* and *niyama* are human values. Lofty human values like truth, non-injury, non-stealing, renunciation, brahmacharya, abnegation, right character and brotherhood are intimately connected with yoga. Through non-injury and non-violence, yoga transmits the message of benevolence and brotherhood for all creatures. It installs the supremacy of truth in society. It inculcates the feelings of self-contentment in man. Renunciation imperceptibly saves society from the vices of stealing, corruption and black marketing. Thus *yama* and *niyama* impart a sound and high character to man. Self-elevation leads to elevation of society as society is nothing else but men taken together. M.K. Gandhi gave the message of truth, non-violence, virtuous conduct and fraternity to the entire world by adhering to the sacred rules of *yama* and *niyama*. Installing truth on a high pedestal, he identified it with God. Similarly, many sages acquiring qualities of character through yoga not only lifted themselves but endeavoured to alleviate the sufferings of humanity.

Discipline is the first need for proper development. Discipline involves those rules and regulations which impart regularity and good arrangement. Yoga teaches the youth contentment. This can help them ward off mental agonies. The inability to gain as sought results in frustrations and mental sickness. So self-contentment acquired through practice of yoga saves a youth from mental and physical affliction. Yoga also treats incurable diseases. Diabetes and diseases pertaining to heart have no permanent remedies in allopathy and other systems of medicines. But yoga provides effective treatment. Costly and pain-inflicting surgery can be got rid of by some special *asanas* and *pranayama*. Brain cells cease to develop after a certain age or point of time and no effort can resurrect it, revive it, recharge it and restart it. In U.S., scientists experimented with some devotees of yogic practice and found that brain cells had shown tendency towards growth — new cells were beginning to develop. In brief, we can say that, yoga can cure many mental and physical diseases and can help maintain equilibrium of body and mind.

Seventeen

Expansion of Consciousness

Kumar Mitra

Human beings should see themselves as one part of the universe rather than its users or rulers.

— Editor

Perhaps it all happened due to the explosive development of human brain. Some fossils of the Oligocene and Miocene era evince that the brain area of a full-grown great ape (the closest ancestor of *Homo sapiens*) was around 300 to 400 cubic centimetres. From the skull-fossil of *Australopithecus Africans* (one of our very ancient ancestors) we have come to know that it took almost 30 million years for the brain area to double (that is, from around 300 to 400 cubic centimetres to around 600 to 800 cubic centimetres). But within the last half-a-million years that brain area has reached up to 1400 to 1700 cubic centimetres in the skull of an adult human being of today. In no other species do we find the brain to have undergone such development. Perhaps it is a sad fact for the human species: we are lonesome travellers on the path of evolution, with no real rival and, that is why, no true friend.

Within a short span of our 'civilized' journey we are facing the danger of destroying all that has been created through our myopic handling of our own technology. Not to speak of the man-made pollution thrust upon every ingredient of our natural environment, we have entered a new millennium to face the horror of nuclear devastation.

What is to be done? As self-protection is a basic instinct,

let us assume that all the conscious activities that conform to this basic instinct are morally acceptable. Let us assume further that we are bound to have moral consideration for those on whom or on which we depend for our sustenance. For the sustenance of oneself, one has to expand the circle (to borrow the phrase from Peter Singer) of one's consideration beyond one's own self. But the question is: How far that expansion has to be made?

To the ancient Greek elites and rulers, the circle was quite narrow. They treated their slaves as raw materials of nature, considered the non-Greeks as barbarians, and did not bestow the infants or invalids any automatic right to live. We may call it a 'naive anthropocentric' viewpoint.

With the advent of Biblical thought in the West, the circle has expanded, at least theoretically, to all human beings. Killing of any human, be that a slave, an invalid, an infant, or a foetus, is wrong because all humans are properties of God; to kill a human being is to deny God's ownership. God, however, has placed all the non-human entities under human custody for human need and enjoyment.[1] So it follows that all non-human entities, animate or inanimate, are only of instrumental value in proportion to their contribution to human well-being. This stance was provided with a new finish in the Baconian-Cartesian-Newtonian paradigm where nature has been treated as a machine over which mankind should gain mastery by means of scientific discoveries and inventions. As a consequence, the general philosophic attitude was that humans alone were morally considerable and hence our environmental policies were evaluated solely on the basis of how these affect humans. We may call it a 'strong anthropocentric' viewpoint. In general, utilitarians, who speak of maximizing the surplus of human happiness over human unhappiness, join this camp. They feel that unless the maximum number of humans get the bare minimum means of living, eco-ethical livelihood will never be possible.

But even here the very concept of 'humanity' appears highly volatile. In practice, moral consideration of humans is vitiated with several attitudinal differences regarding sex, race, class, skin, colour, state, territory, etc. Technological innovations give rise to serious social and ecological problems and new forms of enslavement as well. It is a matter of common experience that from technological innovation the rich gain the most at the expense of the poor — polluting factories, for instance, are most often built near the homes of the wretched.

Amartya Sen goes beyond utilitarianism in the sense that in his welfare-economies he expands the circle, not up to the maximum number of humans, but to all humans, demanding all sorts of economic and social equalities.[2] To widen the circle, he includes the factors of 'capability' and 'entitlement' and to make these factors viable, he asks the state to play its role. Perhaps his analysis is a bit pathological in nature. If the cause of famine in India is the failure of 'exchange-entitlement', then does it not refer to the inherent weakness of market economy or to the neo-colonial extortion? And if that be the case, we shall have to conclude that the factor of entitlement itself is vulnerable. So, the modest statement regarding the aforesaid 'strong anthropocentric' model would be that, at least in comparison to the Greconian model, the circle of moral considerability has expanded a little.

But something more is needed. We should expand our circle of moral considerability to include at least sub-human birds and animals within its periphery. We should treat them, if not as moral 'agents', then at least as moral 'patients' who can, and should, be recipients of moral concern.[3] To set the sub-human living beings on a position at par with the humans, Jeremmy Bentham wrote long ago: "The question is not, can they reason? nor can they talk? but can they suffer?"

We may call this 'weak anthropoperipheral' viewpoint because we agree to step aside from the central position that we have for long claimed for ourselves. In our country, we find Vivekananda, among others, upholding such a viewpoint.[5]

To give a theoretical completeness to this expansion of the circle of moral considerability, we should agree to expand the circle still further to cover the biosphere as a whole. It is true that human beings are very different from every other thing in nature. But difference does not justify apathy. Almost all the ecological problems stem from this apathetic, and often antagonistic, Man-Nature relationship. If by 'living' we mean self-regulating system striving towards some conscious or unconscious goals, we will have to take the whole environment as morally considerable. We may call this 'strong anthropoperipheral' view. The Upanisadic seers, Rabindranath, among modern western thinkers Albert Schweitzer,[6] Aldo Leopold,[7] H. Rolstin III[8] and the like share this viewpoint.

This new perspective gets its force from science with the emergence of Quantum Physics. The barrier between the conscious and the unconscious dwindles. Modern science compels us to accept the relation between ourselves and the environment as internal and never as external. Consequently, we should take it to be a cognitive defect to view human species as the all-important locus of all values and should realize that this cognitive defect leads to a self-destructive practice of treating animate and inanimate natural entities as less important and therefore dispensable. It can be said that such an ethics may have little applicability because still we do not know for certain which human actions will lead to the desired equilibrium of the biotic system. But ignorance cannot be treated as a serious argument, particularly in an age in which we are accumulating so much knowledge at such a great pace.

It is more a matter of realization than of information. We have to feel at heart that the human species is in no way the master of this planet, but just one among many dependent on the environment. Applying our intelligence, we have acquired immense power through science and technology. What is required for our continued existence on this planet is a combination of power with control and intelligence with wisdom.

References

1. cf. The Bible, Genesis I, 29 and IX, 1-3.
2. cf. Sen, A., *On Economic Inequality* (OUP, 1973), and *Famine and Poverty: An Essay on Entitlement and Deprivation*, (OUP, 1981).
3. cf. Frankena, W.K., 'Ethics and the Environment' pp. 3-20 in *Ethics and Problems of the 21st Century*, K.E. Goodpaster and K.M. Sayre (eds.), Univ. of Notre Dame Press, Notre Dame, 1979.

4. Bentham, J., *Introduction to the Principles of Morals and Legislation*, Stafner Press, NY (1789), 1948, chap. 17 fn.
5. cf. Swami Vivekananda, *Karma-Yoga*, Advaita Ashrama, Cal. 1997 ed. p. 72.
6. cf. Schweitzer, A., *Civilization and Ethics* (Part II of *The Philosophy of Civilization*, tr. C.T. Campion,. 2nd ed., London, 1929, pp. 246-47.
7. cf. Leopold, A., *A Sand County Almanac: With Essays on Conservation from Round River*, NY: Ballentine Books, 1966.
8. cf. Rolston III, H., *Environmental Ethics: Duties to and Values in the Natural World*, Philadelphia, PA: Temple Univ. Press, 1988.

Eighteen

Role of the Market in the Health Sector

Prajna Shrivastava

Introduction

Health is an important measure of Human Development.

— Editor

The concept of human development is much wider and richer than can be perceived in the common usage of the word. It means the final goal of human life. The oriental thinking, as evident from the Indian scriptures, reveals that people are born on the earth with a definite goal. That goal is called self-realization or knowing thyself. The more a person comes nearer to this truth, the more developed he is. Human development is thus the perception of the goal with which a person is born. For the realization of that goal a person may adopt any number of means. It may be that while attaining the goal of development one may be lost in the intricacies of means; or the means may become the end unknowingly. If a person attains the goal of self-realization he may become a developed human being. There are examples of developed human beings like Sri Aurobindo and Swami Vivekanand. Unlike common human beings they were great souls. The question before us is how a common person can realize that higher level of consciousness. Lord Buddha, Lord Mahavir and Mahatma Gandhi showed us that path through a high level of tolerance and the nation of 'forget and forgive'.

The UNDP Index of Human Development

The western philosophy of human development has been embodied in the UNDP concept of human development that has led to the development of an index of human development (HDI). This index has ranked the countries of the world on the basis of three indices, e.g. life expectancy, adult literacy and income levels. Amartya Sen analysed the spirit of HDI in terms of 'capabilities' and 'functionings' of human beings (Sen 1987). Later on, Sudhir Anand and Amartya Sen suggested the division of all countries into three groups — low, medium and high levels of human development (Anand & Sen 1993). In the low group the first variable was life expectancy; the medium group included life expectancy and under-5 mortality in the first place along with two other variables, and in the high group was added maternal mortality along with the remaining two. The authors have thus analysed different set-ups for high, medium and low level countries of the world. It means that all countries of the world cannot be measured with the same yardstick of development and that the level of development may not be expected to be the same. In addition, it shows that the component of health, as described above, remains significant at all levels.

References

Anand S. and Sen A. (1993), *Human Development Index: Methodology and Measurement,* UNDP Occassional Papers No. 8.

Sen, A. (1987): The Standard of Living, (ed. G. Hawthorn), Cambridge University Press, Cambridge.

Nineteen

Good Governance

Neelam Trivedi

Spirituality in governance is necessary for human development. Ancient Indian culture has much to offer in this context, as it emphasises the relevance of spiritual thinking and practice in various aspects of human life.

—Editor

At the beginning of the third millennium AD, humanity stands in a situation of extraordinary challenge and openness. The forces of the techno-scientific economy are threatening the very foundation of human life, giving rise to ever more complex social, political and moral questions. At the same time, the old ideas and institutions that have served humanity so well over the past several centuries in its task of survival and advancement seem increasingly irrelevant, unimportant or even counter-productive. People are abandoning old loyalties and building new allegiances shaped by rapidly shifting ideas and hopes.

The model of political authority that is emerging is based on the idea of global responsibility and governance. The 1990s saw a remarkable series of world conferences convened by the United Nations, all addressing problems of a global magnitude. These focused on issues of global well-being and sought to identify ways to link the problems people face at the community level with policies and actions at the international level. The basic argument has been that the world is facing problems that cannot be resolved with action only at the national level. The conferences have dealt with interrelated issues such as environmental protection, well-being of children, human rights and the rights of women, population, unemployment, crime, trade, food security and human settlement.

The call for a 'common framework' for the various initiatives reflects the growing convergence of views that democracy, development and respect for human rights and fundamental freedoms are all interdependent and mutually reinforcing.

The Search for Common Values

It is against this backdrop that the search for common values must be seen.

The report of the Commission on Global Governance in 1995 came out strongly for a 'global civic ethic' as the foundation for cooperation among different societies and cultures facing common global problems. Such a global ethics comprises a common moral minimum of core values shared by all cultures and religious traditions and a set of rights and responsibilities constituting a 'civic code' based on these core values. These values include : respect for life, liberty, justice and equity, mutual respect, caring and integrity. The report also presents a list of rights and responsibilities based on these core values and representing the minimum basis for progress in building a global civil society.

The Spiritual Dimension of Good Governance

Although spirituality is supposed to be an integral part of our religious traditions and beliefs, its secular dimension is crucial in governance.

Indian culture leads in understanding the fascinating aspects of human life, particularly the significance of spiritual thinking. Vedanta and the Upanishads represent our ancient seers' continuous search for knowledge. The vedantic tradition looks at life in this world and tries to find its underlying meaning. The *Rigveda* lays down the dual purpose of human life: we look forward for the emancipation of our souls and also the welfare of the world.

Another concept, which has been cherished thought the long history of our cultural and spiritual existence, is the concept of welfare of all human beings. *Bahujana sukhaya baujana hitayacha* — "the welfare of the many and the happiness of the many." This concept of the happiness of the many has been transformed into the area of public administration as the basic principle. Kautilya says in his *Arthasharstra*: "In the happiness of his subjects likes the king's happiness, in their welfare his welfare. He shall not consider as good only that which pleases him but treat as beneficial to him whatever pleases his subjects."

Two thousand years ago, Tiruvalluvar in Tamil Nadu dealt with the ethics of good administration in his *Thirukkural*. According to him, the king who administers justice and protects his people would be considered as God.

If there is one principle that is fundamental to ethics in administration in India, it is the principle of *dharma*, the principle of doing the right things, the principle of justice. The *Birhadaranyaka Upanishad* points out the basic principle that the responsibility of the king is to protect *dharma*. Only by protecting dharma all citizens get equal opportunities and the weak will not be exploited and harassed by the strong.

The ideal placed before individual was that for a higher or greater interest, lower or personal interest should be subordinated. This idealism is incorporated in a verse in *Hitopadesha*:

"Subordinate the interest of an individual for the sake of the family, of the family to sub-serve the interest of the village, of the village in the interest of the state, of all wordly interest inorder to attain eternal bliss", replacing the last which is concerned with the other world by the words, brings forth the ideas to be followed in the nation's interest.

There is a harmony between the individual and social goals in our tradition. It is this harmony that provides a meaningful basis for ethics in public governance. Every individual has to strive to achieve *moksha* — *aatmano mokshartham*. But at the same his other responsibility is the well-being of the man — *jagat hitayacha*.

The *Bhagawad Gita* is a practical guide for our life. The centrality of the dharma is emphasised by Lord Krishna in his famous observation in the third chapter of Gita — *swadharme nidhanam shreya para dharmo bhayapaha*. Manu is very clear on this subject. Everybody has a tendency to enjoy the material goods in life. It is only the fear of punishment that ensures order. There is hardly an individual in this world who on his own is pure in his conduct. The king's power to punish and teach the people in the righteous path, and the fear of punishment by the king yields wordly happiness and enjoyment.

Tiruvalluvar has also described the same concept of punishment beautifully. The process of the king removing the bad elements from the society, is like the farmer removing the weeds from the field to protect the crops.

The Karma of Public Officials

The term *karma* comes from Sanskrit language with the root *kri* which means "to do", but in its broadest sense it applies also the effects of such actions. The law of *karma* tells us that every action performed creates its own chain of reactions and events, some of which are immediately visible, while others may take a long time to surface. What is important to know is that a right action, generates beneficial results, while an unethical action leads to harmful effects. It is not easy to foresee the consequences of one's actions, but one should be ready either to overcome obstacles that arise due to those actions or to suffer the repercussions.

Once a *karma* has started, its impact will remain with us even though the person who started it all may be dead: his/her *karma* survives in the from of a consequence to the society or to a group of people. In the public domain, the Karma theory is particularly relevant as decisions made by public officials are interconnected to what happens within the society and sometimes even beyond a country's borders. Thus, when an action in the public domain has taken place, those who committed the deed may not face the consequences individually: nevertheless, someone else is going to be burdened with or benefiting from their actions.

By understanding the precepts and relevance of *dharma* and *karma*, a common strategy for public service spirituality and good governance can be developed. Such a strategy depends much upon how those public officials together (a) perceive a common future for their society; (b) act both individually and collectively towards protecting the common good; and (c) realize that they have a moral obligation to support the society's goal since their acts will have repercussions on the future of their society.

The Dharma of Public Officials

The following verse from the *Gita* denotes the role of spirituality in public affairs. Lord Krishna says: "O Partha. That understanding by which one knows that ought to be done and what ought not to be done, what is to be feared and what is not, what is obligatory and what is permitted, leads to the righteous path." (*Gita*, Chapter 18, Verse 30).

That righteous path in Hindu religion is called *dharma*. The term *dharma* can be translated to mean righteousness, a system of ethics and moral duty. A person performing a public duty may be capable of both the good and evil tendencies, so long as he/she remembers that it is his/her duty to sustain the general welfare of all peoples, he/she will act in a righteous manner. But those who deviate from that righteous path will surely endanger the state, and the result would be bad governance, as enunciated by Bhishma in Mahabharata: "The foundation for good governance is Dharma. The King, his ministers and state employees who have taken the oath of their offices to uphold Dharma and take care of the public must not act unjustly or unethically. Because if they do, they will not only destroy the moral basis of governance but in the end will take the state to hell." (Shanti Parva, Chapter 85).

For a public official to act in a righteous manner, it is important for him/her to act in the service of others and to avoid exploiting other human beings. A dharmic public official knows that his/her *dharma* enables him/her to serve others. In so doing, he will be fulfilling twofold duties: one to the self, whereby one seeks inner strength through spiritual actions, and the other to the community-at-large where one works for the common good.

Dharma can lead to mastery over our base characteristics such as greed, exploitation, abuse of power, and mistreatment of people. It requires self-discipline, humility, and above all awareness of the responsibility of holding a public office. Spirituality serves both as a model and operative strategy for the transformation of human character by strenghtening the will to serve the common people. It can provide the incentive for public officials to serve the public.

Toward a Spiritual Governance

The public wants that those offering their services to the state do not commit sinful acts. Ethical violation in public places are encouraged by the absence of fear of being caught, by a tendency to sidestep the voice of conscience, or by the view that if caught, there may be only a mild reprimand. The objective of good governance is to create an environment in which public servants as well as politicians in government are able to respond to the challenge of good governance. That challenge for public officials involves a notion of duty, as well as acting morally and accountably. If these two dimensions can be brought together in public service, it may become possible for a public servant to rise above self-interest. Such a notion creates a shared feeling of public duty among those who govern. This is the essence and basis of moral government.

We believe that by bringing together the domains of moral and procedural accountability, we wage a fight against corruption, mismanagement and bad governance. No nation or society, irrespective of its political and religious orientation, can survive in a spiritual or moral vacuum.

Good Governance in Mahabharata

Gita, an important part of the *Mahabharata*, is known as the source of spiritual thought. But other sections of the epic also throw light on ethical norms ɪor moral life. Some instances are provided below :

1. The eternal duties of kings are to make their subjects happy, to observe truth, and to act sincerely (Shanti Parva, Chapter LVIII, Verse 11).
2. A king guided by righteous conduct (*vyavahar shuddham*) and devoting his life in the service of his subjects acquires fame and immorality both here and hereafter (Shanti Parva, Chapter LXXXV, Verse 2).
3. The foundation of good governance is *dharma* (righteousness). The king, his ministers and state employees who have taken the oath of their offices to uphold dharma and to act in accordance with the common good, must not act unjustly or unethically so as to secure

their private good through selfishness. If they don't behave appropriately, they all will surely go to hell along with destroying the moral basis of governance (Shanti Parva, Chapter LXXXV, Verse 16-17).

4. The main purpose of a king is to protect *dharma* and to bolster righteousness, and to be free from indolence and desires. One should know that a king is the defender of all (lokasya rakshita): (Shanti Parva, Chapter XC, Verse 19).
5. The Lord of Creation, Brahma, has devised *dharma* for the care and well being of all. It is the duty of a king to follow and advance the dictates of dharma (Shanti Parva, Chapter XC, Verse 19).

In Anushasana Parva, Goddess Uma asks Lord Maheshwara to explain to her in detail what duties are assigned to the four castes of men. Lord Maheshwara replies :

1. From the beginning it has been said that the duties of the kshatriya is to protect all creatures. The king gets a fixed share of merits acquired by his subjects. By that means the king becomes gifted with righteousness (Anushasan Parva, Chapter CXLI, Verse 47).
2. The king who rules and protects his subjects piously, acquires, by virtue of the protection he offers to others, many regions of happiness in the next world (Anushasan Parva, Chapter CXLI, Verse 48).
3. Another duty of his is to give punishments proportionate to the offences committed. Properly judging the disputes of litigants before him, truthfulness of speech, and interference for helping the distressed, are the other duties by doing which the king acquires great glory both in this world and in the next (Anushasan parva, Chapter CXLI, Verse 51-53).

In Rajdharmaanushasan Parva, referring to the conduct by which a king can succeed, Bhishma says:

"There are 36 virtues, which a king should practice. He should follow his duties without any malice. He should cheerfully speak out what is pleasant and be brave without bragging. He should make alliances, but not with the wicked. He should never give out his purposes before the wicked persons. He should never inflict punishment without making proper enquiry. He should not entertain malice. He should without pride pay respect to worthy persons, and serve his preceptors and seniors with respect and sincerity. He should serve his elders with humility. He should never strike in ignorance. The king that behaves otherwise is visited by great calamities." (Rajdharmaanushasan Parva, Chapter LXX, Verses 2-11).

Concluding Observations

The essence and basis of the moral state depends on the triangle of those public policies and actions which ought to be undertaken (a) for the general welfare of society, (b) for mainaining and protecting the common good, and (c) securing universal care for all. However, these prerequisites enunciated in ancient times in all civilizations are sadly missing among the leaders and practitioners of governance. The need to operationalize this wisdom through spirituality in governance is imperative. In this task, both the secular and spiritual forces and institutions must work together rather than one fencing out the other. Good governance is not possible without bringing spirituality in the public domain. Although they have different perspectives (one dealing with life here and now, while the other striving for the life hereafter): nevertheless, both are essential for the common good and good governance.

Spirituality in governance means that officials must adhere to the principle of serving others by setting a high standard of moral conduct. Confidence and trust in the liberal democratic system can be safeguarded only when the governing process demonstrates a higher moral tone. The greatest challenge for liberal democratic governance is to rise above a prevailing ethical vacuum, which is a Western legacy to public administration.

Spirituality and governance both have to work together for the common good and good governance. The values of caring and respect for human dignity which are taught by various religious traditions can be our true guide to managing governance problems. It is this author's belief that by bringing spiritual and secular domains together that we can wage a good fight against corruption, mis-management and bad governance.

References

Apel, K.O., The Moral Imperative, *The UNESCO Courier: A Window Open on the World*, XLV, 7-8 July-August, 1992.

Becker, L.C., ed. *Encyclopedia of Ethics*, Garland Publ., New York, 1992.

Bok, Sissels, *Common Values*, University of Missouri Press, Missouri, 1995.

The Commission on Global Governance, *Our Global Neighborhood*, Oxford University Press, Oxford, 1995.

Edwards, Paul, ed. *Encyclopedia of Philosophy*, MacMillan, New York, 1967.

Fleischacker, Samuel, *The Ethics of Culture*, Cornell University Press, Ithaca and London, 1994.

Kung, Hans and Karl-Joseph Kuschel, *A Global Ethic: The Declaration of the Parliament of the World's Religions*, Continuum Publishing Company, 1993.

Schmidt, Helmut, Letter Accompanying 'A Declaration of Human Responsibilities, Proposed by the Inter Action Council', Sept. 3, 1997.

Rio Declaration on Environment and Development, in *Agenda 21*, Published by the United Nations, F. 91.I.11, New York, 1993.

Our Global Neighborhood: Report of the Commission on Global Governance. Oxford University Press, New York, 1995.

Aquinas. St. Thomas, *De perfectione vitae spiritualis*, quoted by Michael A. Smith, 'The Common Advantage and Common Good', *Laval theologique et philosophique*, 1995 (Vol. 51 : 1. pp. 121).

Dwivedi, O.P., Moral Dimensions of Statecraft : A Plea for an Administrative Theology, *Canadian Journal of Political Service*, 1987 (vol. 20 : 4 pp. 699-700).

Dwivedi, O.P., 'Common Good and Good Governance', *Indian Journal of Public Administration*, 1998 (vol. 44. 3 July-September, pp. 253-264).

Dwivedi, O.P. and James Iain Gow, *From Bureaucracy to Public Management: The Administrative Culture of the Government of Canada*, Broadview Press, Peterborough, Canada, 1999.

Frederickson, H. George, *The Spirit of Public Administration*, Jossey-Bass Publishers, San Francisco, CA, 1997.

Hyden, G. and M. Braton (eds.) *Governance and Politics in Africa*. Lynne Rienner, Boulder Co., USA, 1993.

Simon, Yves R., *Philosophy of Democratic Government*, Notre Dame, USA, 1993.

Willa Bruce, Willa and John Novinson, 'Spirituality in Public Service : A Dialogue', *Public Administration Review*, 1999 (vol. 59. 2 March-April. pp. 163-169).

Vittal, N., Central Vigilance Commissioner, Talk delivered at the IMA Seminar on 13.03.2002, Chennai.

World Bank, *The World Development Report*, The World Bank, Washigton DC, 1992.

Part Three

Human Development Index

Twenty

Values and Character

Onkar Nath Tiwari

True development consists of values and character. Income, education and health per se are not central to human development.
— Editor

Human development (HD) cannot be easily defined because of its complex and dynamic character. HD is a comprehensive economic, social, cultural, anthropological and political process. However the religious component of the development, which has equal meaning, has been ignored. Any developmental process involves active participation of the people. The question is, to which factor should we attribute development — the activities, freedom of participation, fair distribution of the benefits or enjoyment of these benefits. The conservatives dwell heavily on abstract notions. They believe in the intrinsic aspect of the development. They see development as enlightened inner self — as ethical values, morals and auto-limitation or self-generated delimited human satisfaction. The other group generally called as modernist talks in terms of determinism in the form of parameters. Development is determined by some extraneous physical or material factors — the availability of these constituting elements in upward movement of human development.

Human rights activists talk only in terms of the availability of its constituting elements. Right to development is today formally accepted as an inalienable right of mankind as a whole regardless of region, religion, caste and creed (General Assembly Resolution No. 41/128, Dec. 4, 1986).

We find a conflict between the modern approach and the 'conservative' or sanatana view. In this article a modest effort has been made to delineate the Sanatan view of development.

II

The term 'Development' derives its force from the attitude, desires and social phenomena. It has never been considered in isolation from prevalent human values.

The sanatana viewpoint is one of values and ethics which guide the entire gamut of human living, thinking and perceptions. Russel contends — "Human society is ethical not political". This holds much strength in the view of the sanatanis. Ethical thinking gives birth to values. Value development is closely related to personality development. Ethics or values emanate from one's inner-self although may factors shape and re-shape them in one's life.

Buddha's Dhammapada says : "Our life is shaped by our minds; we become what we think; suffering follows an evil thought as the wheels of the cart follow the oxen that draw it."

The entire emphasis is on the individual's value-based inner thinking. According to Dada Dharmadhikari the values must be natural to the temperament of the man — Unchangeable, Comprehensive, Universal, Independent and Permanent.

In the Sanatan view development is not seen as craving for material things or possession of the things to feel satisfied, feel pleasure, be human and be ethical. Man has to look into his self and that is the only index of development.

According to sanatanis development is to develop the inner self to a level where pleasure and pain, rather the possession of objects, becomes insignificant. However, to develop one's self or the mind to such an extent is difficult. This is the stage of being sthitpragya or 'neutral' as said in the Gita by Lord Krishna.

III

Values govern the life of an individual and individuals make up a society. When values are self-centred they make a society which is transitory. When values are other than ego-centric they help to build up a society which has its roots in permanence. The most predominant colours the civilisation for centuries.

Those values which lead man towards humanism are the ones to be maintained; those that relegate man to the animal state have to be discarded. The prevailing school of economic thought is based on profit, price, purchasing power, foreign trade, accumulation of wealth beyond one's need and capacity and luxury consumption. Dehumanised development of an individual is the hallmark of the present civilization. There is even a tendency to treat with contempt any mention of human or spiritual values. It is shocking that values of a temporary nature are being promoted even by great scholars. All evaluation is based on the touchstone of 'will it pay?' or 'how much will it pay?'

IV

Does the owning of wealth, luxury goods, plenty of food, multistoried buildings, money in banks, higher education that generates paper qualifications, etc, constitute development? The present era evaluates human development without looking into the inner psyche of the human being. The acquisition of power is the guiding factor of development. Various reports try to ascertain development merely on these lines without any concern for what may be termed 'humanism'. Indexing of development has little concern with man's actual happiness. Indexing is determined by the extraneous measurable items. The advancement of human being is judged by his material possessions, standard of living, educational qualifications and so on. But one cannot measure the level of happiness and joy by the availability of these things.

V

Real development should be judged by the development of values and character in an individual. A society which always hankers for acquisition of material things cannot be said to be developed. A valueless society cannot prevail for long.

Development which does not respect religion, values, ethics, morals cannot be justified.

Sanatana approach to development is based on ethics of sacrifice — nishkam and nivriti. The three dharmas, i.e., kul dharma, varna dharma and lok dharma were the watchwords. Take less and give more, care for the society, have that much which is essential for the life, and sacrifice are a few criteria of the Sanatana approach to human development.

Twenty One

The Inner Self

S. P. Das Gupta

The concept of Human Development as propagated by UNDP fails to deal with the inner-self and related issues.

— Editor

What is Development?

The term 'development' has many connotations. In the usual sense of the word, development is gradual unfolding, or working out in full, like in natural growth or evolution. In a biological sense, development implies the complex process of natural growth and maturation that occurs in living organisms. It also entails some deliberately designed effort towards improvement of human activity. In the field of social sciences, we largely employ the word development in three broad senses, namely (1) philosophical or conceptual, (2) economic geographical, and (3) social or sociological. Let us deliberate upon some of these aspects in our ancient philosophical tradition.

According to the ancient system, sustainable social growth entails continuous production of wealth along with *pari passu* preservation and conservation of natural and human resources as per the doctrine of *yoga-ksema*, that is, literally, the system of value-additive production-cum-conservation. While modern science and efficient technology can lead to higher production, sustainable growth and development can only be achieved by adopting this traditional view of production-cum-conservation of the available natural and cultural endowments and equitable distribution of the same for welfare of all. As per the deterministic school of thought in geography, a community occupying certain territorial space depends for its sustenance upon the environmental resources available from the surroundings within the constraints prevailing in its natural habitats. Habitat, economy and society are intimately related to each other in an extremely complex format, peculiar to mankind and to all other higher order organic systems. Traditional wisdom of India never supports environmentally unsound and socially unequal developmental options.

While developing the available natural resources, it has to be ensured that the means of production adopted for the purpose do not inflict any serious or irreparable damage to the earth and to its component members. The basic principle of sustainable development has been nicely explained in the *Mahabharata* and in the traditional Smriti texts or the ancient law-books of India.

Doctrine of Abhyudaya-nihsreyasa

The ancient system of human resource development was a holistic one and its objectives were focused on the overall improvement of the intellectual make-up of the mind and on value-addition and value-reorientation. This will be evident from the following four objectives of human resource development formulated by Indian traditional thought:

(1) Generation of mass awareness for sustenance of the world-order (*loka-samgraha*), based on dissemination of knowledge and wisdom.
(2) Attainment of wealth, prosperity and exaltation (*abhyudaya* or *abhi-vriddhi*) of individuals, based on permanent value-orientation and intellectual development. A great deal can be attained by way of all-round development (*abhyudaya*) if people learn to work together (*loka-samgraha*) in peace and harmony.
(3) Attainment of knowledge which brings about the highest beatitude and human liberation (*nihsreyasa*) in the inner substratum of human consciousness or human spirit.
(4) Development of a sense of overall physical and ethical well-being and mental peace (*hita-prapti* and *santi*) for all members of the habitat.

The foremost aim of human development is to train people

in such a fashion that they will acquire an urge to rigorously maintain the social order and prevent the break-up of societies. *Loka-samgraha* entails inter-connectedness of the society and unity of the world. A well co-ordinated system of broad-based value education has to be designed to achieve both material wealth (*abhyudaya* or *abhi-vriddhi*) and real spiritual well-being (*nihsreyasa*).

Doctrine of Yoga-ksema

"One must strive hard for generating sufficient wealth, which has not been acquired so far, and also strive for conserving the available resources with utmost zeal. Whatever resource is thus conserved has to be developed further" — states the *Manu smriti* (7/99). It also says whatever "wealth is produced therefrom should then be properly distributed to the deserving persons and to the rightful places." Precisely this is what is known in Indian ethics as the famous doctrine of *yoga-ksema*, that is, the principle of continuous development-cum-conservation of resources. The concept of ecological development of natural resources is in-built in the ancient Indian principle of yoga-ksema. It goes without saying that the world environmental climate would certainly have been much better if we could have followed the above dictum of equitable distribution of resources.

Human Development

There are two dimensions of human development — physical and mental or spiritual — which can be achieved by mental concentration (*samadhi*) and by application of sciences (*vidya*).

While *yoga-ksema* will entail increasing production of goods and services, continued conservation of material wealth and human resources would lead to repeated replacement and recycling of resources *ad infinitum*. The principle of *abhyudaya*-cum-*nihsreyasa* would bring about true exaltation of human life and bliss (*cidananda*) of spiritual liberation (*nihsreyasa*) on the other.

A look at the human development index devised by the UNDP reveals that India is lagging far behind compared to other developing countries. We must pay attention to educational development and health care of the nation and put the people on the path of righteousness (*dharma*) to make India a really strong country.

Growth, Development and Well-being

Technically speaking, 'growth' means higher production, leading to increase in major economic aggregates like national income, consumption, employment, etc. But development demands more than mere material growth. 'Development' truly implies substantial improvement in the social relations as well. Obviously, development implies much higher labour productivity, better management, improvement in human resources, etc.

We need to change over to new technological options in such a manner as to develop the economic and the human resources and improve upon the same without destroying the available natural endowment base. How will it be possible? Let us spell out some of the ideas:

(1) The pattern of economic growth must be compatible with the natural milieu and ecology.

(2) The technological means of production adopted for the purpose must be benign and eco-friendly so as to bring about minimum amount of waste products. There should be neither over-exploitation of the natural resources nor their under-utilization.

(3) In developing natural resources a holistic approach has to be adopted than the existing reductionist or partial attitude. After all, natural endowments are meant for all people and not for a fortunate few.

(4) None can develop in real terms merely by reducing the bounty of nature and by impoverishing the other sectors of the society.

Current Concept of Development

During the 1990s, a new concept of human development has evolved and it is unfolding itself at the global level. It largely corroborates with the ancient Indian concept of *abhyudaya-nihsreyasa* and the doctrine of *yoga-ksema*. The concept of human development is as follows:

> ....the basic objective of human development is to enlarge the range of the people's choices to make development more democratic and participatory. These choices should include access to income and employment opportunities, education and health, and a clean and safe

> physical environment. Each individual should also have the opportunity to participate fully in community decisions and to enjoy human, economic and political freedoms.

One can see here a clear parallel with the ancient Indian goal for attaining human liberty or freedom (*nihsreyasa*). High levels of human development are sought to be achieved within the framework of high levels of freedom of social choice or human liberty (*nihsreyasa*). The second Human Development Report (1991) rightly emphasizes:

> Men, women and children must be the centre of attention — with development woven around people, not people around development. Moreover, development must be participatory, and for this, people must have the opportunity to invest in the development of their capabilities — in health, education and training. They must also have the opportunity to put their capabilities to use — to be fully involved in all aspects of life, to express themselves freely and creatively. Thus construed, development will help enhance everyone's individual and social space — with two caveats. One is, the essence of society is not unrestricted satisfaction of individual choices, but the respect for everybody's potential, possibilities, needs and interests. The second is that the options for the present generation should not be increased by compromising the options for future generations. In short, development must be sustainable.

Human development cannot take place under an environment of *adharma* or lawlessness. People must have easy access to opportunities of education and enhancing their capability to carry out fruitful work for the society. Thus health, education, a good physical environment and human freedom are important parameters of development of the human soul. The key word is development of the individual and not mere economic growth in terms of gross national product. The ancient Indian motto has been — 'development of the people, development by the people, and development for the people'. Human development is not merely 'human resource development' as such or the enhancement of the educational facilities alone. It is much more than that, encompassing the health component of the people and freedom of having own choice in all matters of importance, which are also equally vital components of human development. It is neither the question of mere *garibi hatao* or poverty alleviation. For such development economic growth is also essential, but under a different perspective altogether. The Human Development Report 1991 of the UNDP rightly said:

> Human development requires economic growth - for without it, no sustained improvement in human well-being is possible. But while growth is necessary for human development, it is not enough. High growth rates do not automatically translate into higher levels of human development. And firm policy action is required to forge a close link between economic growth and human development. Just as economic growth is necessary for human development, human development is critical to economic growth. This two-way link must be at the heart of any enlightened policy action.

The Human Development Report emphasised the need for planned generation of *artha* or material wealth for enhancing the human development (*abhyudaya*) as per ancient Indian principles.

Human development has been described by the UNDP (2000) as a "process of enlarging people's choice. Enlarging people's choice is achieved by expanding human capabilities and functionings. At all levels of development, the three essential capabilities of human development are for people to lead long and healthy lives, to be knowledgeable and to have access to the resources needed for a decent standard of living. If these basic capabilities are not achieved, many choices are simply not available and many opportunities remain inaccessible. But the realm of human development goes further; essential areas of choices, highly valued by peoples, range from political, economic and social opportunities for being creative and productive to enjoying self-respect, empowerment and a sense of belonging to a community."

While talking of capabilities, the focus is on the "functionings" that a person can or cannot achieve given opportunities he or she may have. Functionings refer to the various valuable things a person can do or be, such as living long, being healthy, being well nourished, mixing well with others in the community and so on. Income is certainly one of the main means of expanding choices and well-being. But it is not the sum total of people's lives.

Human Development Index

The Human Development Index (HDI) devised by Mahbub ul Haq measures the overall achievement in a country by stressing the basic dimensions of human improvement — (1) longevity, (2) knowledge and (3) a decent standard of living. UNDP has developed a composite index, known as the Human Development Index (HDI), which now largely corroborates with the ancient Indian concept and is principally based on the performance of a country in the field of education in terms of adult literacy, health care in terms of life expectancy, and the levels of national income. It is gratifying to note that several economists of this subcontinent were involved in devising this new socio-econometric Index of Human Development (HDI), notably late Mahbub ul Haq of Pakistan and the 1998 Nobel Laureate in economics, Professor Amartya Sen (1979, 1985, 1992) of India.

UNDP has emphasized on education and health instead of conventional indicators like the Gross National Product (GNP) as indicators of human progress. This is in agreement with the ancient Indian approach. UNDP has devised the human development index (HDI) to assess the development status of each nation of the world. The index is derived from three factors, namely:

(1) Life expectancy at birth in terms of years which indicates the health care status of the country;
(2) Percentage of adult population that are literate, which indicates the spread of education in a country; and
(3) Real Gross Domestic Product (GDP) per capita per annum in dollars adjusted in terms of its Purchasing Power Parity (PPP$).

The three parameters are first reduced in the form of indices and the average index is worked out by calculating the arithmetic mean. The index of a country can vary between zero and unity as per the following equation:

Human Development Index (HDI) = (life expectancy index + adult literacy index + gross domestic product index)/3

Each of the above three indices (longevity, education and GDP) is ascertained by finding the relation of the actual value with the maximum and the minimum values attainable. This is worked out with the following equation:

$$\text{Index} = \frac{\text{Actual value} - \text{Minimum value}}{\text{Maximum value} - \text{Minimum value}}$$

There has been considerable scepticism among economists and other social scientists about the efficacy of the index used in the Human Development Reports. It is indeed impossible to present in one simple number a complex reality in human development and deprivation. Human Development Index (HDI) is undoubtedly a very limited indicator of development. But the old and hackneyed economic concept, the Gross National or Domestic Product (GNP or GDP), is much more crude as an index for the measure of economy. Mahbub ul Haq indeed was frank enough to say, "We need a measure of same level of vulgarity of GNP — just one number — but a measure that is not as blind to social aspects of human lives as GNP is." The Human Development Index (HDI) is a much better indicator of growth and development than mere GNP or GDP.

The measuring rod for GNP or GDP is obviously money. However, the fact remains that money cannot buy everything one needs and some of the most important aspects of life such as a long life and good education can also be achieved without necessarily having a lot of money or high income. It is important to recognize the great achievements made in various countries in these areas.

There are also other aspects of health and education not captured in the Human Development Index (HDI), such as health care for non-life-threatening conditions and quality of education. There are also many other important aspects of life not captured in the HDI or its components such as the issues concerning security, people's participation and environment.

For the first time, in the process of making international comparisons of income levels, an effective use has been made of the Purchasing Power Parity (PPP) concept instead of the usual market exchange rates of currencies in working out the Human Development Index. When comparing the internal purchasing power of incomes, this PPP approach is now an accepted method.

The matter is still debated upon by many but one cannot use income to compare people's standards without also considering the prices they are paying for goods and services they consume. In any case, GDP per capita is not an adequate summary of human life.

It is, however, well recognized that in actual terms, the concept of human development is much broader than the crude Human Development Index as such. It is virtually impossible, perhaps, to come up with a really comprehensive measure, even with a more comprehensive set of parametric indicators, for many vital dimensions of human development are not quantifiable.

TABLE 1
HUMAN DEVELOPMENT IN INDIA AND A FEW OTHER COUNTRIES, 1993

Rank	*Country*	*(1)*	*(2)*	*(3)*	*4)*
	Countries with high human development (HDI > 0.8)				
1	Canada	77.5	99.0	5,947	0.951
2	U S A	76.1	99.0	5,973	0.940
3	Japan	79.6	99.0	5,947	0.938
4	Netherlands	77.5	99.0	5,931	0.938
5	Norway	77.0	99.0	5,946	0.937
	Countries with medium human development (HDI = 0.5 - 0.8)				
58	Brazil	66.5	98.7	5,500	0.796
82	Korea Rep.	71.2	95.0	3,000	0.714
89	Sri Lanka	72.0	89.6	3,030	0.698
108	China	68.6	80.0	2,330	0.609
126	Papua N. G.	56.0	70.5	2,530	0.505
	Countries with low human development (HDI < 0. 5)				
133	Myanmar	57.9	82.4	650	0.451
134	Pakistan	61.8	36.4	2,160	0.442
135	India	60.7	50.6	1,240	0.436
143	Bangladesh	55.9	37.0	1,290	0.365
174	Niger	46.7	12.8	790	0.204

Key: (1) Life expectancy at birth in years
(2) Adult literacy rate in per cent
(3) Adjusted real Gross Domestic Product (GDP) per capita in terms of purchasing power-parity-Dollars (PPPS); and
(4) Human Development Index (HDI) value.

Source: Human Development Report 1996.

The first Human Development Report published in 1990 came out after a period of great crisis in which the concern for people gave way to concern for balancing the budgets and payments. So, the Report met a felt need and was widely welcomed. Since then, the annual Human Development Reports have evoked considerable academic discussion in journals and meetings at different levels. The central concern of the Human Development Reports has since been 'people'. Thus, economic growth, per se, has now been put into its proper perspective. Growth is to be regarded as a means — an important one at that — to serve human ends. But it is not an end in itself. Unless societies recognize that their real wealth is their people, excessive obsession with the creation of material wealth can obscure the ultimate objective of enriching human lives.

The human development approach has tremendous potential for analyzing situation and policies at the national or state level. Many of India's states are large enough to have immense internal diversities in terms of population, resource distribution and regional disparities. The government of Madhya Pradesh was first to come with a state level human development report in 1995 and thereafter in 1998. This helped bring out concern for development into political process and in the state planning effort. As a result, social services, for example, now account for more than 40 per cent of the plan investment, compared with 14 per cent in the previous plan budget. In 1999, Rajasthan, Gujarat and Karnataka followed suit in formulating their own state human development reports.

Parameters of Human Development

Sustainable development can be realized in terms of human development. Its structure may be reduced down to three basic parameters as described earlier. The action required to be taken in this regard can be put down under three steps as detailed below:

(1) Improvement in the spread of literacy and general education within the concerned population;
(2) Improvement in the health care system, so as to raise the expectancy of life span of an individual at birth; and
(3) Improvement in the rate of production of goods and

services per person through appropriate technology and by environmentally viable means.

The only other factor which has to be added and firmly kept in mind as the fourth vital factor is :

(4) improvement in attaining purity of mind, sense of security, peace and stability of the societal structure in which an individual lives and operates.

Ancient Indian Approach

Now let us look into the modern concept of human development a little more closely in the light of ancient Indian approach. The addition of literacy and longevity to the GDP factor yields a somewhat more comprehensive yet a very simple indicator of social development, this small modification is not enough to fulfil the objectives of human development. Greater production or higher GDP per capita eventually leads to wanton wastage and depletion of natural resources and infringement on the human rights. It can lead to unhealthy growth which can trigger off terrible competition, greater concentration of power and even to violence, as the history of human civilization has indicated many a time. The upshot is that higher GDP per capita may lead to *inhuman* development.

Let us look into the ancient Indian attitude towards what is the aim or the objective of life. According to our system (1) righteous deed (*dharma*), (2) mobilization of all available resources (*artha*), (3) dutiful fulfilment of human requirements (*kama*) and (4) attainment of the freedom of choice (*moksa*) are the standard fourfold aspects of life's ends (*purusartha*). This wonderful four-fold (*caturvarga*) scheme of life fulfils the material, spiritual and idealistic craving of man. The only way to attain it is to develop a strong sense of individuality, rational attitude, firm character and manhood of each person.

We have to look into the quality aspect of the general public education instead of simply the number of literates produced every year. In ancient India, education (even though at largely an informal system of deliverance) was widespread so that almost all persons in the kingdom of Ayodhya, for example, were well versed in their respective branch of life. At that period of time, the public education system was so designed that a learner had to pick up not only the science of the fundamentals of things (*vastu-tantra*) but also the basics of the great science of human choice (*purusa-tantra*).

One has to develop the mental faculties to be able to exercise right choices through application of human science (*purusa-tantra*). Purusa-tantra "enables a person to do or undo a thing or to do it otherwise, at will" — has been wonderfully enunciated by Sankaracharya in his interpretation of the Brahma-sutra (1/1/4 *Bhasya*). Thus, purusa-tantra empowers a person to adequately exercise his freedom of choice.

According to the Vedantic thought (*Brahma-sutra* 3/4/5 1), appropriate knowledge can only remove all the obstructions to economic growth and lead to attainment of power (*Adidevananda* 1977). It has been aptly said in the *Chhandogya Upanishad* (1/1/10) — "Only that which is performed with knowledge, conviction and concentration of mind, that alone becomes more and more powerful (*viryavattaram*)."

Material economic growth along with appropriate attitude was seen as imperative. Despite high achievement in application of science, spiritual insufficiency is now crippling us. It has been said in the Vedantic injunction(*Svetasvatara Upanishad* 6/20) — "Men may even roll up the entire firmament, just like a sheet of parchment, still there will be no end of sorrow for them without realizing the luminous source of enlightenment (which lies in one's heart of hearts)."

So, besides production of great amount of material wealth and well-being, there is an absolute need for development of the real human spirit to an adequate level of excellence (*sreyas*) which would lead man to the final liberation (*nihsreyasa*) of the inner self in man. In the first instance, we need to have an-enormous army of young men and women of high determination and great organizing capability. The characteristics of such people have been wonderfully set forth in the following Vedantic passage, enunciated in the *Taittiriya Upanishad* (2/8/1-2), which is a treatise on ancient Indian education system, in a straight-forward language —

> Let there be a young person, excellent and lovely in youth (*sadhu-yuva*), and a great student (*adhyayaka*). Let him be

most efficient in action (*asistha*), most strong-hearted (dridhistha), and be most stoutly built (*balistha*). For him this whole earth will be full of wealth. This is the measure of bliss for one human being. That human bliss, multiplied hundred fold is one unit of measurement of bliss of such persons who have turned into human angels, and so also of the followers of knowledge and wisdom (*srotriyasyaca*), unaffected by desires (*akama-hatasya*)."

This can be achieved by not merely having a good public health service system, but also by making persons follow a contented and tension-free life under a total security cover. It is not a question of how high a proportion of the country's GDP is allocated in the budget for maintaining a hard-to-operate public health service system. It is a matter of how efficiently yet simply and inexpensively a community can live in tune with nature. Frankly speaking, this is non-quantifiable and cannot be wrapped up within a single statistical figure to indicate the level of human development in a country.

The Future Outlook

The paradigm shift at the international level in favour of sustainable environmental development is still in the making. But the general consensus is that development must be people-oriented, equitably distributed and environmentally as well as socially sustainable. New evidence suggests that growth of gross domestic product and equity need not necessarily be contradictory goals. There is strong evidence to show that investment in ecological designs and true human development has been in many a country a springboard for sustainable economic growth. True human development should be kept as the end in view, while the economic growth should be designed to act as a means for that only, while keeping the environment intact.

The aim of sustainable development should be focused on human development through viable economic growth, expansion of education and better health services. How should we get over the ever-widening chasm between the haves and the have-nots of the world? Possibly, the answer lies in promoting eco-friendly traditional skills in different sectors of the economy based on the principles of *abhyudaya*-cum-*nihsreyasa* and *yoga-ksema,* aided by adoption of modern technology. *Yoga-ksema* will entail increasing production of goods and services and conservation of material wealth leading to replacement of resources ad infinitum. At the same time, the principle of *abhyudaya*-cum-*nihsreyasa* would bring about true exaltation and bliss of spiritual liberation.

References

Abid Hussain (1997), 'Science and Technology, a future perspective', Jawarharlal Nehru Birth Centenary Award Lecture (1997), in *Everyman's Science*, Indian Science Congress Association, Volume 32, Number 4, 1998, pp. 158-166.

Adidevananda, Swami (1977), *Brahma-sutras, Sri-bhasya*, Part II, Advaita Ashrama, Kolkata, pp. 434-435

Bose, A. N. (1997), 'Fifty Years of Independence' and 'A Search for an Alternative' in *Fifty Years of India's Freedom*, edited by K. Raghavendra Rao, Ashok K. Maiti, Debabrata Panda, and N. P. Chaubey, Indian Academy of Social Sciences, Allahabad, pp. 116-133

———, (1999), 'India: the Changing Environment in Fifty Years' in *Man and Environment*, Volume 10, edited by S. P. Das Gupta, Center for Study of Man and Environment, Kolkata, pp. 51-59

Das Gupta, S. P. (1997), 'Sustainable Ecological Development: Fifty Years after Freedom of India' in *Fifty Years of India's Freedom*, ed. by Raghavendra Rao et al., Indian Academy of Social Sciences, Allahabad, pp. 70-86

———, (2000 a), 'The Theory of Development' in *Geography and Sustainable Development*, Proceedings of the Seventh Refresher Course in Geography, Calcutta University, ed. S. C. Mukhopadhyay, 2-23 February 2000, pp. 1-7

———, (2000 b), 'Traditional Indian Concept of Sustainable Ecological Development' in *Geography and Sustainable Development*, Proceedings of the Seventh Refresher Course in Geography, Calcutta University, ed. S.C. Mukhopadhyay, 2-23 February 2000, pp. 11-13

———, (2000 c), 'Modern Ideals of Human Development' in *Geography and Sustainable Development*, Proceedings of the Seventh Refresher Course in Geography, Calcutta University, ed. S. C. Mukhopadhyay, 2-23 February 2000, pp. 19-31

Gandhi, M. K. (1956), *Ruskin: Unto this Last: a Paraphrase* translated from Gujarati by V. G. Desai, Navajivan Publishing House, Ahmedabad, pp. 61, 67-68

Hempel, Lamont C. (1997), *Environmental Governance, the Global Challenge*, Affiliated East-West Press Pvt. Ltd, New Delhi, p. 72

Kumarappa, J. C. (1948), *Economy of Permanence (A Quest for a Social Order Based on Non-violence)*, with a foreword by M. K. Gandhi, Sarva-Seva-Sangh Prakashan, Varanasi, 5th edition, pp. iii, 177

Ranganathananda, Swami (1996), *Democratic Administration in the Light of Practical Vedanta*, Sri Ramakrishna Math, Madras, pp. 60-61, 99, 112, 117, 235.

Sen, Amartya (1979), 'Equality of What?', Tanner Lecture on Human Values at Stanford University, reprinted in Amartya Sen, Choice, Welfare and Measurement, Harvard University Press, Cambridge MA, 1992.

———, (1985), *Commodities and Capabilities*, North-Holland Publishing, Amsterdam.

———, (1992), *Inequalities Re-examined*, Harvard University Press, Cambridge MA.

Human Development Report Office on the UNDP (1990), *Human Development Report 1990*, Oxford University Press, New York.

———, (1991), *Human Development Report 1991*, Oxford University Press, New York, pp. 1-21.

———, (1996), *Human Development Report 1996*, Oxford University Press, New York, pp. 1-85.

———, (2000), *Human Development Report 2000*; Oxford University Press, New York

Vivekananda, Swami (1971), *Swami Vivekananda on India and her Problems*, compiled by Swami Nirvedananda, Advaita Ashrama, Kolkata, 6th impression, pp. 26, 35, 40, 64.

Twenty Two

Role of Spiritual Education in Human Development

Mukul Mukherjee

Education for human development must be understood as spiritual education.

— Editor

Ancient knowledge reveals that the purpose of birth of a soul in human form is very different from the birth in any other form. The ancient Indian literature shows that the human body and soul is acquired by a soul after it passes through 84 lakh body forms. These are called *'bhogas'*. The human body form is thus the most precious and the best evolved form of any being. The birth of a soul is purposive unlike the Western concept that the birth of man is accidental. It is only after achieving this body form that the soul can attain *nirvana* or *moksha*. It is therefore expected that while living in this form the most sensible act would be to achieve the goal of nirvana. The extent to which one is nearer or farther from this goal is supposed to be the measure of how developed a human being is.

The Modern Perspective

The modern perspective of human development considers an all-round development of individuals. Man needs education which helps in securing the needs of body, mind and soul. Human form exists at these three levels and the educational system has to cater to the needs at these three levels. The present education system, however, has failed to meet these expectations.

The Human Development Report 2000 of the UNDP combines human development with human rights and emphasises:

* Bold new approaches are needed to achieve the realisation of human rights in the 21st century adapted to the opportunities and realities of the era of globalisation.
* Human development and human rights are close enough in motivation and concern to be compatible and congruous and they are different enough in strategy and design to supplement each other fruitfully.
* The parallel movements for human rights and human development have had distinct traditions and strategies. United in a broader alliance, each can bring new energy and strength to the other.

This balanced report shows the futility of the often politically-motivated debate which has in the past pitted countries against each other, one group arguing that civil and political rights are a pre-condition to development and another maintaining that such rights were the fruit of economic development and could not precede it.

A human rights approach to development accords the highest priority to poverty elimination, integration of women and vulnerable groups in the development process, and to self-reliance and self-determination of peoples and governments, including the rights of indigenous peoples. The Declaration on the Right to Development sees development as "a comprehensive economic, social, cultural and political process, which aims at the constant improvement of the well being of the entire population and of all individuals on the basis of their active, free and meaningful participation in development and in the fair distribution of benefits resulting therefrom."

The tremendous scientific and technological progress being made in present times calls for action to motivate development of human values and qualities along with ensuring economic prosperity. The need is to :

* Associate fully and actively non-state actors and the business community in the promotion, protection and realisation of human rights;
* Identify the different impact of international trade relations

on the enjoyment of human rights and find ways of taking advantage of the globalisation process to fulfil the human rights of the most deprived and vulnerable groups;

* Devise adequate and reliable tools for measuring progress in human rights and comprehensively integrate human rights assistance in development assistance programmes; and
* Address and counter the negative impacts of discrimination, inequalities and racism on sustainable human development.

Certain measures at the political, educational levels can ensure spiritual education and development.

* The voting age should be 25 years. This shall take away the political fervour out of our educational system. The involvement of students in politics has often proved a hindrance to the proper molding of their minds. Moreover, politicians should be put in the care of spiritual heads, and only on the recommendation of such highly evolved personalities should they be assigned responsibilities.
* Each teaching institution should be in the care of some spiritual organisation. It can be any institution that is beyond the fold of religion. The role of such an agency shall be pivotal. A parallel head as vice-chancellor should be there from such an organisation to guide at each level. Or it could be that already existing spiritual organisations be asked to take care of teaching institutions and to direct and guide them.
* There should be a compulsory paper on spiritual practice, necessarily to be attended and passed. Teachers be specially appointed with proper background for the purpose of teaching the course.
* A clear-cut distinction between spirituality and religion should be made. Spirituality begins where religion ends. This has to be understood. By spirituality we mean catering to the needs of the soul. Our prevailing systems do cater to the body, some of it to the mind too, but nothing for the soul. If a little effort is made on this aspect, I am sure we can achieve human development in the real sense at the global level.

* With a view to bring such a highly developed instrument at an optimum level of performance a right kind of a mix of a program is necessary. As in computers we are developing better and better software so we shall have to develop such packages (courses) that will suffice for the need of the human beings as per today's requirement.

Twenty Three

Rabindranath Tagore and Amartya Sen on Human Development

Ratan Lal Basu

Amartya Sen ignores the moral and ethical dimension of Human Development which was the main-stay of Rabindranath Tagore's approach.

— Editor

Introduction

Since the Nobel Prize in Economics was awarded to Amartya Sen there have been attempts to highlight Sen's Santiniketan background and the affinity of his world outlook with that of Tagore's. Unfortunately, a deeper analysis is likely to reveal that Amartya Sen's views (based on Western world-outlook) diametrically oppose Tagore's (based on ancient Indian world outlook), particularly as regards sustainable development and eco-ethical human living. This paper endeavours to highlight these contrasting aspects of the world-outlook of the two Bengalee Nobel laureates.

Tagore on Eco-Ethical Human Living

Rabindranath Tagore's world outlook as regards eco-ethical human living and sustainable development is scattered in various writings (a list is given under References). It is based on ancient Indian view, particularly as revealed in the Upanishads. Tagore considers nature and human life as integral parts of a single entity, the Omniscient, Omnipresent, Ubiquitous (*sarbang khallidang*) Attribute-free (*nirguna*) Brahman. Tagore emphasises symbiosis and balance between man and all other aspects of the material world (plants, other animals, the Earth, atmosphere and all that) and between man and the world beyond (moksha).

In *Aranya Devata,* (R.R. 14.373) Tagore writes that modern man indulges too much in luxurious and profligate living. So long as he used to live in and around the forest he had deep love and respect for the forest and used to live in perfect symbiosis with its plants and animals. As soon as he became a city-dweller he lost his love for the forest which was the source of his sustenance. Wanton destruction of forests in order to supply timber for the city life was a curse on human life. Scarcity of rainfall that resulted endangered human life and rapid spread of deserts engulfed human habitations in various parts of India. Tagore emphasises that we must retrieve our love and respect for the forest and restore symbiosis with the forest in order to save human civilization.

Tagore's views on ecological balance and symbiosis between man and nature have also been elaborated in the article 'Tapavan' (R.R. 7.690-704). The great philosopher-poet does not confine his analysis to the outward manifestations of ecological imbalance alone. He investigates the inner cause of this malady which springs from the *'ripus'* (basic vices) like greed, jealousy, lust etc., residing in the inmost recesses of the human mind. These ripus have their ugly manifestations in commercialism, consumerism and limitless competition. In the article 'Bilaser Fans' (R.R. 6.526-530), Tagore asserts the view that consumerism, which has been eating into the vitals of western societies, has been imported to our country and it has been spreading its horrible tentacles to all spheres of life in India. The motive of insatiable personal consumption has made people in our country lose their social entity and philanthropic attitude and has made most of them mean and self-centred. Pomp and conspicuous expenditure is not a new thing in India. In earlier times it was associated with social activities but now it is centred around purely personal consumption in isolation from the society. Consumerism is not only generating pressure on the purse of the rich but also causing unimaginable hardship to the poor who, goaded by the demonstration effect, are trying to spend beyond their means.

Tagore asserts the view (R.R. 6.529) that revelation of the dazzling wealth does not signify economic prosperity; it shows increasing concentration of wealth at the hands of a few at the cost of the majority.

As regards the perverse effects of competition which is a part of Western society (and is being encouraged in India in recent years), Tagore opines (R.R. 2.711): The motive of competition, which forces one into a mad race for outclassing all other persons around him, leads one to an endless struggle for supremacy and deviates him from the path of responsibility and ethical living. The demonic impulse for going farther and farther ahead knows no limit and makes one's mind ever restless and bereft of stability and peace. Tagore expresses pity for those who consider this mad race as prosperity. In contrast, Indian society, Tagore holds, was based on universal welfare and symbiosis between man and man. It never encouraged this self-destructive competition leading to infighting in human society for individual supremacy.

In 'Samabaya Niti' (R.R. 14.324), Tagore expresses the view that European society is based on the system of exploitation of the majority by the minority. This view is corroborated by Marx and Engels. Tagore admits that ego-centricism, pride, motive of self-advancement and competition within some limit are necessary for the material progress of human society. But if they go beyond limit (as has happened in modern life) they become destructive.

Thus, according to Tagore, eco-ethical human living should be based on symbiosis between man and nature, and between man and man. But manifestation of ripus (greed, lust, jealousy, etc.) through limitless competition, consumerism and commercialism have weakened this symbiosis alarmingly in the modern era. Unless we reverse this trend and restore the objective conditions for eco-ethical human living, the consequences would be perilous.

Tagore on Sustainable Development

Tagore's concept of sustainable development of India emphasises rural regeneration as majority of the population of India live in villages. It has two major planks:

(i) cooperatives; and

(ii) panchayats.

In both the cases, Tagore calls for revival of the spirit of the rural people so that they could be self-sufficient and free from dependence on outside assistance for their economic and social regeneration. Tagore emphasises generation of self-confidence and sense of unity in the minds of the rural people through proper education so that they could on their own remove the maladies afflicting rural India.

If co-operatives and panchayats are imposed on the rural people from outside (say, by the government, political parties or vested-interest groups) they would never be able to generate the process of sustainable development which is possible, according to Tagore, only by reviving the spirit of the rural masses so that they could form cooperatives and panchayats by their own efforts.

In 'Sambaya Niti' (R.R. 14.311-332), Tagore attributes agricultural backwardness of India to subdivision and fragmentation of agriculture plots, problem of marketing and storing, mechanisation of small farms, lack of finance and exploitation by moneylenders. Tagore thinks that all these problems could be solved through co-operatives. He emphasises that the root cause of rural destitution is the lack of self-confidence of the rural people which makes them dependent on outside help and the government. Our primary task is to make the rural people aware of their own strength which lies in unity of the rural people. Tagore stresses : "For this reason, the most urgent necessity in our country is not to place begging bowls at their hands, but to make them confident of their own strength, to make them realise that a man united with others is a complete entity, an alienated individual is but a fragment." (R.R. 14.313).

As regards panchayats, Tagore, in 'Atma Sakti' (R.R. 2.644), opines that the rural panchayat system imposed by the government would be a complete failure. It would engender jealousy and in-fighting among rural people (for the coveted panchyat posts). The members of the Panchayats would be interested in serving more the government officials than their rural brethren. They would virtually become instruments at the hands of the government to suppress rural people. So, panchayats ought to be formed by the rural people by their own efforts and are not to be thrust on them by the government.

Tagore always encouraged the application of modern science and technologies for revival of rural India, but all these should be within the framework of a regenerated rural society based on self-help and freedom from outside interference.

Now let us have a glimpse of Sen's ideas vis-a-vis Tagore's which have been elaborated above.

Tagore and Amartya Sen compared

Amartya Sen's world outlook, notwithstanding his Santiniketan background, springs from the Western paradigm. His major works (a list is given under References) bear testimony to the fact that unlike Tagore (who strongly held the Upanisadic view that ecology and development could by no means be treated in isolation from other aspects of human living and material manifestation of the ubiquitous Brahman), Sen treats ecology and sustainable development as extraneous elements amenable to treatment in the context of market mechanism. Sen treats in detail the problems associated with environment and ecology (1982: 67-68; 1984: 1995-97; 1995: 211-216) and considers these matters on the basis of Western paradigm associated with market mechanism, individual choice and Game Theory. This would be clear from the following excerpt (Sen 1982: 67-68):

> "Suppose it is the case that there are strong environmental reasons for using glass bottles for distributing soft drinks (rather than single-use steel cans) and for persuading the customers to return the bottles to the shops from where they buy these drinks (rather than disposing them off in the dustbin). For a relatively rich country, the financial incentives offered for returning the bottles may not be adequate if the consumers neither worry about the environment nor are thrilled by receiving back small change. The environment affects the life of all, true enough, but from the point of view of any one individual the harm that he can do to the environment by adding his bottles to those of others will be exceedingly tiny. Being generally interested in the environment but also being lazy about returning bottles, this person may be best if the others return bottles, next best if none does, and

> worst of all if he alone returns bottles while others do not. If others feel in a symmetrical way we shall then be in a prisoner's dilemma type situation in which people will not return bottles but at the same time all would have preferred that all of them should return bottles rather than none. To tackle this problem, suppose now that people are persuaded that non-return is highly irresponsible behaviour and while the individuals in question continue to have exactly the same view of their welfare, they fall prey to ethical persuasion, political propaganda or moral rhetoric. The welfare functions and the preference relations are still exactly the same and all that changes is behaviour.
>
> I am not, of course, arguing that a change in the sense of responsibility is the only way of solving this problem, penalizing non-return and highly rewarding return of bottles are other methods of doing this.... The real difficulty arises when the checking of people's actions is not easy.

As regards co-operatives, the following view of Sen as expressed in 'The Political Economy of Hunger (1995: 536) is worth quoting:

> In many countries, the main rural institutions set up by the administration and the political system have taken the form of co-operative structures.... It is no exaggeration to say that rural cooperatives, far from being partners or pressure groups with which the government has to negotiate, are in fact the lower elements of state apparatuses.

Although Sen's observation is related to Africa , the outcome observed is exactly what had been predicted long ago by Tagore in case of Indian cooperatives imposed by the government.

Unfortunately, however, Sen fails to unearth the real cause of failure of the cooperatives and attributes it, wrongly, to colonial legacy and technological backwardness. As solution he prescribes (pp 1995: 542-43): "More precisely, Africa has no choice but to generate and diffuse technological progress at a rate sufficiently rapid to cause regular increase in land productivity."

It is evident that the problems which Africa has to solve in order to trigger off new growth and development impulses in her agricultural sector do not lie wholly in technological sphere. Changes in institutions and in the cultural and political systems will also be required. Moreover, the levels of income and the food security of the smallholder majority in Africa will not be improved unless serious attention is paid to equity issues and distributive effects of agricultural growth-promoting strategies.

Thus, Sen's approach reduces to technological changes and policy measures from outside. The question of moral regeneration of rural mass is totally ignored. This is also evident from his view of technical model building in 'Resources, Values and Development' (1984: 37-89).

In 'On Economic Inequality' (1973), 'Poverty and Famines' (1981) and 'Hunger and Public Action' (1989), Sen has endeavoured to investigate the causes of human deprivation (as regards basic amenities like food, nutrition, health care, education, women's rights, etc.) and analysed them in terms of entitlements and capabilities. Various Human Development Indices (HDIs) have been constructed by the Pakistani Economist Mahbub ul Haq and the United Nations Development Programme (UNDP) on the basis of the concepts of Sen. Sen classifies human deprivations on the basis of these causes into three major groups as:

(i) Those caused by uncontrollable natural calamities like earthquakes, cyclones, etc.
(ii) Those caused by internal vices (*ripus*) of the sufferer.
(iii) Those caused by bad governance, social injustice and economic exploitation of the majority by the well-to-do minority.

Sen emphasises the third category, whereas Tagore would have given more importance to the second category. In an exchange based economy, a man collects his basic amenities through his basic capability, i.e. income ("Exchange Entitlements" according to Sen). Sen deals with, in detail, various human deprivations resulting from lack of capabilities and entitlements. These are the basis of all later deprivation indices constructed by Mahbub Ul Haq (Haq 1997), and the Human Development Reports published each year by the UNDP. According to Sen, policies of the governments of different LDCs and those of the world bodies (World Bank, etc.) are to be reoriented to eradicate human deprivation in various parts of the world. So, in essence, they propose that these authorities are to fill the begging bowls of the deprived. This is an approach most abhorred by Tagore.

It becomes clear that the endeavour to trace Tagorean world outlook (out of Nobel Prize euphoria) as regards eco-ethical human living and sustainable development in Amartya Sen's works, cannot stand close scrutiny. Tagore's world outlook springs from a balanced and perfect view as preached in the Upanishads, whereas Amartya Sen's world outlook is a follow-up of western parochial views sugar-coated with pseudo-humanitarian slogans.

References

Rabindranath Tagore

Rabindra Rachanavali (R.R), 125th Anniversary Education, 1986, Visva-Bharati Publishers Kolkata-17

(i) Vol II, Atmasakti, p. 617, Bharat Varsa, p. 695
(ii) Vol VI, Swadesh, p. 497; Samaj, p. 517; Bilaser Fans, p. 526; Shiksha, p. 563
(iii) Vol. VII, Dharma, p. 447; Santiniketan, p. 521; Tapavan, p. 690.
(iv) Vol. XIV, Samabaya Niti, p. 309; Palli Prakriti, p. 351; Aranya Devata, p. 372.

Amartya Sen

1. 1973, *On Economic Inequality*, OUP, New Delhi, 1999.
2. 1981, *Poverty and Famines*, OUP New Delhi, 1999.
3. 1982, *Choice Welfare and Measurement*, OUP, New Delhi, 1999.
4. 1984, *Resources, Values and Development*, OUP New Delhi, 1999.
5. 1987, *On Ethics arid Economic*, OUP, 1999.
6. 1987 A, *Commodities and Capabilities*, OUP, 1999.
7. 1989, (With Jeam Dreze) *Hunger and Public Action*, OUP, 1999.
8. 1992, *Inequality Re-examined*, OUP, 1999.
9. 1995, *The Political Economy of Hunger*, OUP, 2001.
10. 1996, (Editors : Tean Dreze and Amartya Sen) *Indian Development*, OUP, 1999.
11. 2000, *Development As Freedom*, OUP, 1999.

Others

1. Haq, Mahbub ul (1997), *Human Development in South Asia*, OUP, New Delhi.
2. Marx and Engels (1848), *Manifesto of the Communist Party*, Progress Publishers, Moscow, 1975.

Twenty Four

Moral and Spiritual Index of Human Development

N.M. Lall

A true measure of Human Development would encompass factors such as spiritual, ethical, mental and attitudinal developments.

— Editor

The UNDP defines human development as a process of enlarging peoples' choices, including the urge to live a long and healthy life, to be educated and to have access to resources needed for an adequate standard of living.[1] This approach has been built upon the premise that people are the ultimate beneficiaries of development. National income or economic growth are never automatically transformed into betterment of life. The attainment of high levels of income therefore, occupies a back-seat and is not very important. What is more important is how income is spent to benefit people. In an attempt to measure human development, UNDP has constructed a human development index focusing on the three essential elements of human life viz. longevity, knowledge and income.

Nobel Laureate Amartya Sen has given a new perspective of social choice in approaching human development, taking into account the role played by social, political and economic systems in shaping the social choice.[2] Sen's approach revealed by the Axiomatic Theory of Social Choice is based upon a critical analysis of the utilitarian philosophy and Pareto's negation of inter-personal comparisons of utility. Sen's postulate is more realistic and it has been associated with the ethical norm. This ethical norm has been associated further with the postulate of irreducible level of capabilities in operationalising the philosophy of egalitarianism in a purely democratic set-up. The constraint towards the practical application of social choice on account of Kenneth J. Arrow's 'Impossibility Theorem'[3] has been overcome by accommodating ethical and philosophical postulates. It is a unique social choice where the practical application depends upon the philosophical underpinnings. Sen draws attention to the fact that even a simple probabilistic model would tend to underestimate when compared with realistic presentation. In other words, he has enriched its analytical and conceptual significance by inventing the paradigm of human development oriented towards social choice.

This leads us to a model of sustainable development known as Sustainable Human Development (SHD). SHD stands for that development which generates not only economic growth but distributes its benefits equitably, regenerates the environment rather than destroying it, empowers people rather than marginalising them. The Vedic literature has a very unique role to play in propagation of the concept of SHD. Our Vedas are the only hope in the modern context. There is a need to develop a Vedic paradigm of human development based on SEMI-PACE indicators. SEMI-PACE signify as follows:

S = Index of Spiritual Development
E = Index of Ethical Development
M = Index of Mental Development
I = Index of Intelligential Development
P = Index of Physical Development
A = Index of Attitudinal Development
C = Index of Character Development
E = Index of Economic Development

It is essential to construct the concept of human development as given in the Vedas and attempt to prepare the Vedic paradigm of SHDI in contrast to the UNDP Human Development Index.

References

1. UNDP: *Human Development Report*, 1996 and 1997.
2. Sen, Amartya K.: *Collective Choice and Social Welfare*.
3. Arrow Kenneth J.: *Social Choice and Individual Values*.

Twenty Five

Aesthetic Views of Swami Vivekananda

Tapobrata Sanyal

Art is an integral part of Human Development.

— Editor

Aesthetics is the philosophy of fine arts, the cult of the beautiful. Before we deliberate upon the aesthetic views of Swami Vivekananda, the pertinent question that surfaces is — can a monk who has renounced the world be interested in aesthetics at all? The answer is 'yes' — especially in case of Swami Vivekananda who was a monk of a different sort. Swamiji, despite being a Vedantist to the core, was firm in his view that beauty and bliss are identical and the two culminate in Knowledge Absolute. To a Vedantist, this world is unreal, being susceptible to changes and destruction; it is Brahman — the Existence-Cognition-Bliss Absolute — who alone is real. A Vedantist strives at communion and unification with Him. The state of this union with Brahman is ineffably blissful (*anucchista*), as Sri Ramakrishna was reported to have told Pandit Iswarchandra Vidyasagar. The Upanishads say that Brahman is Bliss Absolute — *anando brahmeti byajanat* (*Taittariya Upanishad* 6/59): Swamiji stated, "If there be a trace of bliss anywhere, be sure of the existence of the ever and definitely blissful God there." (*Vani o Rachana*, II. 368)."

Elsewhere, Swamiji stated that fine arts, science and religion are three separate ways to unveil and unravel the truth (*Vani o Rachna*). Swamiji had a special liking for the fine arts for two reasons — first, to enjoy unalloyed pleasure in appreciating the beauty ingrained in different art forms and, secondly, to have a feel of the truth that emanates from them.

Till a spiritual seeker achieves the Ultimate by becoming one with Him, he has to accept his own entity which is separate from Him in the same way as a devotee worships and adores his deity. For aesthetic enjoyment, there has to be two separate entities — the object of enjoyment, i.e., the art form and the enjoyer. A person who wants to enjoy an art form must have the intellectual and emotional capacity, insight and training to appreciate it. He has to delve deep to understand the truth which the artist has tried to express through his creation, something of the kind of the Upanishadic saying where the truth seeker prays for removal of the golden lid that covers the face of truth (*Isha Upanishad*, 15/16). It also says that what we view with our naked eyes does not represent the Absolute Truth which is, in fact, the Good Ultimate (*Kalyanatamam*). Swamiji was of the view that an artist who is an adorer of beauty and a devotee who is a worshipper of a deity are travelling along the same path. The artist who is a seeker of beauty may see the Beauty Ultimate at the end of his aesthetic journey; a spiritual seeker at the end of his spiritual travel may similarly have a taste of bliss in realizing the Supreme Brahman. The ultimate aim of both is to enjoy bliss.

Swamiji's concept of beauty and truth might have been influenced by the Upanishadic concept of Existence-Cognition-Bliss (*sat-chit-ananda*) which, according to aestheticians, was transformed into the concept of Truth-Good-Beautiful (*satyam-shivam-sundaram*), similar to what Plato propounded and Raja Rammohan Roy accepted later as the motto of the Brahma Samaj. The Truth, the Good and the Beautiful are different facets of the inner Content (*bhava*). An artist views the truth through an object of beauty as he is not content with the bare reality. Truth becomes beautiful when it gives the viewer or the reader a sense of unalloyed joy. An artist considers both the Content and the Concrete. A philosopher is more concerned with the Content (*bhava*) than the Concrete (*bastu*). A scientist is particularly interested in the Concrete and not the Content. An artist comprehends the Content through the Concrete; truth manifests itself through a concrete form. An artist discovers beauty in the form and reaches the truth by unveiling the cover that conceals it.

Swamiji, an erudite scholar, philosopher and poet rolled into one, stated: "Who enjoys a picture — its seller or its viewer? The seller is busy with counting his profit and loss; he wants to reap profit out of a sale — he is only concerned with his commercial benefits. He watches the hammer of the auctioneer and is attentive to the pace at which prices are fluctuating. There is hardly any time for the seller to appreciate the picture. Only he can really appreciate a picture who is unconcerned about commercial gains. He watches the picture and relishes its beauty" (*Vani o Rachana*, II.172). Unless a person gives up his mundane outlook, he can never appreciate a form of art properly. The outlook of the viewer or the reader is important. He must be bereft of commercial passions, unlike the dealer who constantly has an eye on his commercial gains. Swamiji stated that this situation could be likened to a spiritual seeker who is possessed of mundane trivialities. One must develop an unstinted and untainted mind to realize the Ultimate. An appreciator of art should also have a similar mind-set according to Swamiji. He stated elsewhere: "This entire world is His creation. When his desires are expelled, only then can man enjoy the world. He will then not be confined to the petty sense of commercialism, to the wrongful pleasure of possession. The world will then become a beautiful piece of artistry, estranged from moneylenders, sellers and buyers. I have never heard of a more sublime utterance on God than the following — He is a great poet and an ancient poet at that — the entire world is His poetic creation composed out of an infinitely blissful emotional surge and expressed in various forms of verses, metres and measures. If we can make us free from desires, we shall be able to appreciate this poetic world composed by God. Then everything will assume the form of Brahman (*Vani o Rachana*, II.172.)

The outlook of Swamiji stems out of a sense of aloofness from worldly trivialities by its viewer. This alienation from worldly pursuits is a sort of spiritual stoicism (*vairagya*) which may be likened to aesthetic alienation — an attitude of dispassionate aloofness — which a true lover of art is required to cultivate to appreciate an object of art.

Swamiji travelled widely and made it a point to have a look

at the paintings, sculptures and architecture of the countries he visited. He expressed his comments on Greek and Roman architecture, French and German paintings and sculpture, Chinese and Japanese art. His analysis of the above art forms are indicative of his dispassionate outlook — a sort of aesthetic alienation referred to earlier. He commended French art more than the art of Germany and was of the view that Greek art was somewhat of an imitation of real life. According to him, classic Greek art flourished due to the freedom allowed to the artists. France also never imposed any restriction or restraint on the artists (*Vani o Rachana*, VI. 106-143). Swamiji thus corroborated the view that art can flourish only if artists are allowed freedom to create. He also discovered a link between spirituality and reality through the art-medium after analyzing the Attic art of Athens.

Swamiji was all praise for Japanese paintings, which are inimitable and distinctive both in form and content. He used to say, "The Asians have artistic qualities ingrained in them and art is an inseparable organ of their spirituality. The attitude of the Asians — the Indians in particular, is not confined to utility only, unlike the Westerners who seek utility in everything. The attitude of the Asians, on the other hand, transcends utility and looks for beauty everywhere. What is desirable is to blend the two — a combination of art and utility (*Vani o Rachana*, IX.406). This view of Swamiji may not find favour with the conservative aestheticians, but it certainly speaks of his aesthetic farsightedness and clarity. He was presumably prompted by contemporary Japanese art to make the above comment.

According to Swamiji, "Painting is not easy; it is enquiry into and depiction of the reality. A painting must represent the truth. A good painting is like a perfect drama. A work of art should reveal the inner content; the prerequisites are not only perseverance, but earnestness and firmness as well." Swamiji elsewhere compared Greek drama with the Indian. He was of the view that Indian drama had not been influenced by the drama of Greece. He also opined that even the sculpture and architecture of Greece had hardly had any effect on Indian sculpture and architecture .

Swamiji was adept in Indian classical music. While he was abroad, he also had opportunities to listen to Western music. He used to say, "Western music is based on harmony which we lack. Initially, it never appealed to me. But gradually, I started listening to Western music with more attention and ultimately became engrossed in it. A casual glance over a painting is not enough to appreciate its qualities. What is needed is educated eyes." (*Vani o Rachana*, IX.398-399). He also stated that Indian music being shorn of harmony is not expressive of vigour. He was of the view that distortions in Indian classical music had been made after the Muslim invasion. According to him, the Muslim 'ustads' quick-paced the notes of the *ragas* and *raginis* in such a way as to induce elements of discordance in them. They modified our conventional *tappa* form and eliminated its lyrical qualities. Indian classical music could brag of its cadence which France later inducted into her music.

This is an extremely important observation of Swamiji on vocal music. He advocated a harmonious blending of lyrical and musical qualities in a song. This rakes up an aesthetic debate on the dominance of form over content or vice versa in song. Swamiji clearly opted for the middle path which is the most rational approach.

Swamiji's critical appreciation of literature also stands out. He had high regard for the poetic ability of Michael Madhusudan Dutta. He hailed Michael's poetic work *Meghnadabadha* as one of the best in Bengali literature not only because of its special metre and diction, but also for its out-of-the-way outlook for the projection of Ravana's indefatigable valour against odds, resembling Milton's *Paradise Lost* — 'All is not lost, the unconquerable will.'

Swamiji was also deeply interested in the evolution of the Bengali language. He predicted that Kolkata's language would be accepted by the Bengalis ultimately as the standard language. (*Vani o Rachana*, VI. 35-716). His prediction has been prophetic.

Swamiji was of the view that the primary basis of art is nature and ideality. He translated this idea in designing the emblem of the Ramakrishna Mission — a symbolic blending of action, devotion and knowledge which leads one to communion with the Supreme.

Twenty Six

Oneness

Lubna Marium

Human development has to be seen in terms of values, not material wealth. The most important value is that of oneness of all creation

— Editor

At the outset, let me state that I am a humble student of Indian thought, who has embarked on a quest for answers. I place some genuine concerns of these times and some personal musings knowing that we are fellow travellers in this quest. I firmly believe that a responsible and meaningful citizenship requires that people feel a connection to their fellow citizens. In South Asia today, forces inimical to such a people's participation in policy making are constantly endeavouring to create conscious and sub-conscious barriers between the various strata of society. I, therefore, write as a woman, a Muslim woman, a Bangladeshi Muslim woman, but most of all, a Bangladeshi Muslim woman addressing an Indian audience hoping most of all to build bridges between our various identities, so that we can as fellow humans join hands to build a better world for our children.

Much learned comparisons of the Western and the traditional Indian paradigm of 'Human Development' have already been presented. Even a cursory perusal of these comparisons will ascertain that the emphasis on Indian culture is not on the outward manifestation of efficiency, production, acquisition or status, but rather on the inward achievement of harmony, affection, disinterestedness, non-violence and the search for truth. The much told and retold conversation of the sage Yajnavalkya and Maitreyi can be cited as epitomizing the Upanishadic concept of the ideal of chastened perusal of material gain regulated by considerations of morality.

The point I would like to make here is that men are not born with 'goals' in life. They are 'guided', 'influenced' and 'shown the way' by the thinking elite. The instrument of 'publicity' of such knowledge has, in India, been the *katha* and the *natya* which always had an ethical purpose to them. Homilies of sages have filtered into the hearths of people through the social faculty of 'mimesis' via the Epics and Puranas, which have influenced the hearts of men. In a culture where individuality has no value, certain types of individuals came to acquire immense power — the guru, the king, the counsellor, the priest and the state official. The boundless egoism of an Indian in a place of importance and authority has been, with all its vulgarity, as much a part of Indian history down to the present day as has been the endeavour of many unknown people to discipline and then transcend their egos.[1] Only where the individuality of a mass of people is suppressed on one ground or another, can a few people become all important. The question is, how is such a suppression achieved? Indian history is unfortúnately also witness to the influence of money and wealth on sastric laws. The philosopher David Hume was much intrigued by the ease with which the many are governed by the few. This he found surprising because force is always on the side of the governed. He concluded that government is founded on control of opinion, a principle that extends to the most despotic and most military government, as well as to the most free and most popular.[2]

Moving further on, we see the advent of Western learning. No single act of British policy has had a more lasting influence on the evolution of modern Indian thought than the decision of 1835 to use government funds to support education in the English language and to adopt the curriculum prevalent in English schools. A dialogue between two great cultures is in no way to be derided, as long as the motive behind it is an enhancement of wisdom and knowledge.

A vibrant political culture needs community groups, libraries, public schools, organisations, cooperatives, public meeting places, voluntary associations and trade unions to provide ways for citizens to meet, communicate and interact with their fellow citizens. Today the 'neo-liberal' democracy, with its notion of the market, takes dead aim at this sector. Instead of citizens, it produces consumers. Instead of communities, it produces shopping malls. The net result is an atomized society of disengaged individuals who feel demoralized and socially powerless.[3]

South Asia today, where the growth of cable and satellite television is projected to leap to 206 million units by the year 2004 (from 44 million in 1994), being a prime market, is at the brink of this corporate-financed public relations invasion through the electronic media.

It has been acknowledged by social scientists that television has a demonstrative role in rearranging our sense of time and space, fragmenting out cognitive faculty. The screen has become the wish-fulfilling touchstone of the appetites and aspirations of the burgeoning middle class that, in neo-colonial terms, is the counterpart of the comprador (an agent of a foreign power) mentality which looks up to the universally flaunted value systems of the supreme colonizer of our times — the United States of America. The aggressive and almost self-propelled process of colonalization itself is all the more insidious because it is not so much in the physical realm of a land and its natural resources, but operates in the mind of the people. This is not just a crucial fall-out of the system of liberalization, but is one of the instruments of 'neo-liberal' democracy.

Whatever be the methods of government or the paradigm of development adopted (and Reforms are definitely a reality that we cannot do away with), it may be firmly stated that the basic requirement for its success is the 'ethical man'. The poet Iqbal once said, "Religion, which in its higher manifestation is neither dogma, nor priesthood, nor ritual, can alone ethically prepare the modern man for the burden of the great responsibility." That brings us to the problem of defining 'religion' itself. Given its ambiguity, let us call it by another name. A quest for a meaning of our ephemeral lives? For a belief certainly. In Truth, Beauty, the Final Cause, Strings and Black Holes? So many have given this such a lot of thought! Buddha, Jesus, Mohammad, Jalal-ud-din

Rumi, Shankaracharya, Lalon Fakir, Mirabai, Tagore, Einstein, Stephen Hawkins. We have the entire range from aggressive theism, all the way through the mystical quietism of the Sufis and bauls, up to the decomposition of the phenomenal world into the despair of the Existentialists.

Indian thought has maintained that truth is an awareness of a unity between all. For myself, being a dancer, I come face to face with an 'awareness' within myself through my music. It opens doors for me that I can never open with logic and reason. It unites me not just with my fellow humans but with the entire cosmos itself. It makes me look beyond my subjective self and then urges me onwards on this quest.

This is an age of conflict. Conflicts and dichotomies with our egos; open conflicts with others in economic and political life. Yes, there is a surfeit of intellectual activity but unfortunately it makes the path murkier and does not resolve conflicts. At the end of the day all this din just serves to obstruct us from introspection, from looking 'without from within'. In a fine sentence, Tagore says, "Man is defeated when the authority inside him is curbed; curbed by the externals of religion, by tradition and custom, by scripture and ritual." The Sufi and Bhakti movements were just such catholic, egalitarian movements that broke up the exterior shells of Hinduism and Islam, penetrated into the real, common core of mysticism and welded together the two communities, especially the lowest strata of both to a common realization of the Absolute. However, thence, instead of reintegrating forces they thrived in the spiritual thralldom of inaction and renunciation. What attracts me to Indian thought is that all knowledge is translated into meta-ethical norms of social interaction. "*Isavasyam idam sarwam yat kim ca jagatyam jagat,*" says *Upanisad* (1.1), i.e. Is a "(Know that) all this, sentient and insentient, whatever moves in this world is enveloped by God."

If what is in you is also in me, in the countless little street children shivering in the cold, and in the sky and the ocean, and yet again in a wisp of grass or in the bird flying into the sunset, aren't we all then an equal part of the whole? Equals enjoined. Can we ignore the shivering and poverty of the child in the street? When we deface the Narmada do we not then deface a part of ourselves too? A profound thought. The next line of the *sloka*, however, has one of the most down-to-earth pieces of advice. A beautiful commentary by Tagore reads as follows: "When our egos concentrate on the insignificant, it serves only to destroy unity. The part revolts thence against the whole. Thus has renunciation been advocated. However, this renunciation far from taking us towards an emptiness, is assuredly for the purpose of fulfilment. Renounce then the part to gain the whole, renounce the ephemeral for the eternal, ego for love, renounce worldly happiness for bliss."

Is such renunciation of egos possible? Can we overcome the barriers of ritualistic religion and reach towards a universal belief which can enjoin us as responsible, ethical beings moving towards a cosmic destination of human, nay cosmic, unity? Is not that what is really 'human development'? We must decide if we want to make these choices, because the onus is on each one of us, and not on any vague 'political party' or 'political system'.

References

1. Badrinath, Chaturvedi, 'The Place of Individual in Indian Thought and Polity', *Plurality and Individualism*, p. 42.
2. Chomsky, Naom, *Profit Over People*, Madhyam Books, 1999, p. 43.
3. McChesney, R.W; Introduction; *Ibid*.

Twenty Seven

Impact of Greek Philosophy and Christian Theology on Materialistic Concept of Human Development

P.K. Patankar

Present decline in human welfare can be traced to importance of mind in Greek philosophy and the Christian dictum of supremacy of man over nature.

— Editor

The parameters of development prevailing in the Western world were adopted *in toto* by the newly independent developing nations of the world. It was held that if a country lacked resources within its boundaries, it could choose to import them from abroad and pay back from the proceeds of exports. The index of development was arrived at by computing the average amount of consumption of an individual in a given year. In this system, the most developed country is one which records maximum availability and diversity of consumables/products as compared to others. It is obvious that the economic thinking of the Western nations is based upon a strong belief in the supremacy of the forces of consumption. Accordingly, Gross Domestic Product (GDP) and Net Domestic Product (NDP) are computed from the figures of production in a country in a given year for measuring the level of development. These are also used for the purpose of making comparisons. A continued linear growth in GDP is deemed highly desirable in this framework.

In reality, these yardsticks do not measure the actual level of development in the society. There are many other aspects such as the average life expectancy, level of health, literacy, employment etc. which exert a strong influence on development. The per capita consumption figures in themselves cannot provide a true picture of the qualitative aspects of development.

A variety of new indices have been developed to incorporate such factors. They include MEW (Measure of Economic Welfare), NNW (Net National Welfare), QOL (Quality of Life), BHN (Basic Human Needs), PQLI (Physical Quality of Life Index) etc. Despite improvements these indices have failed to measure the development in the true sense. The reason is simple: the indicators are inherently associated with the forces of destruction which are not taken into account while making such calculations. One can study the case of America in this respect. It ranks very high in the list of developed nations. Yet, the state of its society has become a matter of serious concern. The institution of family is under severe strain and almost breaking down. The number of single parent families is rising steeply every year. The percentage of unwed mothers is going up. Cases of suicide and mental illnesses are becoming more frequent. According to an economist, wealth is being accumulated but man himself is getting destroyed from within. The threats posed by environmental pollution and ecological degradation have crossed the danger mark.

The prevailing developmental indices which are based upon the capitalistic economic models and revolve around the consumption levels have proved to be utter failure. Our country too has formulated its developmental strategies on the basis of accepting the validity and usefulness of such parameters. The overall results have been quiet disappointing. The problems of unemployment, poverty, economic disparity etc. have become much more acute. On the other hand, problems like rising crime rates, rampant corruption, environmental pollution, debt, drinking water scarcity, energy shortages, collapse of civic amenities in urban areas, etc. are rapidly getting out of control. Globalisation and liberalization have only ended up in further accentuating the economic exploitation of the third world countries including India. The attempts which are being made to correct this state of affairs perhaps amount to nothing more than curing the symptoms instead of the real causes of the disease. It is, therefore, quite crucial to make an in depth review of the Western parameters of development.

The parameters of development do not arise in a vacuum. They reflect a clearly identifiable, social, cultural and political context. A close scrutiny reveals that the genesis of this consumer-minded, selfish and soulless civilization lies in the Greek epistemology theory of the method or grounds of knowledge.

According to the Greek philosopher Aristotle, man is endowed with the capabilities of thinking logically and hence logical mind should be employed for understanding the world. He particularly stressed upon accepting logic as the final decisive factor while arriving at conclusions. This theory continued to dominate people's mind for the next 1500 years. Later, Christianity spread far and wide, rejecting the notion of supremacy of intellect and declaring that it was the root cause of all problems. It laid great stress on faith and thinking. This put a full stop to the process of free thinking. However, there was no controversy for a long time due to many commonalities between the Aristotelian worldview and the Biblical accounts. The progress in physical sciences, nonetheless, came to a grinding halt. In the 15th century, Galileo proposed that the earth was constantly revolving around the sun which actually remained in a fixed position. As this view did not accord with the Biblical narrative, Galileo was subjected to torture and suffering. Subsequently, many other thinkers freed themselves from the stranglehold of the church. They had found a new way of learning. A method for conducting objective analysis based upon direct observations, formation of hypothesis and verification through experiments was developed.

Rene Descartes was a famous 17th century French mathematician and philosopher. According to him, the survival of man depends upon his mental progress. Mind occupies the driving seat in the body and controls its activities. In philosophical terms, this amounts to saying that a thinking being can control and run nature itself. The seeds of exploitation are contained in this thought since it means that a powerful and imaginative mind can also dominate a mind which is much weaker in comparison. Rene Descartes divided the human personality into two separate parts.

He also paved way for creating a system of understanding life by subdividing it.

This ideology received further impetus from Newton's discoveries of the laws of motion. Newton also put forward the theory that the entire universe is a giant machine which is functioning on the basis of certain laws. If man discovers these laws, he will also achieve the capability of controlling the whole universe. Subsequently, many other scientists claimed that since the man was capable of becoming the master of the universe there was no reason for believing in God. The new approach of science gave a tremendous boost to the confidence and ambition of mankind. Rapid advances were made in the areas of science and technology. Science had totally rejected the 'Faith'. The scientific discoveries and technological inventions also resulted in a manifold increase in the sensory ability of man apart from the capacity to perform.

A separation between science and Faith had definitely taken place. Nonetheless, the Christian views on the relationship between the man and the universe do have something in common with the scientific thinking on the subject. According to Christianity, God has sent man to earth with the command that he may enjoy all its fruits. The idea that man and nature are two distinct entities is implicit here. Christianity also preaches that man occupies the highest position in the universal order. Nature is his slave. It has not created him. It is also concluded that man is nothing but a bundle of a variety of desires. His happiness, therefore, lies in fulfilment of these desires. The concept of God, afterlife, moral considerations, etc. were pushed into the background as being of little value while the tendency towards unchecked consumption received much encouragement. Limitless consumerism demanded a higher and higher level of production and productivity and industrialization became a pressing necessity. It can be thus seen that the modern parameters of development have been fuelled by (1) the Christian views on the relationship between man and the universe, and (ii) the materialistic bias in the sciences. Such was the foundation on which the social and economic superstructures of the Christian world were built up.

The industrial revolution sharply accelerated the pace of

production. The problem of finding larger markets to absorb the surplus production was solved by making use of the colonies. A new international economic system came into existence. The motive of higher profit demanded faster rates of production as well as consumption. Consumerism received encouragement in all possible ways. In order to boost the consumption of a product in the fiercely competitive market place, it became essential to rapidly upgrade its design and quality. In the process, the long cherished belief in the eternal human values and lasting human relationships had become irrelevant. In the new scenario relationships were formed and sustained purely on the basis of mutual usefulness. This new order had the following key features:

1. Struggle for existence.
2. Survival of the fittest.
3. Exploitation of Nature.
4. Individual rights.

Such was the worldview adopted by the scientists, sociologists and the philosophical thinkers of the West. This world view has had a far reaching impact on all facets of human life.

This worldview developed by the Western world is only about 200-300 years old. In the earlier period, people of different nations had evolved their own worldviews which formed the basis of their social life. It is remarkable that these nations had never resorted to colonial exploitation in the entire course of their history. They did not even exploit the natural resources abounding within their own territorial limits. And yet, these countries, including India, China, Japan etc. were very prosperous.

Tibet and several nations of Africa are examples of countries where the nature has been far from being bounteous. Human societies there, however, responded by choosing to lead a simple and undemanding life. They never invaded other countries to gain control over their natural resources.

The developmental approach of all these societies radically differed from the European viewpoint. So far as India is concerned, its ideas about development reflected the underlying objective of achieving harmony and balance between various aspects of life.

The Indian thinkers held that the apparent diversities found in living or non-living constituents of the universe are actually only expressions of the underlying unity in different forms. The discovery of this truth is indeed a unique contribution of the Indian philosophy to the word. It has also been instrumental in the evolution of a holistic approach towards the quest for knowledge. In fact, our social order is also based upon this worldview.

According to the Indian thinkers, there is no struggle for existence in the world. Since the entire creation is manifestation of one single truth, there cannot be any scope for conflict and struggle.

References

1. M.B. Brown, *The Economies of Imperialism.*
2. K.L. Kedia and A. Sinha, *Gender Assumption of Growth and Development Theories.*
3. Paul Harrison, *Inside the Third World.*
4. Meadows & Meadows, *Limits to Growth.*
5. K.C. Sudershan, *Ubharte Vaicharih Adhistan.*
6. Mahatama Gandhi, *Grass Swarayya.*
7. Dilip Kulkarni, *Samyak Vikas.*
8. Pt. Deen Dayal Upadhyaya : Ekatma Manav.
9. K.L. Kedia & A Sinha: Drishti Dhosh To Vikalp Kaise?

Twenty Eight

Gandhi's Approach to Human Development

Raj Kumar Sen

Right to work is an integral element of Human Development. Economic Growth must be sacrificed to create employment for this purpose.

— Editor

I

According to traditional Indian thinking, a man after completion of his studies (*bramacharya*) should enter into the second stage of his life (*grahasthya*) when he should carry out his earthly duties. His objectives should be to acquire money or material well-being (*artha*) and to enjoy conjugal life (*kama*). But both *artha* and *kama* are based on the first objective of righteousness (*dharma*), the basis of which has been established in his first stage of life through his learning. In other words, the basic objective of education is to build up one's life as per directions of *dharma*. Even during the *grahasthya* stage of life, one has the right to acquire only the amount required to fulfil his basic needs. If he acquires beyond that level then he is acting as a thief and he should be punished accordingly. In the third stage of life he discards both *artha* and *kama* and even his normal social life and adopts *banaprasthya* or self-exclusion from all earthly activities. It has been advised that one should go for *banaprasthya* when one is above fifty. But to achieve his final objective—*moksha*, he has to embrace *sannyasa*, i.e., complete detachment from everything, after *banaprasthya*. Of course, in reality ordinary people were never perfect and could not follow rigidly the way of life as prescribed in the scriptures. But even then spiritually a man was under the fear of committing a sin. Moreover, due to the absence of a middle income class in the Indian society there were only two classes viz. very rich and the very poor. The handful of royal and aristocrat families including a few big merchants spent their lives in luxury and the rest of the society consisted of innumerable people toiling in the fields and in the cities to maintain their lives at the subsistence level. Due to the absence of modern transport and communication system and mass media and the prevalence of widespread illiteracy, the poor could not obtain any correct idea of the very high level of living enjoyed by the rich. This was a two-stage type simple consumption dualism. This could not give birth to consumerism because of nearly homogenous production structure and very little corruption among the masses though crime and violence were not unknown. Whatever consumerism and corruption were there, they were confined to the small rich class only and could not affect the society at large where the religious and ethical values were quite strong to control the individual and social vices.

It is with the advent of the British education system and as a consequence of industrial revolution and technological progress that the money economy expanded, traditional values eroded and a strong middle income class emerged bridging the gap between the standards of living enjoyed by the few rich on the one hand and the vast majority of poor and destitute on the other. The British system of education also imparted religious education but that was not imposed on the natives. At the same time, the basic education was not based on religion. Thus, the ground was prepared for a religion-neutral and value free education system in India and the educated Indians started, as the British rulers desired, to look down upon their own culture, religion, history and literature. The middle income class aspired to uplift their living standard to the level of the rich while the poor aspired to reach their standard of living. To make this dream come true, no step was considered as unethical or wrong in a world of eroding values. The end justified the means and naturally, the doors to the world of corruption were thrown open in this process of uplifting the standard of living of the respective classes. In this situation human objectives remained confined to achieving *artha* and *kama* only and the other goals of *dharma* and *moksha* became irrelevant. Even *kama* i.e. the basis of a conjugal life, became dependent on *artha* and for *artha, kama* could be sold in the market as services.

The feature of consumerism became widespread especially in the 20th century when several scientific inventions changed the world and the outlook of its people. Waves of inventions—aeroplane, electricity, radio, telephone and telegraph, nuclear weapons, computers, television, life-saving medicines, genetic engineering and so on—led to extremely rapid change of technology and its innumerable diversifications. One result was the flooding of the market with consumer goods pertaining to every aspect of life. Everyone wanted to raise his standard of living irrespective of his class in society.

Economics identified the goal of the consumer as that of maximising utility i.e. satisfaction through consumption of goods and services, while the goal of the producer was to maximise profit. In the fulfilment of these objectives, the consumer faces only one constraint viz. income, which he always tries to overcome by raising his level by any means, fair or foul as there is no ethical principle or religious norm to control him beyond a tolerable limit. The producer also tries to maximise profit by any means, even by adulteration of the goods or services he sells. Here also, morality has no place. There are some regulatory authorities to prevent economic crimes but gradually they also become purchasable with a few pieces of silver. Gradually, people begin to accept such corruption as part of life and bribe adopts respectable names like speed money, grease money and so on and there are economists who promptly develop models showing how such things lead to efficiency in the production system in material terms.

In India, the political system after independence, beginning with the lofty ideals of parliamentary democracy, rapidly degenerated into a system which started to increasingly depend on money and muscle power to influence popular support. Thus, the criminalisation of politics and collection of money as donations from businessmen became the rule of the day. The legal system could not prevent persons of dubious character from getting elected. The situation continues to worsen : for instance, recently, exhibiting rare unity, political parties obstructed attempts for election reforms, instituted by the Election Commission of India under the Supreme Court's instruction, involving declaration of properties, criminal records by candidates.

The situation in India has worsened since her adoption of the policy of so-called economic liberalisation in 1991. Among other things, there is now no upper limit of income for the corporate houses. There has been a wage explosion comparable to international standards releasing demand for consumption of goods and services of international standard. The production structure of the economy is already skewed under the influence of the nuovo-rich with an abundance of consumer gadgets while the threat of food insecurity looms large in the horizon. Increasingly, most human values like honesty, truthfulness, compassion, love etc. are being sacrificed at the altar of money. Money has also become the main source from which flows power, respect, honour and comfort coveted by all. Corruption reigns high in this situation and India ranks high in terms of corruption among the low-income economies of the world.

We find that there is an unending craze for increasing the standard of living in terms of material well-being only. This craze does not take into account any ethical norm nor is it eco-friendly in nature as it feeds itself on continuous exploitation of natural resources leading to environmental pollution and degradation. A man can increase his consumption provided he has the required amount of money and his satisfaction is maximised through maximisation of consumption. The technological revolution and the demonstration effect through the mass media has led to consumerism of an unsustainable nature. This single-minded craze for money compels one to acquire black money through corruption.

II

Let us study the economic views of Gandhi and see how they can help restore an eco-ethical standard of living in the interest of the Indian economy and the world as a whole.

Truth and non-violence are the two well-known principles of life that govern all Gandhian thoughts. Gandhi was not an economist and hence had no economic theory as such in narrow sense but he had a philosophy of life covering all of its aspects. Both Gandhi and Marx, in the ultimate analysis, depended chiefly on the development of the inner traits of human life to achieve their ideals, though, through completely opposite paths. Gandhian ideas always concentrated upon the possible ways of uplifting the levels of living of the downtrodden. In fact, the level of living to be enjoyed by an individual plays a vital role in formulating Gandhian prescription for determining the course of economic development of India in particular and developing countries in general. In the Gandhian economy there will be a fairly even standard of living by material standards for everybody. This economic order will strive to provide a simple life, the chief characteristics of which would be truthfulness, non-violence, equality of status and of opportunities, fairly equal distribution of wealth, necessities and comforts of life, and minimum state control with decentralisation. Only necessary mechanisation will be allowed. There would be an upper limit for income and the wealthy would follow the principal of trusteeship following our traditional values. It aims at provision of a decent minimum level of living for all and improving this living while controlling the inequalities, again within decent limits. This is also conducive to environment protection, supremacy of truth and honour to all religions. Gandhian ideas centred around the upliftment of everybody (*sarvodaya*) and not the maximisation of national income without any control on distribution, which always benefits the few and harms everybody else. Under *sarvodaya*, emphasis is laid on *antyodaya* i.e., upliftment of the weakest. Here poverty alleviation starts from the bottom and is not concentrated at the periphery as observed in the current official policies of poverty alleviation in India where resources are subject to numerous leakages and the target is maximisation of the number of poor to be uplifted above the poverty line. Gandhi was always against the abject poverty of the masses which was not only materially harmful but also morally degrading.

That employment is the best remedy of poverty is clear in Gandhian economics. He preferred production by masses for consumption goods rather than mass production by large scale industries which cater to consumption but do not lead to enhancing purchasing power of the masses. Our economic planning along non-Gandhian lines has followed the model of highly mechanised and centralized large scale industries. We could neither alleviate mass poverty nor could provide mass consumption goods nor provide employment for the large number of our people.

Gradually, the world is realising that the present type of consumption-oriented industrialisation is not sustainable in the long run. Appropriate policies need to be adopted without delay for the protection of environment. Gandhi favoured the use of current economic resources which are renewable in nature in preference to the reservoir economy resources where stocks are limited. This strategy may be called eco-friendly. According to Gandhi, one of the factors leading to increasing violence in different parts of the world was their craze for using the reservoir economy resources, abandoning current economy. Gandhi preferred production of goods meant for home consumption rather than of goods required for exchange so that the level of living could be increased domestically. Production of goods for exchange, he said, would lead to inequality and ultimately violence. In Gandhian economics there is no place for violence. In the name of export-led growth strategy, we are always trying to export the best we can produce while depriving our countrymen from consuming them. The example of exporting basmati rice while importing inferior quality of rice to meet the domestic needs may be cited. Gandhi preferred organic fertilizers and pesticides to chemical ones as the latter increase the fertility of the soil in such a manner that it is permanently exhausted and has many undesirable side-effects. He did not prefer the creation of infrastructure which led to further exploitation and inequality. Thus, for irrigation he preferred dug-wells and tanks to large hydro-electric projects. His well-known emphasis on small-scale, cottage and agro-industries will lead to decentralised industrialisation, raising the level of living of the masses and reducing the inequality in the income distribution and mass poverty. This will also reduce the growth rate of population. Economic history proves that through raising the standard of living population growth rate can be slowed down and not by population control measures when mass poverty is prevailing. Gandhi was for industrialisation which would lead to the increased welfare of the common masses measured in terms of daily necessities of life. He never supported industrialisation for its own sake.

It is sometimes claimed, wrongly, that through the 73rd Amendment of the Constitution, the Panchayati Raj system was made strong in India, empowering the people as dreamt by Gandhi in his concept of *Gram Swaraj*. This Panchayati Raj system has seen the emergence of a third tier of governance imposed from above (the other two being the centre and the state) with a partisan election system leading to the rule of majority even at the lowest level. The rule of majority is always against the principle of *sarvodaya* and definitely bypasses the *antyodaya* principle as here the beneficiary is not only weak but also voiceless, being in absolute minority. In Gandhian village republic democracy is a participatory one without involving the political parties. Power evolves from the bottom and is not granted from above. The panchayats are to be self-sufficient as far as possible and independent of financial aid from outside. This will motivate the people to generate their own resources, exploit fully their potential and restrict their aspirations to the limit of their capacity and capabilities. The present system of dependency on grants and aids imparts a uniform pattern of development paradigm everywhere irrespective of the local perception. This has caused irreparable harm to the tribal and hill communities in particular. It has resulted in spread of corruption on a massive scale among the rural people. Thus, corrupt practices have been generated among the common people, who no longer consider such an economic offence to be bad. This is much more dangerous than corruption at the top that has been exposed through various financial scams.

The concern for equity in the Gandhian system has led to what is known as consumption planning. This can not only restrict the wastage of resources, but also limit the ever increasing aspirations of higher standard of living due to absence of demonstration effect from the neighbourers. The present aggressive advertisement system through mass media and television in particular is creating a false perception of happiness through acquisition. It creates a two-fold adverse impact on the life of the common people. On the one hand, the increasing costs of competitive advertisements artificially result in a high cost economy, creating hardship for the ordinary people. On the other, it also infuses dissatisfaction with one's level of living through a very strong demonstration effect perpetuated in most of the cases through a false or exaggerated representation of the advantages to be enjoyed from the product that is advertised. This also leads to erosion of values including treating women as commodity for promotion of sales. Such vices of market economy are absent in Gandhian Socialism. The economic wealth must be distributed among all equitably, if not equally. There should be no one suffering from want of food and clothing. Everybody should be able to get sufficient work to enable him to make the two ends meet. This ideal can be universally realised only if the means of production of elementary necessities of life remain in the control of the masses. They should be freely available to all as God's air and water are or ought to be.

The current prescription to impart environmental studies and value education in the curriculum is a move towards the right direction. It is only natural that such attempts will be opposed by the vested interests. But, as believed by Gandhi, attempts even at the level of a single individual with nobody else to follow him will surely lead to progress towards achieving the goal.

References

1. Sen, Raj Kumar, 'Level of Living and Gandhian Economic Theory', *International Journal of Social Economics*, Vol. 24, No. 7-9, England, 1997.
2. Sen, Raj Kumar, 'Sustainable Policy Options for Structural Adjustment Strategy in India: A Gandhian Alternative'. Sen, R.K. (ed), *Liberalisation, Adjustment and Reforms in India*, Bodh Publications, Kanpur, 1996.
3. Sen, Raj Kumar, 'The Unsanctioned Economy and Consumption Dualism' in Monga, G.S.& Sanctis, V.J. (eds) *The Unsanctioned Economy*, Himalaya Publishing House, Mumbai, 1983.
4. Sen, Raj Kumar, (2000): 'Looking Back at Gandhi: An Economic Perspective', Invited Lecture at Gandhi Charcha Kendra, Rabindra Bharati University, Calcutta.
5. Juergensmeyer, M, 'The Gandhi Revival — a review article', *Journal of Asian Studies*, Ann Arbour, MI, 1984.
6. Agarwal, S.K, *Gandhian Plan of Economic Development for India*, Padma Publishers, Mumbai, 1944.

7. Sen, Raj Kumar, *Parallel Economy and Economic Dualism in India*, Indian Economic Association Conference Volume, Jabalpur, 1982.
8. Sen, Raj Kumar, *Utility, Marshall and Development Economics*, Indian Economic Conference Volume, Ahmedabad, 1990; Das, D.K.(ed), *Economic Ideas of Six Great Economists*, Deep & Deep Publications, New Delhi, 1994.
9. Sen, Raj Kumar, 'Decentralised Planning in India and the Market Economy' in Sen, Raj Kumar (ed), *Indian Economic Issues: Essays in Honour of Prof. Santikumar Ghosh*, Rabindra Bharati University, Calcutta, 2000.
10. Sen, Raj Kumar, 'Political Economy of Development Paradigms in LDCs with reference to India,' Paper presented in the Indian Economic Conference, Trivandrum, 2000.
11. Sen, Raj Kumar, 2000, 'Consumption Pluralism, Erosion of Values and Corruption in India'. *Corruption and Development*, Department of Economics, Rabindra Bharat University, Calcutta.

Twenty Nine

Social and Moral Role of Education

Meenakshi Mishra

Education is an input to jobs and wealth. That is fine. But other moral and social dimensions should be added so that education becomes liberating rather than entrapping.

— Editor

The chief aim of modern education is to provide employment and not development of personality. Keeping in view the need for material and spiritual advancement and for performance of duties and responsibilities in an orderly manner, education has been given due importance right from the dawn of civilization. Its necessity and importance cannot be denied. Intellect and wisdom gained and sharpened by education is the real strength of man. Ancient Indians had a lot of faith in the efficacy of education. "Education imparts humility, humility grants expertise and with expertise man acquires wealth. Dharma and comforts are created by wealth." For ancient Indians, the goal of education was all-round development of man's personality.

Today education is acquired simply to brighten one's chances of earning livelihood and getting better jobs and gaining a higher standard of living. Undoubtedly in the past, basic education did have this aim but to acquire education with this aim alone was condemned (Kalidasa Mal Mitram).

Values change with times. A student of the ancient period in India did not have to worry about getting a job or financial independence the way a student has to do today. But when this goal of financial independence becomes the sole aim of acquiring education, the aim of developing one's personality is pushed to the background. It disturbs the equilibrium. We are facing a peculiar situation today. Personality development has been neglected both in the man who has got employment and who has not. Modern educational system has failed to make man understand that getting a job is not the ultimate aim of education.

The sole aim of present education being provision of a job, it has been limited to bookish knowledge. In this age of cut-throat competition, to excel, students utilise and spend major portions of their energy in preparing from the syllabus.

Character building is neglected. After getting a job one remains busy in making one's financial position strong. This single aim of material progress inculcates many blemishes in man and they, in turn, tell upon his health. The aim to amass more and more wealth compels man to do extra labour and he takes to intoxicants. Such mode of living adversely affects personality. It is said in the *Gita* — "Yoga kills out all pain for him who is regulated in eating and amusement, regulated in performing actions, regulated in sleeping and waking" (6/17).

Self-control results in reasoning, wisdom, intelligence and power of justice. Man is able to distinguish between truth and falsehood. He develops a discerning intellect. All these traits play a vital role in inculcating a sound personality.

These is a need of introducing compulsory professional and vocational courses for students so they can acquire vocational training of their choice. Students would thus be able to follow their own cherished professions and earn livelihood easily. The provision to make students experts in their hereditary vocations was there in the educational system of the past. Division of labour produced experts and this gave impetus to social progress and it kept the social equilibrium intact.

Modern educational system lays emphasis on character building and personality development along with providing opportunities to get jobs. But this is only in principle. In practice, livelihood remains the end of life. The need of the hour is to lay full emphasis on personality development through well-planned educational norms. Responsibility for this lies both on educational institutions and the society.

Thirty

Poverty Index

Shekhar Mukherji

Poverty and unemployment are crucial factors leading to low human development.

— Editor

Introduction

Abject poverty and widespread illiteracy among women and men are ground realities in India. This paper is concerned with the causal linkages between poverty and consequently high level of fertility and infant mortality in the country, especially in poor villages and urban slums.

Although the recent National Family and Health Survey (NFHS, 1992-93) has collected data about women's demographic behaviour and use of health services or family welfare, it has little information on people's income, consumption, or their poverty level. Without the study of people's economic condition, it is most difficult and unscientific to explain India's high fertility or infant mortality levels. Thus, a great need was felt to devise some alternative ways to estimate people's poverty condition.

Based on surrogate measures, this paper computes Poverty Index at the state level as well as at the individual level, and through canonical model analyses its causal effect upon fertility and infant mortality rates particularly in the three relatively developed states (Goa, Kerala and Tamil Nadu) and six less developed states (Andhra Pradesh, Bihar, Madhya Pradesh, Rajasthan, Uttar Pradesh and West Bengal).

Method of Computing Poverty Index at the State Level

The United Nations Human Development Report (1997, Technical note, Appendix 1) has devised ways of computing Human Development Index and Poverty Index for different nations. For Poverty Index they have used certain measures like: (a) life expectancy at age 40, (b) female illiteracy rate, (c) per capita Gross National Product (GNP), (d) proportion of people not getting health services, and (e) proportion of people lacking essential drinking water facilities.

Methodology of Computing Poverty Index at the Individual Level

Individual level measure of poverty index is computed on the basis of the following five indicators because data for their income is not available:

(1) female illiteracy,
(2) whether the respondent woman is living in a *kuchha* house,
(3) non-availability of drinking water in the house,
(4) non-availability of toilet facility in the house, and
(5) non-availability of health facilities to the women respondent and/or her children anytime during the four years previous to the survey date.

If answer to the questions is yes, then the woman respondent is given a score on each such measure; otherwise she is given a zero score. The sum total of all such yes scores gives her poverty index at the individual level. This index varies between a value of zero (when she is assessed as not poor) and a value of maximum score (when she is in the poorest category). So far as is known, no such attempt of computing individual level poverty index has been made previously. This poverty index is computed for all 90,000 women respondents surveyed for all major sates of India (Mukherji 1997b 10-145).

Canonical Analysis between Poverty, Fertility and Mortality

Canonical analysis is made at both the levels : (a) for all-India level, by taking states as units of observation, and (b) at state-level, by taking individual women respondents as units of observations. Analysis was first made at all-India level. In the next step, for each of the 25 major states of India, canonical analysis was made separately, by using data of the poverty index and NFHS data of individual respondent's demographic variables (like children born, infant mortality index, child mortality index, and population programme variables like contraceptives ever used, number of child immunization courses completed, female sterilization done or not, etc). Out of 25 states, findings of only nine states are presented here. All data here refer to individual units. Sample size sometimes exceeds 6500 or more cases for a state (Mukherji 1997b: 1-126).

Canonical Analytic Model

Canonical analysis is a higher form of regression analysis. Instead of a single dependent variable as in a regression model, it deals with a matrix of dependent variables, and a matrix of independent variables, and instead of one, yields a set of solutions in a single run of the test, as many as the minimum number of variables in the two sets. In short, canonical analysis can do in a single shot what hundreds of regression analysis cannot do. (Hotelling 1937: 321-377; Cooley and Lohnes 1962: 45-65; Mukherji 1979: 1-80; Mukherji 1992: 1-92).

Canonical analysis usually yields a set of solutions as large as there are patterns in demographic (dependent) and socio-economic plus policy (independent) matrices, whichever has the smaller number of variables. Since there were only three variables in demographic or dependent matrix, only three pairs of canonical vectors or canonical varieties, are extracted successively from dependent and independent matrics with decreasing order of predictability in the same manner as in principal components analysis. As can be seen from each such canonical inter-relationship, a particular type of socio-economic-cum-policy variables is causally linked with a specific kind of demographic variables, and in each case, the canonical correlation between the pair of vectors is maximized (see Tables 1 to 8).

With reference to Canonical Structure Matrix (Tables 1 to 11), here the following points are noteworthy (Mukherji 1997b: 21-178):

a. *Canonical varieties:* are separate patterns of relationships between input factors (or variables).
b. *Canonical loadings:* degree and direction of relationship of the specific variables with canonical variate pattern.
c. *Canonical Correlation:* Statistical dependence between each matched pair of variates.
d. *Trace Correlation:* General statistical overlap between two sets, dependent and independent.

The overall statistical overlap or Trace correlation is also quite high, which indicates the extent to which the independent set has explained that portion of total variance in the dependent set. There are successively three significant relations which have emerged in each analysis, with canonical values.

Findings at Canonical Analysis of Individual Level Data.

With reference to Table 5, the complicated canonical linkage equation for the first pair of variables for the state of Andhra Pradesh can be written as follows based on only high-loadings (usually above 0.40):

0.991 (Children ever born, CEB) = 0.668 (Poverty Index) – 0.55 (Female sterilization) + 0.33 (No ANC care given)

This can easily and meaningfully be interpreted as Poverty index will increase with high level of CEB, especially when female sterilization is lacking and when no ANC care is given. Canonical correlation between this matched pair of canonical variates is 0.32 indicating that one single factor, alleviation of abject poverty condition among the people, will be greatly conducive to reduce fertility rate in backward states like Andhra Pradesh. This factor has emerged as the strongest determinant of fertility behaviour amidst a total of nine variables. Conspicuous absence of many other important variables in the first linkage is also noteworthy (like family planning and immunization).

In like manner, successive canonical correlations, loadings, and corresponding patterns of causal relationships between demographic behaviour set and socio-economic variables-cum-policy set can be easily interpreted. Remaining canonical relationships are briefly stated in the summary Table No 1 and are detailed in Tables 2 to 11.

All these canonical linkage equations are not only statistically significant, but are also practically very meaningful. These canonical results are interpreted as follows:

Part I: Findings from Six Less Developed States

The findings are detailed in Table 1 to 7 and are summarized in Table 1. The most important canonical linkage from each state is highlighted as follows:

	State	*Most important Canonical Linkage Equation*
1.	AP	High poverty, high no. of children ever born per mother (CEB).
2.	Bihar	High poverty, high CEB;
3.	MP	High poverty, high CEB;
4.	Rajasthan	High Poverty, High CEB, also no ANC available;
5.	UP	High poverty, high IMR, as little immunization;
6.	WB	High poverty, though some ANC was available.

The results are self-explanatory. State after state repeats the same causal relationship between poverty and high fertility. Further details of other canonical linkages are elaborated in summary table 4.

Retrospect

Two noteworthy aspects may be mentioned.

First, the measurement of Poverty Index at the individual level is a unique contribution in the study of human development index. It provides a simple but meaningful and operational index of deprivation of the individuals. The basic data may be easily collected in common surveys, and this poverty index can be easily computed for the individuals, especially for the females. This will indicate the degree of their deprivation. So, more use of such an effective index will enhance population research and geographic research.

Secondly, apart from this poverty index, this paper has repeatedly demonstrated many meaningful and causal relations between poverty index and fertility rates and infant mortality rates, which are eye-openers as they prove the basic fundamental causal relations between widespread poverty and high fertility in India. More such meaningful research is henceforth required.

Policy Implications

One of the most fundamental findings that emerges is that poverty is the very important cause for increasing high rate of fertility in different states of India. Canonical linkage shows almost a one-to-one relationship between the two. It clearly emphasizes that in India, it is the abject poverty which is the cause and high fertility the effect and not vice-versa. As many canonical linkages have demonstrated, compared with poverty index, other variables have contributed very little in determining fertility (Mukherji 1997c; Mukherji 1997d: 1-43).

Policy import of these very fundamental causal relations is clear. It highlights the most urgent need for providing universal and massive (functional) literacy to all girls and to all adult women of India (as illiteracy is the most important indicator of poverty index), and for direct poverty alleviation programmes, if we are truly serious about ensuring fertility decline and for reducing infant mortality rates (Mukherji 1997e: 1-12). Concrete programmes for fighting out widespread female illiteracy will do wonders. Various poverty elimination programmes should be carried out immediately by creating widespread employment-generating programmes among the poor masses, especially among the poor women. Irrigation development, multiple cropping, cash cropping, intensive cultivation, and creation of village industries, cottage industries, and agro-industries will generate massive employment. These may be attempted in the villages. Small-scale industries may be set up in urban slums. This employment generation programme, both in rural areas and urban slums, alone will do the miracle. It will greatly bring down the levels of fertility and infant/child mortality, as various canonical linkages have clearly demonstrated.

Secondly, as many canonical linkages have testified, there is a urgent need to revamp the family planning programs, as well as augment the ANC care, child immunization programmes.

Thirdly, the crucial relationship between poverty among the mothers and very high level of infant deaths has emerged time and again; so also the causal relations between high ITR and abject poverty.

TABLE 1
SUMMARY OF RESULTS OF SIX SEPARATE CANONICAL ANALYSES. AP, BIHAR, MP, RAJASTHAN, UP, AND WEST BENGAL (1992-93 DATA)

State	*Canonical Linkage pairs*		
	1	*2*	*3*
AP			
Meaning of Canonical Linkages	High poverty, high CEB.	High IMR, as no ANC, & FP not used, though some sterilization	High CMR in rural areas, because less immunization moderately high poverty, though some ANC
available			
Bihar			
Meaning of Canonical Linkages	High poverty, high CEB; high IMAR as NO ANC	High CEB in urban areas, where No sterilization, though some immunization	High poverty, high CMR; even in urban areas though some ANC available
MP			
Meaning of Canonical Linkages	High poverty, high CEB, high IMR, high CMR, as No ANC	Moderately high poverty, high CEB, even in urban areas, though less immunization	High CMR in rural areas where FP not used and little immunization, though some ANC available
Rajasthan			
Meaning of Canonical Linkages	High Poverty, high CEB, as No ANC	In rural areas, high CMR where little Immunization	High IMR in rural areas where no ANC care given, though some immunization available
UP			
Meaning of Canonical Linkages	High poverty, high CEB, high IMR, as little immunization	Mod. poverty even in urban areas, high CEB, though some FP used	High poverty, high CMR though some ANC was available
WB			
Meaning of Canonical Linkages	High poverty, High CEB, though some ANC available	High IMR, in rural areas, where some sterilization done, but no ANC, nor FP used	High CMR, where FP not used, though ANC available, but low immunization completed

TABLE 2
CANONICAL STRUCTURE MATRIX, ANDHRA PRADESH, 1992-93, NFHS DATA (NO. OF CASES: 1593)

Variables	*Canonical Variate*		
	1	*2*	*3*
A. DEMOGRAPHIC MATRIX			
(Dependent Set)		Canonical Weights	
1. CEB (Children Ever Born)	.991489	–.319171	–.147071
2. IMR (Infant Mortality Rate)	–.090750	.895386	–.315260
3. CMR (Child Mortality Rate)	–.093351	.310506	.937540
B. SOCIO-ECONOMIC-CUM-POLICY MATRIX			
(Independent Set)			
4. Urban Residence	.243382	–.273196	–.567941
5. Poverty Index	.668801	.120726	.463620
6. Female Sterilization	–.553892	.488043	.144893
7. No Antenatal Care	.378589	.648319	–.464523
8. Fam. Planning Ever Used	.197612	–.442000	.414541
9. Number of Immunization	.065523	–.238584	–.232119
C. CANONICAL CORRELATION	.319280	.127498	.071920
D. MEANING OF CANONICAL LINKAGES	High poverty, high CEB	High IMR, as no ANC, & FP not used, though some sterilization	High CMR in Rural areas, because less immunization, moderately high poverty, though some ANC available
E. Trace Correlation	.2027871		
Wilks Lambda	.8788921		
CHI Square	205.1291000		
Significance	.0001		

TABLE 3
CANONICAL STRUCTURE MATRIX, BIHAR, 1992-93, NFHS DATA (NO. OF CASES: 2909)

Variables	*Canonical Variate*		
	1	*2*	*3*
A. DEMOGRAPHIC MATRIX			
(Dependent Set)		Canonical Weights	
1. CEB (Children Ever Born)	.833318	.652737	.253361
2. IMR (Infant Mortality Rate)	.516901	-.451623	-.734191
3. CMR (Child Mortality Rate)	.195943	-.608252	.629898
B. SOCIO-ECONOMIC-CUM-POLICY MATRIX			
(Independent Set)			
4. Urban Residence	.24446	.437485	.598375
5. Poverty Index	.845937	.013165	.583788
6. Female Sterilization	-.115369	-.655273	-.067891
7. No Antenatal Care	.478617	.310090	-.508682
8. Fam. Planning Ever Used	.010334	.313362	.161500
9. Number of Immunization	-.203231	.429766	-.108126
C. CANONICAL CORRELATION	.237481	.074632	.040955
D. MEANING OF CANONICAL LINKAGES	High poverty, high CEB high IMR as NO ANC	High CEB in urban areas, where No steriliza- tion ,though some im- munization	High poverty, high CMR; even in urban areas though, some ANC available
E. TRACE CORRELATION	.145653		
WILKS LAMBDA	.936773		
CHI SQUARE	189.6716000		
SIGNIFICANCE	.0001		

TABLE 4
CANONICAL STRUCTURE MATRIX, MADHYA PRADESH, 1992-93, NFHS DATA
(NO. OF CASES: 2980)

Variables	*Canonical Variate*		
	1	*2*	*3*
A. DEMOGRAPHIC MATRIX			
(Dependent Set)		Canonical Weights	
1. CEB (Children Ever Born)	.595836	.635192	-.578922
2. IMR (Infant Mortality Rate)	.665436	-.765178	-.019018
3. CMR (Child Mortality Rate)	.449638	.105046	.815161
B. SOCIO-ECONOMIC-CUM-POLICY MATRIX (Independent Set)			
4. Urban Residence	-.010364	.529382	-.427701
5. Poverty Index	.779504	.560438	.082983
6. Female Sterilization	-.188535	-.344240	-.007398
7. No Antenatal Care	.589691	-.398284	-.665499
8. Fam Planning Ever Used	.051251	.335555	-.595139
9. Number of Immunization	.079733	.126241	-.114246
C. CANONICAL CORRELATION	.239017	.125008	.095537
D. MEANING OF CANONICAL LINKAGES	High poverty, high CEB high IMR as NO ANC	Moderately high poverty high CEB even in urban areas, though less immunization	High CMR, in rural areas where FP not used and little immunization, though some ANC available
E. TRACE CORRELATION	.165210		
WILKS LAMBDA	.919665		
CHI SQUARE	249.142700		
SIGNIFICANCE	.0001		

TABLE 5
CANONICAL STRUCTURE MATRIX, RAJASTHAN, 1992-93. NFHS DATA (NO. OF CASES: 2433)

Variables	*Canonical Variate*		
	1	*2*	*3*
A. DEMOGRAPHIC MATRIX			
(Dependent Set)		Canonical Weights	
1. CEB (Children Ever Born)	.989073	-.385099	-.099961
2. IMR (Infant Mortality Rate)	-.125984	.258893	.942344
3. CMR (Child Mortality Rate)	.076568	.885818	-.319368
B. SOCIO-ECONOMIC-CUM-POLICY MATRIX			
(Independent Set)			
4. Urban Residence	.133129	-.850191	-.353977
5. Poverty Index	.705261	-.341655	-.635102
6. Female Sterilization	-.254434	-.029067	-.121937
7. No Antenatal Care	.620790	.055051	.431189
8. Fam. Planning Ever Used	.173514	-.269573	.219544
9. Number of Immunization	-.068257	-.289658	.471544
C. CANONICAL CORRELATION	.239179	.082968	.040291
D. MEANING OF CANONICAL LINKAGES	High poverty, high CEB as NO ANC	In rural areas, high CMR where little immuni-zation	High IMR, in rural areas where no ANC care given, though some immunization available
E. TRACE CORRELATION	.148002		
WILKS LAMBDA	.934783		
CHI SQUARE	163.7455000		
SIGNIFICANCE	.0001		

TABLE 6
CANONICAL STRUCTURE MATRIX, UTTAR PRADESH, 1992-93, NFHS DATA (NO. OF CASES: 6395)

Variables	*Canonical Variate*		
	1	*2*	*3*
A. DEMOGRAPHIC MATRIX			
(Dependent Set)		Canonical Weights	
1. CEB (Children Ever Born)	.778957	.710938	-.024445
2. IMR (Infant Mortality Rate)	.609617	-.596254	-.471621
3. CMR (Child Mortality Rate)	.146946	-.372891	.881462
B. SOCIO-ECONOMIC-CUM-POLICY MATRIX			
(Independent Set)			
4. Urban Residence	-.225118	.689856	.130967
5. Poverty Index	.625487	.491843	.724796
6. Female Sterilization	-.169928	-.134474	.164942
7. No Antenatal Care	.722776	-.021295	-.583734
8. Fam. Planning Ever Used	.034605	.465266	-.237117
9. Number of Immunization	.074906	.217210	-.182599
C. CANONICAL CORRELATION	.247593	.136526	.031361
D. MEANING OF CANONICAL LINKAGES	High poverty, high CEB, high IMR, as little immunization	Moderate poverty even in urban areas, high CEB, though some FP used	High poverty, high CMR, though some ANC was available
E. TRACE CORRELATION	.164241		
WILKS LAMBDA	.920295		
CHI SQUARE	530.7607000		
SIGNIFICANCE	.0001		

TABLE 7
CANONICAL STRUCTURE MATRIX, WEST BENGAL, 1992-93, NFHS DATA
(NO. OF CASES: 1877)

Variables	*Canonical Variate*		
	1	*2*	*3*
A. DEMOGRAPHIC MATRIX			
(Dependent Set)		Canonical Weights	
1. CEB (Children Ever Born)	.980197	-.565490	-.157681
2. IMR (Infant Mortality Rate)	.147718	.734204	-.452601
3. CMR (Child Mortality Rate)	.131883	.375721	.877661
B. SOCIO-ECONOMIC-CUM-POLICY MATRIX			
(Independent Set)			
4. Urban Residence	.121832	-.440914	.208942
5. Poverty Index	.884971	-.171161	.230622
6. Female Sterilization	-.251119	.501562	-.047486
7. No Antenatal Care	.344931	.414490	-.608669
8. Fam. Planning Ever Used	.133467	-.566011	-.696611
9. Number of Immunization	-.046172	-.180455	.212504
C. Canonical Correlation	.328511	.110641	.033751
D. MEANING OF CANONICAL LINKAGES	High poverty, high CEB though some ANC available	High IMR in rural areas, where some sterilization done but no ANC nor FP used	High CMR, where FP not used though ANC available, but low immunization completed
E. TRACE CORRELATION	.201081		
WILKS LAMBDA	.880156		
CHI SQUARE	238.9718000		
SIGNIFICANCE	.0001		

Part II: Findings From Three More Developed States

The first most important canonical linkage pair that emerged from subsequent canonical analyses of relatively developed states are shown in Tables 9-11, and are summarized in Table 8. The first most important canonical linkage pair are shown below:

States	*The most Important Canonical Linkage Pair*
1. Goa	Little poverty, and much sterilization, so low Children Ever Born per mother (CEB);
2. Kerala	Less poverty, less CEB;
3. Tamil Nadu	Less poverty, and high sterilization, so low CEB.

TABLE 8
SUMMARY OF RESULTS OF THREE SEPARATE CANONICAL ANALYSES: GOA, KERALA, AND TAMIL NADU

State	*Canonical Linkage Pairs*		
	1	*2*	*3*
Goa:			
Meaning of Canonical Linkages	Little poverty, and much, sterilization, so low CEB	High Immunization, low IMR, though mod, high CMR	Where no ANC, and little immunization, quite moderately notable IMR
Kerala:			
Meaning of canonical Linkages	Less poverty, less CEB	More sterilization, less CEB, though some IMR also	Mod. high CMR, where immunization less, though ANC given
Tamil Nadu:			
Meaning of Canonical Linkages	Less poverty, & high sterilization, so low CEB	Less poverty, low IMR, where though some ANC given, but little immunization	Quite high CMR in rural areas, even when some immunization and some ANC available

TABLE 9
CANONICAL STRUCTURE MATRIX, GOA , 1992-93, NFHS DATA
(NO. OF CASES: 1099)

Variables	*Canonical Variate*		
	1	2	3
A. DEMOGRAPHIC MATRIX			
(Dependent Set)		Canonical Weights	
1. CEB (Children Ever Born)	-.976832	-.395453	-.384185
2. IMR (Infant Mortality Rate)	-.199520	.329149	.868086
3. CMR (Child Mortality Rate)	-.077406	.857483	-.314369
B. SOCIO-ECONOMIC-CUM-POLICY MATRIX			
(Independent Set)			
4. Urban Residence	-.065549	.153813	.187397
5. Poverty Index	-.719217	.101863	.220810
6. Female Sterilization	.629252	.275895	.569308
7. No Antenatal Care	-.280280	-.171380	.724488
8. Fam. Planning Ever Used	-.054463	-.206982	-.169254
9. Number of Immunization	-.030808	.904232	-.196175
C. CANONICAL CORRELATION	.447803	.233268	.163233
D. MEANING OF CANONICAL LINKAGES	Little poverty, and much sterli-zation, so low CEB	High immuni-zation, low IMR; though mod. high CMR	Where no ANC, and little immunization, quite mode-rately notable IMR.
E. TRACE CORRELATION	.3063693		
WILKS LAMBDA	.7358271		
CHI SQUARE	335.5955000		
SIGNIFICANCE	0.0001		

TABLE 10
CANONICAL STRUCTURE MATRIX, KERALA, 1992-93, NFHS DATA (NO. OF CASES: 1499)

Variables	*Canonical Variate*		
	1	*2*	*3*
A. DEMOGRAPHIC MATRIX			
(Dependent Set)		Canonical Weights	
1. CEB (Children Ever Born)	-.911381	-.596698	.053004
2. IMR (Infant Mortality Rate)	-.384443	.683488	-.518136
3. CMR (Child Mortality Rate)	-.146932	.420471	.853654
B. SOCIO-ECONOMIC-CUM-POLICY MATRIX (Independent Set)			
4. Urban Residence	-.087526	.097520	-.251692
5. Poverty Index	-.825998	.256187	.285778
6. Female Sterilization	.287017	.909844	.052666
7. No Antenatal Care	-.476195	.147742	-.638093
8. Fam. Planning Ever Used	.003364	-.256103	-.379745
9. Number of Immunization	-.030228	.098110	-.548488
C. CANONICAL CORRELATION	.378878	175083	.043728
D. MEANING OF CANONICAL LINKAGES	Less poverty, Less CEB	More sterilization, less CEB though some IMR also	Mod. high CMR where immunization less, though ANC given
E. TRACE CORRELATION	.242291		
WILKS LAMBDEA	.828611		
CHI SQUARE	280.8795000		
SIGNIFICANCE	.0001		

TABLE 11
CANONICAL STRUCTURE MATRIX, TAMIL NADU, 1992-93 NFHS DATA
(NO. OF CASES: 1427)

Variables	*Canonical Variate*		
	1	*2*	*3*
A. DEMOGRAPHIC MATRIX			
(Dependent Set)		Canonical Weights	
1. CEB (Children Ever Born)	.991435	.371915	-.120074
2. IMR (Infant Mortality Rate)	.074597	-.852871	-.346543
3. CMR (Child Mortality Rate)	.107200	-.366456	.930317
B. SOCIO-ECONOMIC-CUM-POLICY MATRIX			
(Independent Set)			
4. Urban Residence	-.034311	-.026550	-.660628
5. Poverty Index	-.425644	-.560179	-.009272
6. Female Sterilization	.813676	-.596547	-.040050
7. No. Antenatal Care	-.381561	-.438383	-.605524
8. Fam. Planning Ever Used	-.057716	.273923	.100228
9. Number of Immunization	-.081619	-.249825	.430320
C. CANONICAL CORRELATION	.444541	.173360	.104530
D. MEANING OF CANONICAL LINKAGES	Less poverty, high sterilization, so low CEB	Less poverty, low IMR, where though some ANC given but little immunization	Quite high CMR in rural areas, even when some immunization and some ANC available.
E. TRACE CORRELATION	.282015		
WILKS LAMBDA	.769765		
CHI SQUARE	372.0941000		
SIGNIFICANCE	.0001		

References

1. Cooley, W.W. and Lohnes, P.R. (1962), *Multivariate Procedure in the Behavioural Sciences*, Wiley, New York, pp. 35-45.
2. Hotelling, Harold (1936), 'Relations Between Two Sets of Variate', Biometrika, 28, pp. 321-377.
3. Mukherji, Shekhar (1977) 'Assessing Interrelationships between Population Policies, Social Systems, and Demographic Behaviour in India: An Analytical Framework', *Demography India*, 6, Nos. 1-2, pp. 250-266.
4. Mukherji, Shekhar (1979), 'The Mobility Field Theory: A Spatial Behavioural Foundation to Movement Dynamics, with Application to Indian Situation', IGU working Group on Transformation of Rural Habitat and National Geographical Society of India, Research Monograph No. 25, Banaras Hindu University, Varanasi, pp. 1-80.
5. Mukherji, Shekhar (1983), *The Demographic Field Theory: Population Policies and Demographic Behaviour in India*, Thinkers Library, Allahabad, pp. 1-141.
6. Mukherji, Shekhar (1989), "Application of the Demographic Field Theory to Study Demographic Behaviour, Socio-economic Systems, and Population Policies in India", in *Dynamics of Population and Family Welfare*, K. Srinivasan and K.B. Pathak (eds.). Himalaya Publishing House, Bombay, Chapter 18, 343-373.
7. Mukherji, Shekhar (1992), 'Application of the Demographic Field Theory to Developing and Developed Countries', International Institute for Population Science Research Monograph, Bombay, pp. 10-92.
8. Mukherji, Shekhar (1994), 'Poverty and Fertility in Uttar Pradesh: Strategies for Poverty Alleviation and Better Health Services', Background Paper, Seminar on Population and Development in Uttar Pradesh, December 1994, pp. 1-18. pub in seminar Volume, — *Population and Development in Uttar Pradesh*, B.R. Publishing Co, New Delhi, 1996.
9. Mukherji, Shekhar (1997a), 'Poverty and Fertility in India: Results of Findings of the Demographic Field Theory — Linking Demographic Behaviour, Socio-economic System, and Population Policies in India', in IIPS Newsletter, Bombay, 1997, January, No 4-6, pp. 1-6.
10. Mukherji, Shekhar (1997b), 'Application of Demographic Field Theory to India: Linkages between Demographic Behaviour, Socio-economic systems, and Population Policies', Himalaya Publishing House, Bombay pp. 1-185 (in press).

Rummel, R.J. and Mukherji, Shekhar (1981), *Analyzing Population Policy and Demographic Change*, Prajna, Calcutta, pp. 1-80.

U.N. (1997), *Human Development Report*, Appendix, New York, N.Y.

Thirty One

Human Development Index (HDI) in Madhya Pradesh: Reassessed

A.S. Dey

The district-wise computation of Human Development Index in the pattern developed by UNDP ignores many crucial factors and leads to lopsided ranking.

— Editor

Introduction

According to the UNDP (1993), "Human development is the development of the people, for the people, by the people. Development of the people means investing in human capabilities, whether in education or health or skills, so that they can work productively and creatively. Development for the people means ensuring that the economic growth they generate is distributed widely and fairly. Development by the people means giving everyone a chance to participate."

The contemporary discourse on human development is framed around the twin notions of capability and deprivation. The capability approach maintains that resources have no value in themselves apart from their role in promoting human functioning. So, human development has two sides. One is the formation of human capabilities such as improved health, knowledge and skills. The other is the use people make of their acquired capabilities for productive purposes.

In this context, the UNDP has played a lead role in developing and framing an index for human development known as Human Development Index (HDI). The index is comprised of the unweighted average value of a set of three different categories of human capabilities: longevity, as a proxy for health-related capabilities; education, as a proxy for information and knowledge-related capabilities; and income as a proxy for capabilities to obtain a particular level of living. Since 1990, the UNDP's yearly report is providing HDI indicator for different countries around the world. The index value ranges from 0 to 1 and countries can be compared in terms of their relative index with one another. In 1998 among 174 countries, India is located at the 128 position, having a HDI value of .563. Among the neighbouring SAARC countries, Sri Lanka (.733) and Maldives (.725) are better placed than India.

Few countries computed HDI for their sub-regions explicitly within the human development framework of UNDP. In India, few studies (Tilak 1991, S. Kumar 1991, Probhu and Chatterjee 1993, EPW Research Foundation 1994, Population Foundation of India 1995) computed state-wise indicators of HDI. All these five studies indicated a poor value of HDI for Madhya Pradesh. Among 15 major states, Madhya Pradesh ranked 13 in the four studies and 15 in the other studies. Kerala ranked first in all the five studies.

The Government of Madhya Pradesh has made an attempt to compute district-wise HDI using the same framework as adopted by UNDP. Among the three components of human capabilities, education is represented by literacy rate and school enrolment ratios, health is represented by IMR and income is represented by per person income and rural poverty. The detailed description of computation methodologies can be seen from the Human Development Report in Madhya Pradesh (1995). This method here is termed as 'Method-I'.

Objective

In this paper an attempt has been made to reassess district-wise HDI of Madhya Pradesh by introducing, apart from capabilities related variables, other human development related variables like employment, communication, infrastructure and banking as well as other development related variables.

Further, instead of giving equal emphasis to all the variables, weighted mean of the indices according to their contribution to the human development are taken into view. To know weightage of different variables, the factor analysis model is attempted. Here, this method is termed as 'Method-II'.

Data Used :

The 33 variables which are in some way related to human development are as follows:

Economical

- Percentage of workers engaged in non-agricultural sector, 1991
- Percentage of cultivated land is irrigated, 1995-96
- Value of agricultural produce per hectare area (Rs.), 1995-96
- Per person food grain produced (kg), 1995-96
- Percentage of population below poverty line, 1992-93
- Per person consumption of electricity in rural areas (kilowatt/hour), 1995-96
- No. of registered industries per lakh population, 1995

Education

- Female literacy rate (excluding 0-6 age-group), 1991
- Percentage of population middle and above level education, 1991
- No. of students per teacher in SSC/HSC schools, 1995-96

Social

- Population Density (per sq. km.), 1991
- No. of females per 1000 males (sex ratio), 1991
- Percentage of Tribe population, 1991
- Percentage of villages having electricity, 1995-96
- Percentage of village having drinking water facility, 1995-96

Communication

- Length of metalled road per 100 sq. km. area, 1995-96
- No. of regd. vehicles per 1000 population, 1995-96
- No. of people covered per post office, 1995-96

Demographic

- Total fertility rate (TFR), 1984-90
- Contraceptive prevalence rate (CPR), 1996
- Under-5 mortality rate.

Health

- Percentage of target achieved in DPT, 1997
- Percentage of target achieved in OPV, 1997
- Percentage of target achieved in BCG, 1997
- Percentage of target achieved in Measles, 1997
- No. of hospital beds per lakh population, 1995-96

Geographic

- Percentage of total land having forest, 1995-96
- Percentage of total land is cultivatable, 1995-96
- Rainfall (mm), 1995-96

Banking

- Per farmer loan recvd. from agri co-operative society (Rs.), 1995-96
- Per person money deposited in co-operative banks (Rs.) 1995-96
- Per person money deposited in scheduled commercial bank, 1995-96
- Per person loan received from scheduled commercial bank, 1995-96

Different sources for data information are district-wise socio-economic indicators of Madhya Pradesh, 1995-96, Statistics of Madhya Pradesh in Brief, 1998; Directorate of Health Services, For Immunization Indicators Census of India, 1991; Registrar General of India, 1997.

Factor Analysis Model

The factor analysis model is chosen for this study for two reasons: first, for constructing the weight of each variable, and second, to reduce the number of variables.

For constructing the weight of each variable, the First Principal Component Method of Factor Analysis was used to compute composite index of human development index. This technique justifies its application as it explicitly takes into account the problem of multi-colinearity among the original variables by orthogonalizing the whole set of variables through a process of linear transformation and assigns objective weights to the included variable.

The composite index representing the level of human development of ith district is presented as

$$HD_i = \sum_{i=1}^{33} \frac{a_j}{\lambda} \cdot \frac{X_{ij} - X_{min,j}}{X_{max,j} - X_{min,j}}$$

Where,

HDi = Human Development Index of the ith district

a_j = First Principal Factor Loading of jth variable

λ = Latent Root of the First Principal Component

X_{ij} = The value of the jth variable in the ith district.

$X_{min,j}$ = Minimum value of the jth variable

$X_{max,j}$ = Maximum value of the jth variable

The value of the First Principal Factor Loading of the 33 variables is provided in Table 1.

Table 2 presents district wise HDI as observed in the two methods. The first two columns of the table provide HDI values as observed in the two methods. The last two columns show the respective rankings of the HDI values among different districts in the two methods. In the table, districts are arranged in order of HDI values of Method-I from highest ranking to lowest ranking. The group of first 15 districts is termed here as 'High HDI' districts, the next 15 districts as 'Medium HDI' districts, and the last 15 districts as 'Poor HDI' districts.

Method I: The districtwise values of HDI show highest ranking for Indore (.619) followed by Bhopal (.609) and Durg (.519). Only three districts have HDI value of more than 0.50, 29 districts have between 0.3 to 0.5 and 13 districts have less than 0.3. The least value of HDI is noticed in Tikamgarh district (0.156).

Method II: The reassessed value of HDI based on factor analysis shows highest ranking for Indore (0.666) followed by Bhopal (0.632), Gwalior (0.513) and Ujjain (0.460). Like Method I, three districts have HDI value more than 0.5, 31 districts between 0.3 to 0.5, and 11 districts less than 0.3. The least value of HDI is found in Bastar district (0.202).

Comparison between Method I and II: The correlation between two sets of values is seen as 0.709. The correlation among 'High HDI' districts is 0.715. The corresponding value among 'Medium HDI' and 'Poor HDI' districts is 0.786 and 0.695 respectively.

If we compare ranking of HDI values in the two methods, we can see that among 45 districts, the HDI rankings of 12 districts are more or less similar. A difference of two points is hardly noticed, e.g. rank of Durg in the first method was third, as compared to fifth in the second method. The first method provided a better ranking for 14 districts, while second method yielded a better ranking in the remaining 19 districts.

A closer look at the table shows that as one moves from 'High HDI' to 'Poor HDI' districts, more dissimilarity in ranking is noticed. Among the first 15 'High HDI' districts, more or less similar ranking is observed in seven districts. The first method provided a better ranking in seven districts, and the second method provided a better ranking only in one district (Mandsour). The corresponding value in the 'Medium HDI' districts are 2, 6 and 7, and in 'Poor HDI' districts are 3, 1 and 11 respectively.

The highest discrepancy is observed in the Raisen district: the first method provided seventh rank to it as compared to its 29th rank in the second method. Let us look into socio-economic characteristics of Raisen district. Per capita income of the district is highest (Rs. 7201) followed by Indore (Rs. 4508) and Bhopal (Rs. 4485). Industrial belt of Mandideep near Bhopal has increased the business and transportation activities of Raisen and this is mainly responsible for high income of the district. But, the district is lagging behind in many indicators when compared to other districts. The female literacy rate is 25 per cent as compared to 29 per cent for the state. Length of metalled road per sq. km. area is 10.2 km. (MP 17.3 Km.), registered vehicle per thousand population is 19 (MP 30), number of telephone connections per lakh population is 609 (MP 829). Moreover, 61 per cent of families in rural area and 23 per cent in urban area are below poverty line. The corresponding values for the state are 62 and 17 respectively. It seems that the second method which ranked Raisen district relatively lower than its position the first method seems to be justified.

Secondly, Factor Analysis is used to reduce the number of variables (i.e., 33) by describing each linearly in terms of new, uncorrelated factors. The factors provide a parsimonious description of the observed data by retaining the most important information contained in the original data. The model extracts the maximum variance of the data explainable by the underlying factors that describe the structure and pattern of the original variables. Within this strategy, the variables enter the factor model without the grouping of the variables into any a priori structure. Here, orthogonal rotation using the varimax technique is used where factors are assumed to be independent, i.e., uncorrelated.

Table 3 shows the relative effect of the factor on human development. These values are referred to as factor loading. The table also indicates the commonality of each variable — that is, the proportion of the variance in the dependent variable that is explained by the various components of development. The rotation reduced the number of factors to six having eigenvalue more than

1. The extracted factors explained about 73 per cent of the variance. A description about six factors is given below.

Factor 1 associates human development with Economic (including Education and Banking) related variables. A high factor loading (between 0.58 to 0.94) is noticed in nine variables as can be seen from Table 3. All other 24 variables have factor loading less than 0.5. It is the principal factor, has an eigenvalue of 9.9 and explains 30 per cent of the variance in human development.

Factor 2 correlates human development with health related variables like Percentage of Coverage in DPT, OPV, BCG and Measles. All the four variables have factor loading between 0.78 to 0.96. All other 29 variables have factor loading less than 0.27. This factor has an eigenvalue of 4.8 and explains 15 per cent of the variance in human development.

Factor 3 associates human development with geographical resources related variables. High factor loading is seen in variables like Proportion of Forest Land (-0.821), Proportion of Cultivable Land (0.814) and Rainfall (-0.680). One variable, Proportion of Villages having Electricity, which is not strictly a geographical variable and has high factor loading (0.746), is included in this category, which may be due to its association with other variables in this category. It has an eigenvalue of 3.2 and explains 10 per cent of the variance in human development.

Factor 4 associates human development with demographic variables like Total fertility Rate (TFR), Contraceptive Prevalence Rate (CPR) and Under-5 Mortality Rate. The factor loading of the three variables is seen as -0.730, 0.815 and -0.544. It has an eigenvalue of 2.7 and explains eight per cent of the variance in human development.

Factor 5 associates human development with social development related variables like Proportion of Scheduled Tribe Population, Proportion of Population Lying Below Poverty Line and Sex Ratio (No. of females per 1000 males). It has an eigenvalue of 1.8 and explains six per cent of the variance in human development. The factor loadings in the three variables are seen as -0.606, -0.611, and -0.659. An unrelated variable, Proportion of irrigated land is noticed in this category having high factor loading, 0.769.

Factor 6 associates human development with infrastructure development related variables like Population Coverage per Post

Office, and Proportion of Villages Having Drinking Water Facility. The factor has an eigenvalue of 1.6 and explains five per cent of the variance in human development.

The factor analysis model adopted here has enabled reducing of the number of variables from 33 to 6. Moreover, while reassessing the district-wise values of HDI, it has taken care of the inherent deficiencies of the earlier method.

TABLE 1
VALUE OF THE FIRST PRINCIPAL FACTOR LOADING OF THE 33 VARIABLES

Variable No.	*Variable Name*	*Factor Loading*
1.	Percentage of workers engaged in non-agricultural sector in 1991	-.052
2.	Percentage of cultivated land is irrigated, 1995-96	.520
3.	Value of agricultural produce per hectare area (Rs.) in 1995-96	.606
4.	Per person food grain produced (kg), 1995-96	-.126
5.	Percentage of population below poverty line, 1992-93	-.493
6.	Per person consumption of electricity (kilowatt/hour) in 1995-96	.602
7.	No. of registered industries per lakh population	.804
8.	Female literacy rate, 1991	.763
9.	Percentage of population middle and above level education, 1991	.865
10.	No. of students per teacher, 1995-96	-.258
11.	Population Density (per sq. km.), 1991	.879
12.	No. of females per 1000 males (sex ratio), 1991	-.324
13.	Percentage of tribe population in 1991	-.530
14.	Percentage of villages having electricity, 1995-96	.522
15.	Percentage of villages having drinking water facility, 1995-96	.047
16.	Length of metalled road per 100 sq. km. area, 1995-96	.540
17.	No. of regd. Vehicles per 1000 population in 1995-96	.908
18.	No. of People Covered per post office	.391
19.	Total fertility rate (TFR), 1984-90	-.224
20.	Contraceptive prevalence rate (CPR), 1996	.268
21.	Under-5 mortality rate, 1991	-.433
22.	Percentage of target achieved in DPT, 1997	.339
23.	Percentage of target achieved in OPV, 1997	.341
24.	Percentage of target achieved in BCG, 1997	.273
25.	Percentage of target achieved in Measles, 1997	.250
26.	No. of hospital beds per 1000 population, 1995-96	.463
27.	Percentage of total land having forest, 1995-1996	-.547
28.	Percentage of total land is cultivatable, 1995-1996	.584
29.	Rainfall (mm), 1995-96	-.234
30.	Per farmer loan recvd. from agri co-operative society (Rs.), 1995-96	.664
31.	Per person money deposited in co-operative banks (Rs.), 1995-96	.658
32.	Per person money deposited in scheduled bank	.859
33.	Per person loan received from scheduled bank	.887

TABLE 2
HDI VALUES AND RANKINGS IN METHOD I AND METHOD II

District	HDI Value		Rank	
	Method I	Method II	Method I	Method II
Indore	0.619	0.686	1	1
Bhopal	0.609	0.632	2	2
Durg	0.519	0.442	3	5
Gwalior	0.497	0.513	4	3
Ujjain	0.466	0.460	5	4
Chhindwada	0.461	0.366	6	17
Raisen	0.456	0.327	7	29
Dewas	0.444	0.373	8	14
Bhind	0.440	0.389	9	10
Mandsour	0.405	0.411	10	7
Balghat	0.401	0.316	11	30
Bilaspur	0.387	0.339	12	26
Dhar	0.385	0.374	13	13
Raigarh	0.384	0.283	14	38
Vidisha	0.382	0.346	15	23
Seoni	0.377	0.284	16	37
Damoh	0.374	0.316	17	31
Sehore	0.372	0.355	18	18
Morena	0.371	0.355	19	19
Hoshangabad	0.371	0.377	20	12
Ratlam	0.363	0.403	21	8
Jabalpur	0.357	0.431	22	6
Raipur	0.350	0.372	23	15
Narsinhpur	0.336	0.394	24	9
Datia	0.332	0.384	25	11
Mandla	0.331	0.248	26	43
Surguja	0.323	0.211	27	44
Bastar	0.319	0.202	28	45
Rajnandgaon	0.312	0.280	29	39
Shajapur	0.309	0.366	30	16
Betul	0.308	0.301	31	34
Khandwa	0.304	0.346	32	22
Sagar	0.299	0.345	33	24
Khargaun	0.277	0.347	34	21
Shivpuri	0.260	0.293	35	35
Sidhi	0.256	0.264	36	41
Guna	0.251	0.315	37	32
Jhabua	0.229	0.284	38	36
Satna	0.225	0.352	39	20
Sahdol	0.220	0.261	40	42
Chatarpur	0.216	0.332	41	28
Rewa	0.213	0.306	42	33
Raigarh	0.179	0.342	43	25
Panna	0.175	0.266	44	40
Tikamgarh	0.156	0.337	45	27

Method I: As computed by Government of MP.
Method II:Reassessed value of HDI using Factor Analysis Method.

TABLE 3

FACTOR LOADINGS, EIGENVALUES, VARIENCE EXPLAINED AND ACCUMULATED VARIANCE EXPLAINED AS OBTAINED FROM ORTHOGONAL ROTATION IN FACTOR ANALYSIS USING THE VARIMAX TECHNIQUE

Var. No.	Variable Name	Factor 1	2	3	4	5	6	Commo-nality Value
1.	Percentage of workers engaged in non-agricultural sector, 1991	-	-	-	-	-	-	0.79
2.	Percentage of cultivated land is irrigated, 1995-96	-	-	-	-	.769	-	0.81
3.	Value of agricultural produce per hectare area (Rs.), 1995-96	-	-	-	-	-	-	0.85
4.	Per person food grain produced (kg), 1995-96	-	-	-	-	-	-	0.83
5.	Percentage of population below poverty line, 1992-93	-	-	-	-	.611	-	0.84
6.	Per person consumption of electricity in rural areas (kilowatt/hour), 1995-96	-	-	-	-	-	-	0.69
7.	No. of registered industries per lakh population, 1995	.665	-	-	-	-	-	0.82
8.	Female literacy rate (excluding 0-6 age-group), 1991	.789	-	-	-	-	-	0.84
9.	Percentage of population middle and above level education, 1991	.893	-	-	-	-	-	0.94
10.	No. of students per teacher in SSC/HSC schools, 1995-96	-	-	-	-	-	-	0.85
11.	Population Density (per sq. km.), 1991	.876	-	-	-	-	-	0.97
12.	No. of females per 1000 males (sex ratio), 1991	-	-	-	-	-.659	-	0.88
13.	Percentage of Tribe population, 1991	-	-	-	-	-.606	-	0.82
14.	Percentage of villages having electricity, 1995-96	-	-	-	-	-	-	0.79
15.	Percentage of village having drinking water facility, 1995-96	-	-	-	-	-	.352	0.76
16.	Length of metalled road per 100 sq. km. area, 1995-96	.587	-	-	-	-	-	0.80
17.	No. of regd. Vehicles per 1000 population, 1995-96	.904	-	-	-	-	-	0.94
18.	No. of people covered per post office, 1995-96	-	-	-	-	-	.753	0.73

(Contd...)

(Table 3 Contd...)

		(1)	(2)	(3)	(4)	(5)	(6)	(7)
19.	Total fertility rate (TFR), 1984-90	-	-	-	-.730	-	-	0.81
20.	Contraceptive prevalence rate (CPR), 1996	-	-	-	.815	-	-	0.72
21.	Under-5 mortality rate.	-	-	-	-.544	-	-	0.78
22.	Percentage of target achieved in DPT, 1997	-	-	-	-	-	-	0.96
23.	Percentage of target achieved in OPV, 1997	-	0.957	-	-	-	-	0.96
24.	Percentage of target achieved in BCG, 1997	-	0.862	-	-	-	-	0.86
25.	Percentage of target achieved in Measles, 1997	-	0.783	-	-	-	-	0.78
26.	No. of hospital beds per lakh population, 1995-96	-	-	-	-	-	.493	0.72
27.	Percentage of total land having forest, 1995-96	-	-	-.821	-	-	-	0.85
28.	Percentage of total land is cultivatable, 1995-96	-	-	.814	-	-	-	0.87
29.	Rainfall (mm), 1995-96	-	-	-.680	-	-	-	0.66
30.	Per farmer loan recvd. from agri co-operative society (Rs.), 1995-96	-	-	-	-	-	-	0.78
31.	Per person money deposited in co-operative banks (Rs.), 1995-96	.727	-	-	-	-		-0.83
32.	Per person money deposited in scheduled commercial bank, 1995-96	.939	-	-	-	-	-	0.96
33.	Per person loan received, from scheduled commercial bank, 1995-96	.923	-	-	-	-	-	0.94
	Eigen Value	9.99	4.80	3.19	2.69	1.86	1.66	
	Varience Explained	30.3	14.5	9.7	8.1	5.6	5.0	
	Accumulated Varience Explained	30.3	44.8	54.5	62.6	68.3	73.3	

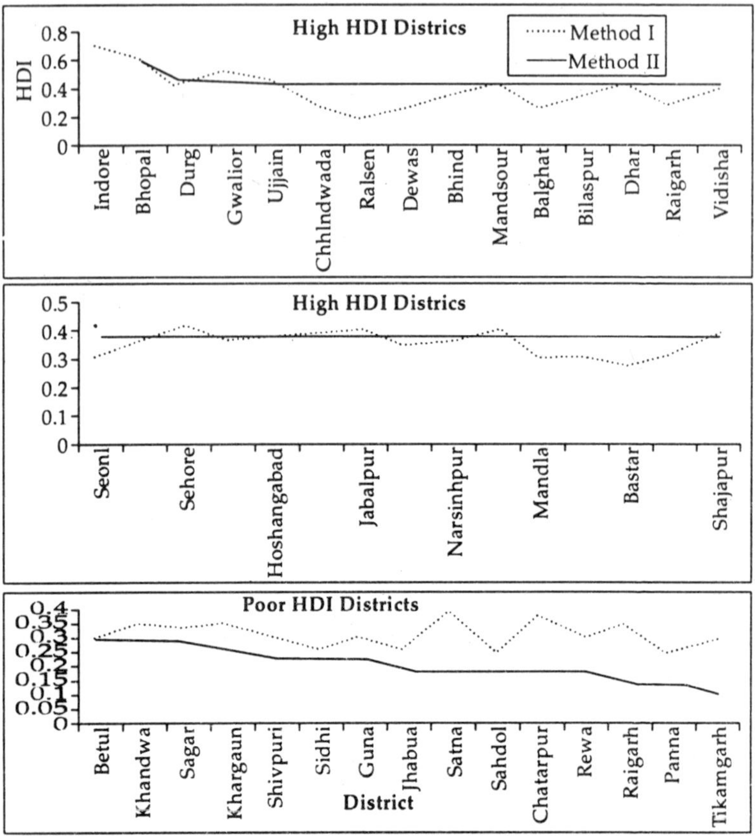

References

District-wise socio-economic indicators of Madhya Pradesh, 1995-96, Directorate of Economic and Statistics, Govt. of Madhya Pradesh, Bhopal.

E.P.W. Research Foundation, 1994, 'Social Indicators of Development for India'. *Economic and Political Weekly,* May 14, 1994.

Harry H. Harman, *Modern Factor Analysis, 1967,* University of Chicago Press, Chicago.

Madhya Pradesh Human Development Report, 1995, Directorate of Institutional Finance, Govt. of Madhya Pradesh, Bhopal.

Nussbaum, Martho, 1995, Introduction in Martho Nussbaum and Jonatha Glover (eds.), *Women, Culture and Development: A Study of Human Capabilities,* New York, Oxford.

Sen, Amartya, 1972, *Inequality Re-examined,* New York, Oxford.

Statistics of Madhya Pradesh in Brief, 1998, Directorate of Economic and Statistics, Govt. of Madhya Pradesh, Bhopal.

UNDP 1993, *Human Development Report 1993,* New York, Oxford University Press.

Part IV

Social Organization for Human Development

Thirty Two

Human Welfare in Hindu Scriptures

S.K. Dixit

This paper outlines the rules suggested in the Puranas and Vedic literature for the attainment of human welfare.

—Editor

Man has made great progress in every sphere of life in the modern times. He has now entered into the Space Age and is looking for presence of life on other planets. An enormous increase in the availability of means for satisfying his needs and ambitions has taken place. This has, however, also meant that he is becoming even more dependent on physical resources. He himself now somewhat resembles a machine devised by science and technology.

Favourable geographical conditions are generally deemed essential for helping a country achieve economic and social development. This include factors such as extensive plains, proper climate and access to sea coasts which can promote trade and commerce. The availability of minerals and other resources provide a solid foundation for industrial development. But, it is now being felt that nations are not able to make economic and social progress despite having most favourable geographical conditions. This is because of a continuous moral decline in society. Man has developed an attitude of neglect towards essential values of human existence. The development of a society is directly linked to the moral values. It is essential to work for moral progress in the society and sensitise the individual towards human values. Lasting progress would not be possible otherwise.

Economic development has given rise to many distortions in

the moral values. These include rise of individualism, the desire to become instantly rich and prosperous, over-dependence on material resources, uncontrolled exploitation of natural resources, the culture of industrialization and urbanization, lack of sensitivity and social awareness, lack of patriotism, decline in moral values, emergence of consumerism, tendency towards social injustice and crime, racial divisions and class conflicts.

Remedies to these problems can be found in the ancient Indian treaties — the Vedic texts, Smritis, Puranas and the epics. The literature of this era is full of moral teachings and the right code of conduct for man. They deal with protection of the earth and its environment, ways to bring about human welfare, and inculcation of a patriotic spirit among the members of the society.

Human Conduct:

The ancient Indian literature contains many directives concerning human behaviour and conduct:

* The cause of *dharma* is upheld through truthfulness. Cleaning protects the utensil. Dignity and propriety in behaviour saves the family and the clan.
* Life of living beings is uncertain. Wealth and youth are subject to change. There is uncertainty about a man's wife, son, etc. but his fame, glory and dharma have a lasting permanence.
* The man who wants to achieve his objective must always have the company of good people. Bad company will never bring about welfare either in this world or in the world beyond (*Garuda Purana*).
* The Grihastha, i.e. the family man must make effort to learn and practise the Vedas. He should organise *yajnas*. He should not only discharge his domestic chores but also take out time for worship (*Kurma Purana*).
* A person who only speaks truth and who has conquered the feeling of anger that lies within becomes like the Great Being, the Brahman. A man who bathes daily, worships regularly, studies regularly and who is soft spoken and able to keep his senses in check, achieves great heights in this world and in the world beyond (*Kurma Purana*).

* The man who gives away a fixed portion of his wealth in charity and is endowed with kindness and piety is to be called a *grihastha* in the true sense. One should keep away from evil deeds and perform such deeds, which have been recommended in the scriptures to the best of his abilities (*Kurma Purana*).

The world can be conquered through a conduct based on truth. Truth is the highest stage. To describe something exactly the way it is, is truth, say the learned sages. The control over physical instincts and senses is called *dama*, while the control over mind is called *shama*. (*Kurma Purana*).

No violence should be done to any creature. Falsehood should never be uttered. Words which are not liked or may cause harm should never be spoken. If one steals even a twig, leaf, dust or water belonging to someone else, he is sure to be doomed.

Daily Life

The Pauranic literature contains many directions for governing the daily life and activities of a man — his food, clothing, sleeping, etc. These need to be followed by the human community in the present times. The Puranas say that man should not succumb to ill temperament. Jealousy and attachments are fit to be given up. Greed, pride, condemnation of knowledge, condemnation of others, drunkenness, sorrow etc. should be given up too with due effort. Never inflict pain on others. If the son and students are punished it should be with the righteous intention of making them able. (*Kurma Purana* 16.50.61).

Food Habits

Kurma Purana has given a detailed account on what is fit to be eaten and what should not be consumed. The man who accepts its advice will succeed in leading a long and healthy life.

A Brahmin should not touch wine in any form. The man who drinks loses morality. He becomes unfit for conversation. Man also falls by eating and drinking that which should not be eaten or drunk. A happy life demands abstinence.

Student Life

A student should give up laziness, sleep, false speech and speaking ill of others. He should leave his home and reside at a spot which has been cleaned up and purified (*Kurma Purana*, 27.19).

Protection of the earth and its environment

Destruction of shrubs, creepers, plants and trees bearing flowers or fruits or other useful products is prohibited. Killing of cow is prohibited; even harming it in any way is prohibited. There is no way of repentance if this sin is committed (*Kurma Purana*, 32.57).

Rivers are divine and placed in the ranks of gods. Their well-being has been desired through prayers. According to *Kurma Purana*, the river water should not be polluted. No one should indulge in excessive consumption or misuse of the produce of the earth. One should not point his feet towards a cow, a brahmin, fire, teacher, sun or the moon.

Human Welfare

The Indian 'Smritis' pray that "may all attain happiness, may all enjoy good health and be free of diseases, may every one enjoy complete well-being, may no one be unhappy and sorrowful."

A famous Vedic prayer seeks: "May all that which brings well-being and may all that is righteous and pure and brings greatness and is never defeated, come to us from all directions. May the Gods who never obstruct progress and who protect us everyday keep us free from all obstructions. May we benefit from the kindness of the gods. May we receive the wisdom of the gods who transverse on a straight path. May we receive the friendship of gods. May god make us long lived. May the air bring us comfort and health. May the gods increase our wealth and prosperity. May the gods secure us. May the god who has never been defeated grant us bliss. May he become our guardian."

A Rigvedic verse goes thus — "May we tread on the everlasting beneficent path, going as the sun and moon who are eternally engaged in following their duty. May we travel on the path shown by the scriptures with a sense of mutual love for each other." (*Rigveda* 5.51.6).

Yajurveda (30.3) prays, "O Lord of the Universe! Rid us of all the pains and sorrows, grant us all that which brings happiness and welfare."

Shathapatha Brahman, (14.1.1.30) seeks: "Take us away from the untruth towards the truth, from the darkness towards light and from death towards immortality."

Patriotism

Progress of a man is possible only when the nation progresses.

The views related to the development of the nationalistic spirit as found in the *Rigveda* (10.91.2) are: "O Lord, please grant us that wisdom which would make us live in harmony with each other and move ahead. May we all possess a similar sweet voice. May we all feel alike and may all have equal share in the produce of our nation and enjoy it together. May our disposition be free of blemish. May our disposition be such as to promote the feeling of love and concern for each other."

Another verse goes like this: "O Lord, grant us such off-springs who are endowed with excellence and who can bear mighty weapons. May they have the capability of defending themselves as well as their country. May we lead our nation with full alertness. May noble thoughts visit us."

Thirty Three

Varna and Caste

Dharmender Kumar Misra

Varna is based upon one's inner inclination. Caste or *jati* is practically based on inheritance and has become outdated. The correct varna system must be re-established.

— Editor

The caste system has proved a bane to Indian society. Some give religious sanctity to the system by citing illustrations from the *Gita* in favour of it. But the *Gita* does not contain any verse creating for endorsing chasms and divisions among human beings.

If our scriptures are not to be blamed for the emergence of the caste system the question arises, who created the caste system in Indian society? Why is caste considered to be the main basis of Indian social superstructure? It is a fact that caste system has spread its shadow in all spheres of life in India — social, cultural, economic and political. Analysis of castes is indispensable for the study of Hindu life.

Caste and varna are two distinct entities denoting different set-ups. They are to be defined separately. The hub of Indian social organisation is varna system. Division of labour is indispensable in the society. Proper division of labour is possible when it is based on the nature, bent of mind, qualities and inclinations of individuals. Ancient Indian society had group-wise division of labour where every group was assigned a particular varna. Conduct and duties of the members of each group were subjected to particular standards and evaluation. This was the varna system.

Sri Yaskacharya says that the word 'varna' originates from

the root *vri* denoting selection or varna (colour). We can deduce from this that varna is that which man selects according to his nature and work.

Only one hymn in the *Rigveda* mentions varna. This hymn explains the origin of four varnas from the four different organs of Prajapati. The Brahman was his mouth, his arms were the Rajanyah (Kshatriyas), his thighs became the Vaishyas. From His feet were born the Sudras. Dr. Radhakrishnan has accepted the symbolic meaning of this verse. Purushukta description of the Indian system of varnas depicts unity underlying diversity. Different organs of body social work in sympathy and in loving cooperation with one another in spite of differences of position, of shape, of characteristics and of functions. So also different varna.

Brhadaranyaka Upanishad says that Prajapati did not create all the four varnas simultaneously — at one go. In the beginning, he created only Brahmans. Finding Brahmans incapable of performing all the necessary functions of society, He created Kshatriyas. Still, many functions remained undone. When all the work could not be thus accomplished smoothly, He created Vaishyas in the shape of Vasu, Marut, Rudra and Aditi. In the end, to bring about completion in the social life, He created Sudras.

Chhandogya Upanishad believes that there is intimate relationship between varna and past life. Deeds done in the past life determine the quality of the next birth. Combination of deeds and qualities entitle men to the status of a particular varna.

According to the *Mahabharata*, Prajapati initially created all human beings as equal. But in due course of time those who displayed different traits were allotted different varnas based upon their distinct deeds and qualities. Brahamans who displayed wrath, anger and pride were called Kshatriyas. Brahmans who became indifferent to their *dharma*, who engaged themselves in agriculture and rearing of various domestic animals became Vaishyas. Brahmans who followed falsehood and whose conduct become shredded in doubt and who showed traits of greed and sexual indulgence became Sudras.

Colours of different varnas depict their respective qualities. White colour of Brahmans symbolises sacredness. Red colour of Kshatriyas indicates anger and royal qualities. Yellowish shade of

Vaishyas displays mixture of wrath and vices (passions of love and pleasure). Black colour of the Sudras symbolises vices and impurities. Janaka, in order to get his doubt clarified, is said to have asked Guru Parusharam: why there was difference of colour in human beings although they had been created equally by Prajapati. Guru Parusharam admitted that all human beings had been equal in the beginning and of single colour. But just as the change in soil and seed changes the shape of farming, similarly change in deeds of man changes his colour.

In Vana Parva Yudhisthira opined that qualities should determine the varna — Brahmans or Sudra. In the *Gita*, Lord Krishna says to Arjuna:

> The four varna were created by me, by distributing qualities and acts. Know me to be the creator of them (*Gita* 4/13).

Smritis put forward different view-points regarding the varna system. One *sloka* of *Attri Smriti* presents a view-point similar to that put forward by the *Gita*. It says that people taking birth on this earth are Sudras. Sacraments, qualities and actions put them on the higher or lower rungs of the social ladder. *Yagnavalkya Smriti* opines that all are born equal from mothers. Investiture with the sacred thread makes one Brahman, Kshatriya or Vaishya. This ceremony is performed in the 8th year, in the 11th year and in the 12th year of the Brahman, of the Kshatriya and of the Vaishya respectively. For sudras this ceremony is not performed.

Manu Smriti concurs with the theory of birth of varnas as illustrated in the Purusha Sukta of the *Rigveda*. Brahmans form the head of the social order. They are members with intellectual bent of mind and they think. Their main function is to accumulate knowledge and distribute it. The function of the arms is to protect. In the social set-up, we have people whose main quality is their physical strength. They are called Kshatriyas. Responsibility of administration and of good social arrangement lies on their shoulders. From the thighs are born the Vaishyas. The function of stomach and thighs is to store and distribute. Ploughing, rearing and protection of kines, trade, donation giving, study and performance of *yajna* are the duties of Vaishyas. Sudras in society represent the feet of body social. Function of the feet is to move, work and to carry the weight of the body. Sudras representing feet are not capable of serving the society in any other way than by doing labour and service. Their duty is to serve the other three varnas.

Varna was determined on the basis of qualities and actions up to the *Mahabharata* age. After the *Mahabharata* age, composers of Smritis tried to interpret the Purusha Sukta in such a way that varna system come to be considered to be a God-made set-up. The varna system became entangled in the mesh of the caste system. Gradually, the varna system based on qualities and actions transformed into the caste system based on birth.

Let us count merits and demerits of both the systems.

The varna system was an intelligent and intelligible division. It was a unique system of division of labour and specialization. Performance of duty was known as varna dharma. Religious tinge was given to duties and responsibilities. So man got encouragement and spiritual satisfaction while doing his job. No one was superior to another. All occupations were equal and honourable in so far as they were not in conflict with morals. A scavenger had the same status as a Brahman. It was possible for a Sudra to become a Vaishya. Transformation from one varna to another was possible. The concept of the varnas was linked to power of four types:

1. Power of knowledge.
2. Power of administration and army.
3. Power of property and service.
4. Power of labour and service.

Endeavour was made to provide a system of checks and balances in the varna system. Through division of labour effort was made to ensure that all the four powers did not accumulate in the hands of some people or a group of people. All the four powers were divided keeping in view the maintenance of equilibrium in society.

There appear to exist some demerits of the system as well. Equality, liberty and truth are three pillars of a social set-up. They provide stability. In the birth-based caste system they are ignored. This system is based on double standard of morality. It is not to treat some people as stupid, unholy and idiotic by birth as compared to other persons. It is based on monopolistic notion. Maximum privileges were given to the powerful persons.

Restrictions were imposed when some other group of men tried to rise on the social ladder. This stemmed social progress and inculcated rivalry, jealousy and unnecessary bickering.

How did the conception of caste emerged after the *Mahabharata* period? How and why did caste system come into being? These questions need to be answered.

Origin of caste is perhaps in the Sanskrit word *jat* which denotes more importance being given to man's birth and his family. Many scholars have stressed upon the structural and functional aspects of castes while others have laid emphasis on its origin. Kule says, when a group strongly and stauchingly adheres to heredity it becomes a caste. According to another scholar, caste is a group where man links his birth with his fate and where his social status is predetermined in entirety. Herbert Rizzle says that caste is collection of families or groups of families which have a common name and boast of their origin from an imaginary forefather or god. They lay emphasis on single traditional occupation. Hattan has come to the conclusion that caste is an arrangement where the entire society gets divided into self-centred units different from one another. Relations of these units are determined by traditions based on high and low.

This brings us to the conclusion that caste is a hierarchical structure based on birth. It enjoins restrictions on its members regarding modes of eating and drinking, marriage, occupation and social interactions. Scholars agree that the caste system is variable and restrictions imposed by it are not final. On the basis of wealth, status, power and honour one can change one's caste.

Let us see what are the bases of change of caste? Do we come across such instances in ancient times and have they been sanctioned by society? Caste system has been undergoing change from time to time. These changes can be classified in six periods:

1. Vedic period (6000 BC - 2000 BC).
2. Post Vedic period (upto the end of 3rd century AD).
3. Dharma Sastra period (upto 11th century).
4. Medieval period (upto late 18th century).
5. British period (from middle of 18th century to the beginning of 20th century).
6. Modern period (after Independence).

Vedic period

This period was the longest in the history of caste system. Knowledge of this period is available from the Vedas, Upanishads and Brahmana *granthas*. Society was divided into different varnas but relations among them regarding marriage, occupation and modes of eating and drinking were not very rigid and hard. *Chhandogya Upanishad* has many illustrations to show that in the matter of matrimonial relations, there were no restrictions. Shama Shastri is of the opinion that before the period of Buddha, there were no regulations regarding inter-caste eating and drinking and matrimonial relations. Man could change his varna on the basis of his qualities, actions and nature (inclination). According to *Satapatha Brahmana* Kshatriya King Visvaratha became a Brahman—sage Visvamitra. In *Shiv Purana*, we can find many instances where Vaishyas changed their varna and became Brahmans. Three Vaishyas — Bhala Nanda, Vatsa and Sankila — compiled mantras and became Brahmans.

Post Vedic Period

In the beginning of this period, the Brahmans, to secure and stabilise their position, separated duties of different varnas from one another. They denied investiture with the sacred thread and study of scriptures to the Sudras. Many thinkers like Gautama, Bodhayana and Apaslamba created codes of conduct and compilation of hymns, testaments which gave maximum rights and privileges to the Brahmans. This period also saw maximum growth of Brahman *granthas*. Dr. R.C. Saxena says that Kshatriyas, Vaishyas and Sudras perhaps did not accept the varna system at this time. With the rise in the influence of Jainism and Buddhism these three varnas raised the banner of revolt against the varna system.

In 148 B.C. a Brahman king named Shunga ascended the throne for the first time. It was the time when fanatical revolts started against Jainism and Buddhism. Perhaps this period also saw the creation of *Manu Smriti*. It presented an outline of a new Hindu religion incorporating religious ceremonies in abundance. New practical rules and regulations denigrated hybrid castes. This resulted in a rapid growth of sub castes and their membership soon swelled.

Dharma Sastra period

Dharma Sastra era starts at end of the third century AD. Brahman purohits played a vital role in the formulation of state policies and state administration. According to Dr. Narmdeshwar Prasad, Purohit ministers had completely crushed Kshatriyas and other castes in the Gupta period. They had practically severed all connections with the Vedas and established the laws propounded by the *Manu Smriti* as practical ideals. Duties of different varnas were determined partially on the basis of *Yagnavalkya Samhita, Vishnu Samhita, Prashara Samhita* and *Narada Samhita.*

Medieval Period

This period starts with the end of the 11th century AD. Two significant changes occurred in the society — rise and downfall of Rajput kings and complete acceptance and adherence to the Brahmanic set-up. B.N. Dutt says that in this age religious ceremonies, faith and rituals became all powerful. Strong administration was absent. That is why Muslims, treading distances of hundreds of miles, facing no opposition on the way, plundered and looted the Hindu temples. Centralised power was missing and religious bigotry prevailed over state affairs. Many changes crept into the Dharma-shastras and Puranas and their decrees were made different from the decrees of the Vedas. Decrees were incorporated in the scriptures which declared Brahmans to be *bhoopati* and *bhoodeva,* lords of lands and their worship was made obligatory for the king and his subjects. Penance was made compulsory for the sins committed. Penance for different sins and offences was fixed. So much so, provisions were made to observe penance by giving gold to the Brahman equal to the weight of the deceased. Religion was made a thing to be feared. Priests became deputies of God. This made caste the sole basis of social life of the Hindus. No doubt, many reformers and great souls like Kabir, Gurunanak, Balbhacharya and Chaitanya raised their voice against the bigotry and religious ostentation. They tried their best to usher in some reforms and bring religion back to its natural form but by that time society had gone so dormant. The efforts of these great souls could not exert any major influence.

British Period

The British encouraged and gave patronage to the caste system. Financial objectives were behind this move. They could gain handsome revenue through entry taxes imposed on temples, pilgrimages and holy places. Moreover, the Indian populace were kept pitted against one another so that they would not find any time to raise the banner of revolt against the British. For this purpose, they encouraged untouchability also. In 1767, the East India Company sanctioned setting up of caste courts. This resulted in separate village assemblies of castes and sub-castes.

In the last years of the 18th century reformatory sectarian and religious societies like the Brahma Samaj, Arya Samaj and Ram-krishna Mission began opposing fanatic casteism. But by that time roots of casteism had gone very deep into the soil of Hindu society and it proved difficult to uproot the system.

In the first half of the 20th century casteism experienced well-organised opposition. Credit for the campaign goes to Gopal Krishna Gokhale, Lokmanya Tilaka, Ranade and M.K. Gandhi.

Modern Period

Today, state determines the structure of the social set-up. Religion and rituals have lost their grandeur. This has made the status of the Brahman equal to the status of others. Brahmans have adopted other professions. Social status of a person is not measured by his caste today. His abilities, qualities, expertise, leadership qualities and economic prosperity play vital role in this regard. A poor and novice Brahman stands nowhere before a prosperous and proficient Sudra. In the metropolitan cities, one can attach to his name any caste and nobody bothers to verify its authenticity.

Matrimonial conceptions are changing rapidly. Inter-caste marriages are gaining ground. Pedigree, race and exalted family have lost their importance. The aim of marriage is no longer to satisfy certain religious demands but to lead a harmonious domestic life. The daily newspapers are filled with matrimonial advertisements displaying prominently the tag of 'Caste No Bar.'

Modes of eating and drinking have slackened. Brahmans do not hesitate to consume eatables prepared by the members of other castes. Brahmans mix with the members of other castes in restaurants, hotels and tea parties. Birth does not determine the status of a man today. Prosperity, boldness, intellect and riches command respect and honour in the society.

Equal rights of education and rapid spread of literacy have sounded the death knell for the mythological parables which gave a religious tinge to the caste system.

However, even today some Hindus think that the caste system can support the crumbling society. In the rural areas, this system is still being given due respect and people think it is for their welfare. Seventy-six per cent of India's population still lives in the villages. Industrialization and westernization have brought about a change in the thinking of less than 24% of the population which resides in cities. This percentage is not sufficient to change the entire social set-up. The need of the hour is social revolution and only then can casteism be totally abolished.

Thirty Four

Importance of Varna System in the 21st Century

Mala Pyasi

The varna system in ancient society helped in meeting the people's multifarious needs. What is required today is adoption of the varna system while getting rid of casteism.

— *Editor*

Explaining the peculiarity of the varna system, Dr. Radhakrishnan opined that every man is a Sudra or unholy at the time of birth. Only by his good deeds he achieves the status of a Brahman or other higher strata. Mahatma Gandhi was also of the same opinion. He was of the view that varnas symbolise duties and not rights. They confer no privileges. Moreover, varnashrama teaches self-restraint. It is clear that varna of a person is determined by his qualities and his good or bad deeds and actions, not by birth.

The ancient Indian society was divided into varnas on the basis of qualities and deeds. It was an idealistic society. But in modern society, varna and caste have become synonymous. In reality, they are two distinct identities.

Acharya Yaska opines that the word 'varna' originated from the root 'vrin' (*varno vrinoteh*) (Nirukta 3.2), which means to select. In the *Rigveda* (2.12.4 and 1.96.5) varna denotes colour and class of men. Vāman Shiv Ram Apte is of the view that the word varna means colour, worship, to light, to marry, to spread or scatter. Verses from the *Rigveda* convincingly establish that the word varna was not used to denote a social arrangement. It rather denoted a tradition to adopt any vocation freely and without any restriction.

Members of a family used to undertake any work or enterprise as per their wishes and inclinations.

The Rigvedic sage says: "I am a poet, my father is a physician and the mother a grinder woman." The *Vayu Purana* also depicts that there was no need of varnashrama in Satyuga (*Vayu Purana* 8.60).

The Rigvedic was a simple society where there did not exist a system of varnas.

The tenth portion of the *Rigveda* where the Purusha Sukta verse mentions Brahmin, Kshatriya, Vaishya and Sudra simultaneously for the first time (Rig 10.10.12) is of later origin. Here too, the word varna is conspicuous by its absence. It is all clear that in the Vedic age, these four words did not denote four varnas. But still this verse does describe the process of social development.

The description about the origin is simply symbolic. Main duty of the Brahmins was to learn and teach, to perform yajnas and other religious rites and all these acts were done through the mouth. So their origin was ascribed to the mouth of Prajapati. The main duty of the Kashtriyas was to protect the people and here arms occupy the most vital and important place. So their origin was ascribed to the arms of Prajapati. Vaishyas were mostly engaged in trading. Trading made them travel from one place to another. So their origin was ascribed to the stomach and the thighs of Prajapati. The function of the feet is to carry the weight of the body from place to place. So the origin of the Sudras is ascribed to the feet of Prajapati. The seeds of the four subsequent varnas, however, were definitely sowed by this time. With the passage of time and with the advancement of civilization and culture, needs of man multiplied and multifarious activities cropped up. To meet the exigencies and new requirements a clear-cut social structure came into being.

Varna was determined on the basis of birth and this gave birth to casteism. The word *jati* is from the root *jana* meaning birth or origin i.e., birth symbolises high and low, difference and disparity. Ultimately these castes divided into sub-castes and hybrid castes were formed. Occupations and vocations gave birth to many castes. In due course of time these castes multiplied. The divisions and subdivisions of castes emerged only after the downslide of Buddhism and Jainism when water-tight compartments of holy and unholy thoughts were created through rites and rituals. As a result, every caste started following its own rites and rituals pertaining to modes of living, occupation and marriage and this inculcated the feeling of aloofness and separation. By the advent of the middle ages bonds of casteism had become impregnable. It was difficult for a man to change his caste. People entering into inter-caste marriages were excommunicated.

History testifies that the march from varna system to casteism had ushered an era of downfall. The evil impact of casteism is evident.

We, however, see that the varna system had acted as a prop for our ancient society, meeting multifarious needs of the people for centuries together. Elementary needs of life are knowledge, protection, finance and medical assistance. The varna system met these needs in a balanced way. Poet Kalidasa has spoken high of this system and favours sincere adherence to it (*Raghu* 14.67).

If we adhere to the varna system and reject casteism, many ills of the present-day society would end. The basis of a well-planned society lies in the varna system in its original form. The notion of birth determining caste should be done away with. Only qualities and work should matter. If we adhere to the concept of the four varnas only, chasm between man and man would disappear and harmony would rule the world.

Thirty Five

Good and Bad in Varna System

Mamchand Rewaria

Varna system was based on division of labour. There is a need is to allow each person to select his varna according to his work. Birth-based varna system is both incorrect and unacceptable.
— Editor.

The Indian caste system is unique among systems of social stratification. Caste is connected with economic differentiation. Individual could move from one varna to another. Varnas have degenerated into *jatis* (castes). They continue to grow in number extending the division of labour. Caste is an endogamous group. J.H. Hutton suggests that the original Aryans invaders of India, with their distinct ranks, introduced the principle of social stratification into a society already divided into exclusive tribal groups.

Karma and *dharma* constitute a doctrine which is undoubtedly one of the principal sustaining forces of the caste system. The grip of the traditional caste system is still firm and people from lower castes or others with humble origins must behave with considerate tact and discretion if they seek to enhance their influence and importance in the community. Overt caste discrimination has certainly diminished.

Varna is not a mere institution made by man but it is a law discovered by him. Evil is not in the law or the institution itself but it lies in the doctrine of superiority and inferiority which are added to it.

The four varnas define duties and they confer no privileges. All are born to serve God's creation — Brahman with his knowledge, Kshatriya with his power of protection, Vaishya with his commercial ability and Shudra with his bodily labour. It does not mean that a Brahman is absolved from bodily labour or the duty of protecting himself. There is nothing again to prevent the Sudra from acquiring all the knowledge he aspires.

Division of labour and economic compulsions led to the creation of the system of varna. Work culture was the criterion for varna. *Manu Smriti* clearly elucidates this. One of the verses of *Yajurveda* describes the process of social development. The verse explains the division of society, comparing it to the different organs of the human being. In the human being the function of the head is to think. In the social-set up we have people with intellectual bent of mind. They are Brahmans. In the human being, the function of arms is to protect. In the social set-up, we have people whose main accomplishment is their physical strength. They are called Kshatriyas or Rajanyas. In the human being the stomach and thighs store and distribute. In the social set-up, some people store and distribute. They are Vaishyas. Function of the feet is to move, labour and work. In the social set-up also, we have people who labour and work. Feet carry the burden of the weight of the body. They are called Sudras. Lord Krishna assigns duties to four varnas as under:

"Serenity, self-restraint, austerity, purity, forgiveness, uprightness, wisdom, knowledge, belief in god are the duties of the Brahman.

"Prowess, splendour, firmness, dexterity, not flying from battle, generosity, are the traits of the Kshatriya.

"Ploughing, protection of kine and trade are the duties of Vaishya.

"Sudra's duty is service."

Man attains perfection by doing his own duty. Manu assigns different duties to different persons according to their qualities. He has classified duties ordained to various varnas as under:

Brahman — to learn and to teach, to do *yajna* and perform *yajna*, to give and take donation.

Kshatriya — to rule justly, impartially and to honour the best and abjure the rogues, to utilise wealth for education, to serve the deserving ones, to study the Vedas, to remain strong in soul and body by conquering senses.

Vaishya — to trade, to plough, to protect kine and to feed the people, to arrange money for the propagation of education and Dharma.

Sudra — to serve all the three varnas and earn his livelihood thereby.

It is clear that varnas were created on the basis of work and labour and not on the basis of birth. Manu adds that even a Sudra can become a Brahman, a Kshatriya, a Vaishya by the sheer force of his actions and work. Thus varna is determined as per the ability and quality of a person. In the same way a Brahman degrades himself by his misconduct. If a Sudra lives and conducts himself like a Brahman he is a Brahman in the real sense of the term. *Satyarth Prakash* denounces Brahmans who created perversions in such a wonderful, lofty and beautiful varna system. Their ego and selfish interests corrupted the system.

In ancient times offsprings of all the four varnas used to be educated in the *gurukula* under one roof. After the completion of education a person used to join a varna as per his ability and do his duty there.

The lofty conception of *varnashrama* became degraded and came to be identified with empty ceremonials and assumption of superiority by some and imposition of degradation upon others. The assumption that the varna is determined by birth has resulted in divisions in society and animosity among the divided groups. A Brahman remains a Brahman even if he indulges in degraded deeds. A Sudra remains a Sudra even if he conducts himself like a Brahman. This outlook has damaged our social fabric beyond repair. The root of the evil lies in the peculiar social system exclusively based on the principle of heredity.

Politics of casteism rules the scene. Leaders mushroom in the name of caste and creed. Associations trying their level best to preserve the lofty traditions and prestigious institution of *varnashrama* are looked down upon. Respect and honour are showered on the corrupt and criminals.

Fighting in the name of caste is on the rise. The politics of vote has disintegrated the society. The downtrodden are being suppressed in society. Atrocities and brutalities against the exploited are multiplying. Change of religion is the natural outcome. The notion of superiority has become an essential component of the thinking of the upper castes. They cannot tolerate if a downtrodden raises his head and tries to conduct himself like them. Poor, hapless and exploited people have to undergo untold miseries and degradation. Women belonging to lower castes are sexually assaulted.

The need of the hour is to re-establish the ancient varna system in its purest form. All impurities should be purged. Men of character working selflessly can fight the demon of casteism. Inter-caste marriages based on mutual love, respect and common outlook can work wonders. Only then society can get rid of casteism. Casteism disfigures the individual psychologically. Dalits and downtrodden, Sudras so to say, are condemned to misery. Casteism encourages nepotism, favouratism and makes a man partial and his vision blurred. Members of the same caste, if large in number, establish their own monopoly.

The varna system based on ability and quality brought about harmony and unity. The false notion of superiority made the life of people belonging to different castes miserable when they refused to do menial jobs because their castes did not allow it. This created a sense of insecurity in society. With the passage of time distinctions and dogmas have established themselves firmly. Casteism has made the Sudras wary of expressing themselves in society. Mass conversion to Buddhism is a warning.

If the persecution in the name of caste continues, the persecuted would embrace other religions and it is a dangerous signal for Hindism. We must nip the evil in the bud otherwise it would be too late.

Thirty Six

Impact of Casteism

Raj Pal Singh 'Raj'

The varna system in the beginning was based on division of work but it later came to be determined on the basis of birth. Notions depicting hatred and separation inherent in the *Manu Smriti* became the source of ills plaguing the Hindu society and prevented its unification.

—Editor

Study of scriptures and the ancient history of India reveals that India was at the zenith of glory in the fields of learning, knowledge, science and commerce at about 2000 B.C. At that time India was called a treasurehouse of gold. It was a land of plenty, peace and prosperity. Here the highest ideals of religion and philosophy attained their culmination. But this lofty culture and civilization underwent a change with the advent of the Aryans who came from Central Asia, Northern Europe or the Arctic regions. These Aryans through deception, knavery, craft and cunningness defrauded the then Asura emperor Bali. The emperor was taken in by three cleverly crafted utterances of the Aryans. They finished him off and took over his throne. B.S. Gautam has written about this episode: "Vishnu, in the guise of a Brahmin tactfully and deceptively acquired the rights of education, administration and commerce from King Bali."

With the passage of time they coined new words. Persons acquiring learning were named as Brahmans, power-wielders were named as Kshatriyas and traders were given the name of Vaishyas. Thus originated the varna system.

German scholar Max Muller opines that the Aryans compelled the enslaved natives to adopt their rituals, customs and traditions. Setting aside three varnas — Brahman, Kshatriya and Vaishya — for themselves, they fought brutal battles with the natives for over 1500 years. This battle is called *Devasura Sangram* in the *granthas*. Defeated non-Aryans were enslaved and were assigned the sole duty to serve the three varnas. They gave them the name of Sudras. Famous Hindi scholar Acharya Bihari Lal also mentions this battle between the Aryans and the natives in his creation, *Devasura Sangrama*. A relentless and bloody battle continued for hundreds of years. Customs and traditions of both the warring sides got fused into a heterogenous mass. Asura king Bali was exiled and the Aryans started the varna system which is prevalent even today. The varna system is illustrated in the *Rigveda* (10.70.12) — "From Prajapati four varnas originated. The Brahmin was his mouth, His arms were the Rajanyah (Kshatriyas); His thighs became the Vaishyas. From his feet were born the Sudras." Valmiki endorses the the *Rigveda* regarding the origin of *varnasharma*. Whatever Lord Krishna said in Shanti Parva is similar to what is propounded in the Vedas and *Ramayana*.

Notions of hatred, separation and disparity inherent in the *Manu Smriti* are blocks in the path of unification of Hindu society. To say that the Sudras originated from the feet of Prajapati is derogatory. It is perhaps a deliberate attempt to put across the idea that the place of the Sudras is at the feet. The *Manu Smriti* asks for repentance from a Sudra if he happens to kill fowls and insects. No such repentance is enjoined on the so-called superior varnas. A Sudra's position is worse than that of an animal's. Strict penance is prescribed for the Sudras. Should this be the position and condition of the person who serves society selflessly and who thinks that service is his dharma?

The *Attri Smriti* presents a miserable picture. It says if a Sudra dares to conduct himself like a Brahman he is to be put to death because his action invokes the wrath of the gods and it would destroy the entire empire as water consumes fire. Is it justified? The story of the decapitation of Shambuka, a Sudra, by Lord Rama is alarming: Rama cut off his head because Shambuka dared to become a sanyasi. So deliberate attempts were made to subjugate and suppress the Sudras. Whenever they tried to rise in the social ladder, they were tortured or eliminated.

Vishnu Purana presents a similar fate of the Sudras and thinks them to be objected, abhorred and kicked like a mongrel. "Food of a Sudra is worth taking provided he offers his life, wife and money to the Brahman, otherwise in no case his food is to be touched," propounds *Vishnu Purana*. *Hareet Smriti* presents an obnoxious picture of the Sudras — "Sudra is to wear old clothes only, eat only the leftover by a Brahmin, love his own woman and should refrain from any other woman.... If a Sudra abides by these rules by speech, deed and mind his sins can be destroyed and his punyas would fetch him the throne of Indra." The theory of *punya* and *papa* was coined to keep the Sudras religiously intoxicated. One can find very derogatory utterances for the Sudras even in the Upanishads. The *Teittiriya Brahmana*, *Panchvish Brahmana*, *Satpatha Brahmana* and *Aitreya Brahmana* also clearly state that the only duty of the Sudra is to serve the other three varnas. This is the duty assigned to them by Prajapati himself.

In the varna system duties are given preference over rights. But women were always in a disadvantageous position. A Brahman could sleep with women from all the four varnas. A Kshatriya could marry women from the Vaishya varna and the Sudra varna. Vaishya was allowed to have his life partner from the Sudra varna but a Sudra was denied such privilege. He could marry a woman only from his own varna.

In the beginning the varna system was based on division of work or labour but with the passage of time the condition changed and varna system began to be determined on the basis of birth. Once born a Sudra, he was always a Sudra and even his lofty deeds failed to elevate him in the social hierarchy.

After Independence, India pledged to uproot this casteism, a slur, a stigma, but the reality is otherwise. Roots of casteism are going deeper and deeper into the social soil and establishing themselves firmly. This unfortunate rise of casteism disturbs national integration. The germs of this disease have spread and entered into the very polity of India. It has mushroomed into many sub-castes and *gotras*. Disintegration of society is inevitable. Segregation in society is on the increase. Many ills have been let loose by this tendency.

1. Jealousy and hatred among different castes and *gotras*.
2. Conversion of religion.
3. Discrimination against untouchables and downtroddens.
4. Paucity of sympathy and cooperation.
5. Caste to be determined by birth.
6. Downfall of hereditary occupations.
7. Monopoly on education by privileged classes.
8. Ever increasing evil.
9. Cut-throat competition.
10. Competition of lifestyle.

In the present democratic set up, discrimination on grounds of religion, caste, creed, race, sex or place of birth is prohibited. Any such discrimination is unethical and unjust. Fundamental doctrine of international law of human rights bestows the right to end such discrimination. Constitution and laws try their utmost to fight against such discriminations but change is not round the corner. Discrimination still persists. They are like the Phoenix. Atrocities, brutalities, inhuman treatment and torture, physical and mental, are perpetrated in the name of religion, creed, colour, race and sex.

Impact of casteism is evident. It has played havoc and created enmity between man and man. It has filled the drains with blood of the innocent. It has let loose untold miseries. The earthquake of casteism has sent its vibrations throughout the globe. Only recently members belonging to a dominant caste butchered innocent children, women and men of Khanda Tutsi caste in Africa. Such brutalities continue to raise their ugly heads in one corner of the world or the other. Under the aegis of the U.N. a conference was held from August 31 to September 7, 2001 in Durban, South Africa to arrest this trend. Intellectuals under the leadership of Shri N. Pal Diwakar registered their protests for not including the Indian caste system in the agenda of that conference. The Indian Government did not want to get this included in the agenda saying it was a domestic problem. About 200 Dalit intellectuals went to Durban. The statement prepared by the National Human Rights Commission condemned discrimination on the basis of caste and race. Sri Bharat Jhoonjhunwala in his scholarly write-up titled 'Why fear discussion on casteism in Durban' has clearly mentioned that we must present the varna system in its true colours and perspective before the international community.

Thirty Seven

Evolution and Function of Varna System

Brij Bhushan Rajvanshi

The Varna system has evolved gradually. Its purpose is to create social cohesion. The present birth-based caste system has little connection with the varna system.

—Editor

Varnashrama of the Vedic age and caste system as is perceived today are quite different entities. In the beginning of the Rigvedic age, Aryans were not divided. Words *panchjanah* (Rig 1.89.10) and *panchkristya* (Rig 2.2.10) denote five main sub-castes namely Gandharva, Dasyu, Dasa, Pani and Dev i.e., singers and artists, non-Aryans (enemy class), serving class, trading class and ruling class respectively. But later on this very word *panchjanah* in the Indian context was substituted for the five classes of descendants of the five sons namely Anu, Yadu, Druhaya, Turvashu and Puru of Yayati of the Lunar (*chandravansh*) dynasty. The Vedas also mention other clans such as Bharata, Tritsu and Srinjaya. It simply means that with the spread of the descendants of Yayati in India different clans emerged.

The Solar (*suryavansha*) dynasty founded by Manu had kings like Ikshvaku, Sharyati, Namanedishtha and Karoosh. The son of Ikshvaku named Nimi who established Aryan colonies was not given the name of clan. The denomination of a person's 'colony' or 'state' was used with traditional blessings for the people belonging to the Solar dynasty.

In the beginning, the social condition of the people of every clan, colony or state of the Aryan community was the same. All were parts of the same general multitude. But with time, differences in their situation surfaced.

Primarily two types of division in human society can be seen as natural: intellectual superiority and strength and bodily ability. As a result, even in the ancient Vedic age Brahmans and Kshatriyas began looking distinct from the general multitude. Sages and the persons performing religious rites came under the category of Brahmans. Warriors who protected the people from foreign invasions and from the non-Aryans and who ensured peace and prosperity in society were called Kshatriyas. That is the reason that if Purusha Sukata is left out we would fail to find any mention of Brahman, Kshatriya, Vaishya and Sudra in the *Rigveda*. Modern scholars opine that the Purusha Sukta (10.90.12) was added to the *Rigveda* at a later date.

Though Brahman and Kshatriya castes originated from the same general multitude yet they were put on a higher pedestal of status because of the respect and honour they commanded at that time. The common members remained as Vaishyas. They contributed to the production of wealth through agriculture, rearing of kines, trade, different vocations and industry and helped in the income-increasing enterprises for the augmentation of the means of government. Primarily the classification of Brahman, Kshatriya and the remaining members of the community was not on the basis of birth. Intellectual ability and expertise in warfare made the position of these people a privileged one. It put them on a higher pedestal than the Vaishyas. Still, in the Rigvedic age, Aryans were a single unified ratial lot.

Even in that Rigvedic age there were Dasas, *yakshas* and other advanced and skilled artisan communities different from the Aryans. The Aryans and Dasas sometimes combined to fight their common enemy, the Dasyus (non-Aryans). After their assimilation with Aryans, the art and practical purposes of these people did not dry up. They continued following their respective trades. But for practical reasons they remained on the lower rung of the social ladder and were treated as 'Dasas'. In due course of time these so-called 'Dasas' came under the nomenclature of Sudras. This class because of its ability to serve in different ways became part and parcel of the varna system of society. Aryans and Sudras even had matrimonial relations and this resulted into hybrid races especially in southern India and they were called 'Vratyas'.

Although Sudras enjoyed somewhat lower status in society yet they were not untouchables. Brahmans used to visit their houses, perform *yajnas* and other religious rites and rituals, and accepted donations from them. Sudras were allowed to practise oblation to the deities like the other varnas.

Increasing Significance of the Four Varnas in Later Vedic Period

There took place a tremendous increase in the religious ceremonies, laws and regulations of the Aryans when they settled down permanently in India. The ancient simple set-up slowly and steadily became complex. Many verses of the *Yajurveda* and the *Atharvaveda* give clear-cut indications of the four varnas. This proves that during the Vedic period the varna system had got itself established firmly. The Purusha Sukta of *Rigveda* explains the division of society, comparing it to the different organs of human body. The Brahmans in society represent the head (thinking organ). The function of the arms is to protect. The Rajanyas or Kshatriyas in society symbolise the arms. The function of the thighs including the stomach is to store and distribute. The Vaishya represent thigh and stomach. The function of the feet is to carry the burden of the weight of the body and to carry man from place to place. The Sudras represent the feet. In the human being the function of the head is to think. In the social set-up we have members with intellectual bent of mind. They are Brahmans. They stand for the head of social being. There are people whose main accomplishment is their physical strength. They are Rajanyas, the protectors. They represent the arms of the social being. Similarly, the Vaishyas represent thighs and stomach. They are to store and distribute. The feet's function is to move, labour and work. The Sudras correspond to feet. They are not capable of serving the society in any way other than by doing labour and service. This description visualises the natural and scientific order of the society. Whenever this equilibrium is disturbed, the society disintegrates. Any component in trouble diminishes the ability, capability and strength of the whole body social. Complete internal cooperation in a living body is must. So is the case with social body. Mechanical uniformity of position, of rank and of function amongst all members of society would cause disintegration of society. Difference of function is the sign of life. Only in death uniformity can be seen. Our modern leaders are playing the dirty game of factionalism, ignoring the real meaning of cooperation and coordination in the body social. They argue that the word feet means the downtrodden. If the feet refuse to work and if they go stiff the whole body would get rotten. Similarly, if the labourers and the persons engaged in body labour shirk their duties there would be chaos in society.

In the later Vedic period, offsprings of the first three varnas acquired learning and education according to their traditions and remained ever eager for a second birth involving investiture with the sacred thread. It is a recognised fact that learning imparts a second birth to man. Contrary to this, the fourth unit of society remained engrossed in the service of society. Verses Nos. 6 to 10 and 16 and 17 of the 30th chapter of the *Yajurveda* mention different nomenclatures for different members of society according to their ability and capacity to work. Varna by birth had nothing to do with it. The system prevalent in the past was flexible enough and it depicted no class-wise structure. The Sudra varna never denoted present-day scheduled castes.

Varna Variation in the Sutra-Granthas in the Post Vedic Period

The subject matter of the Vedas is concerned with singing the praise of the *yajna* and religious rituals and exploits of the kings whereas the Upanishads and other *granthas* are concerned with the Brahma Sutra. Sutra Granthas and Smritis followed Brahmana Granthas in the order of creation such as Gautama's *Dharmasutra*, Vashistha's *Dharmasutra*, Bodhayana's *Dharmasutra* and Katyayana's *Sarotasutra*. The *Manu Smriti* and *Yagnavalkya Smriti* also made their appearance at a later stage. Now varna was determined by birth and not by profession or vocation.

Gautama *Dharmasutra* declares that the king is no doubt the best but the Brahman is at the highest in the social ladder. Kshatriyas came down to the second position in the social hierarchy. But as neither the Brahman nor the Kshatriya could do without one another, they developed a strong union between one another The Vaishyas and the Sudras, categorised on the basis of birth and not on the basis of profession or occupation, received a setback and their condition worsened over time. The Vaishyas, because of their well-earned and accumulated wealth, started becoming targets of exploitation. Being in the category of workers the Sudras' condition became that of serfs and slaves. Listening to the Vedas and the ritual of the investiture with the sacred thread were denied to the Sudras. The legal system too became varna-oriented. The lofty conception of *varnashrama* became degraded and came to be identified with empty ceremonials and assumption of superiority by some and the imposition of degradation upon others. Varna disparity surfaced visibly. Varna based on birth came in vogue and it encouraged exploitation of the Sudras. Slokas Nos. 41, 42, 43 and 44 of the 18th chapter of the *Gita* explains the work culture of the four varnas. The duties of Brahman, Kshatriya, Vaishya and Sudra have been distributed according to the qualities born of their own nature.

The brahman's duty concerned serenity, self-restraint, austerity, purity, forgiveness, wisdom, knowledge and belief in God.

The kshatriya's duty concerned prowess, splendour, desterity, generosity and firmness.

The vaishya's duty concerned protection of Kine and trade.

The sudra's duty concerned service.

Sloka No. 47 of the second chapter of the *Gita* declares:

"The business is with the action only, never with its fruits, so let not the fruit of action be thy motive, nor be thou to inaction attached."

Sloka no 13 of the fifth chapter has made everything lucid:

"The four castes were created by me, by the different distribution of qualities and actions." Sloka No. 32 of the seventh chapter condemns Vaishyas, Sudras and women to menial birth; only Brahmans and Kshatriyas are sacred by birth and actions. If Vaishyas and Sudras want elevation they are advised to remember and sing praises of God and give up actions. Thus the Brahman and Kshatriya are privileged ones and heaven is reserved for them whereas the Vaishya and Sudra are condemned to hell.

Varna and Caste in the Present Context

Varna and caste are not synonymous. Varnas are four but castes are numberless. There are many castes which do not even fit in any varna. Kayastha caste is a glaring example. It is a hybrid caste. Actually, the rise of castes in India has been altogether independent of the varna system. Whenever clans or tribes amongst Aryans settled down in an area permanently they established their own state-like set-up and with the passage of time such *janpad* units assumed the garb of separate and distinct castes. Khatri, Arora, Aggarwal, Rohtagi, Kori, Saini and many other castes developed and saw their growth in the same manner. Weavers, carpenters, ironsmiths, goldsmiths, washermen, barbers and many others formed guilds and their own rules and regulations pertaining to their professions. Their associations were very strong and it was difficult for any member to violate the established rules and regulations of his community. In due course of time these professional classes assumed distinct colouring and sprouted into distinct castes. No effort was made to put them under any varna. This established their distinct identities all the more. From time to time many foreign invaders came and, adopting Indian religion and culture, became part and parcel of Indian society. Their varna status was not fixed. But some Smritikars did try to categorise them into hybrid castes.

It is essential to keep in mind the glaring difference between varna and caste. Division of four varnas into numberless castes on the basis of birth was a step contrary to the original motive and spirit inherent in the Aryan culture and its traditions. It was an unparalleled instance in world history whereby superiority and inferiority in the social hierarchy surfaced and the notion of the untouchability originated. Atrocities perpetrated by castes hampered the harmonious growth of the Indian society.

Thirty Eight

Caste Associations

Ram Swarup

Democratic associations of all castes should be made to provide security to their members. At the same time inter-caste marriages should be encouraged.

— Editor

The numerous castes and clans of India have had their own identities, distinct differences and sanctions which have been safeguarded by, among other means, little or no intermixing. Generally marriages are not solemnised outside the ordained castes. So class- and caste-ridden society has become a fine example of narrow-mindedness. The ones to suffer the most are the Harijans who cannot find an escape from the degradation and suffering inflicted on them by other members of the society. It is time that all castes and clans unite their efforts to fight against injustice in society, particularly against the abuse of women and children and spread of evil practices.

Creation of associations of castes and clans right from the village level to the national level is the need of the hour. The leaders of such associations should be elected or selected unanimously as per their abilities and qualities of character. They must have organisational expertise to mobilise the common members for common cause. It should be obligatory for every family to contribute at least one percent of its income to the associations so that they became monetarily viable and strong. A proper directory of all the members of the association should be prepared and maintained. This directory must have all the possible entries regarding a family.

Lists of orphans, widows, widowers and handicapped parents having no young sons to support them should be prepared and maintained properly. Community centres run by the associations should look after the needs and upbringing of all destitutes. They should be given food, shelter, clothing and medical aid. They should be engaged in creative work. They should be provided with all kinds of facilities and opportunities so that they can perform to their best in whatever field they choose.

Parents of talented wards should be given soft loans. Poverty-stricken members of the association should be given proper financial assistance to start their own business and thereby be made self-dependent. The need is to create a congenial atmosphere of trust where the loanees could repay their loans willingly. Special training should be imparted to the young to protect womenfolk. Young maidens should be infused with courage and boldness to protect themselves. Training should be given to make our young men and women rise above the considerations of power and pelf. Fear, deception, greed and other inducements should not make them victims.

Every community should appoint learned men to guide it at every step to bring about and maintain mutual respect and love among families. Every member of the association should be well informed about the matrimonial needs and educational needs of every other member.

Inter-caste marriages should be welcomed and they should not be frowned upon. The terms 'superiority' and 'inferiority' should be discarded.

It is the pious duty of the community to ensure that demand of dowry does not raise its ugly head. Secondly, protection of the honour of girls and women should be the paramount duty of the community. Associations should try to eliminate vices of drugs and wine, meat and egg. Women can play a vital role in cementing familial relations and inculcating mutual trust and respect.

There should be continuous rapport amongst associations. Frequent meetings are a must to ponder over different problems facing the people. Jatiya Sneh Sabha having its own constitution can be established on a permanent basis. This sabha can play a vital role in bringing about harmony and unity in the association.

Thirty Nine

Contradiction of 'Dalit' Literature

Sharad Singh

There is a contradiction in dalits denying the idea of birth-based caste and insisting that only a dalit by birth can write dalit literature.

—Editor

Twenty centuries have been buried deep into the fathomless chasms of oblivion. They have become part and parcel of history. We can appreciate and criticise them but we cannot remold them. Present and future can be remoulded but history cannot be. Statistics can undergo a change, history can be rewritten but episodes which have happened cannot be changed.

We look determined to do away with the varna system. Efforts have been made over the last two centuries to eliminate the varna system and bring all sections of society on a common platform. Social and literacy campaigns have been launched during the 19th and 20th centuries to end the kind of discrimination against the lower castes that has ripped apart the Indian social fabric. In this context, the fact that Dalit literature gained popularity in the latter half of the 20th century is quite perplexing. It appears to indicate that efforts done to eliminate the varna system have been half-hearted. The natural result being growth of literature of the trampled by the trampled. Literature, after all, mirrors the society.

What do we mean by Dalit literature, literature of the trampled by the trampled? When did it come into circulation? We have to turn the pages of Hindi literature of the bygone ages. Conception of Dalit literature is inherent in Marathi literature.

Writers from the trampled and exploited sections of society, to establish their own separate identity, called their works 'Dalit Literature'. In Marathi, this nomenclature surfaced with the campaign of the downtroddens in 1960. By 1980, it came to be of substantial importance. A seminar on Dalit literature was organised at the national level in Nagpur in 1996. This left an indelible mark on the hearts of many writers. The Dalit awareness and experience gained a significant identity. Today the word 'Dalit' has assumed the shape of a symbol of the exploited, tortured and tormented, ignored and unprivileged people. Under the editorship of Kamleshwar, two special issues of *Sarika* on Dalit literature came out in 1975. In October 1997, the Institute of Higher Studies, Shimla organised a seminar on the subject 'Dalit Sahitya and Asvet Lekhan — Contemporary Trends'. Many Hindi writers now prefer to be called Dalit writers. Om Prakash Balmiki, Jai Parkash Kardam, Sushila Takbhore, Shyoraj Singh Baichein, Lal Chand Rahi and many others are some famous Dalit writers. It is a matter of personal freedom and liberty to attach any name to one's own but it ceases to be a personal matter the moment literature is named on the basis of varna. The question is, is it just and proper to call a part of Hindi literature 'Dalit literature' because its writers consider themselves Dalits?

We must remember that Buddhist saints who created literary works in Hindi were originally *chamars*, washermen, tanners, weavers, scavengers, vendors, oilmen, non-Aryans and so on. They were bitter against the anomalies found in the Vedas and the Puranas. By the 12th century, the social set-up had become so defective that the downtrodden were denied the right to education. Kabir, Raidasa, Peepa, Sena and Sadan then adopted the verbal tradition to present their thoughts in verse and their verses were passed on verbally from one generation to another.

Strangely enough, the side which admits that man is high or low by his actions and not by his birth tries to evaluate literature on the basis of its origin. It asserts that literature born from the mind and brain of a person belonging to the Dalit class automatically becomes Dalit literature. Is it not commiting the same mistake in literature that Manu committed in society?

To link literature to class, gender and colour is to make its utility for society doubtful. Dalit litterateurs admit the monopoly of Brahmanistic elements in literature. They admit that the syllabi do not prescribe their writings. Jai Parkash Kardam's view that Hindi literature "abounds in such writing as smack of Sawarna mentality", published in the collection on Dalit literature in the June 1999 issue of the progressive magazine *Sanchetna* edited by Maheep Singh, does carry weight. This collection contains views of Ramnika Gupt about persons who decry Dalit literature. Ramnika Gupt unfolds a tactic adopted by Sawarna litterateurs to degrade writers from the Dalit class. He says they rank Premchand or Nirala as equal to the Dalit writers. It is done just to nullify the importance of the Dalit writers. For the lamp has no significance before the sun. These views expressed by J.P. Kardam and R.Gupt throw light on two important aspects. One, absence of proper evaluation of literature especially named as Dalit literature is a grouse among Dalit writers. In reality, Dalit literature is not a separate identity but it is the result of nepotism, favouritism and factionalism prevalent in society and especially in Hindi literature. It is a bad corollary also in the sense that the literature which helped society to rise above the narrow and shallow mesh of the varna system by infusing awareness is seen surviving on the crutches of the varna system. How tragic it is!

Secondly, it depicts the anguish of Dalit litterateurs because monopolistic tendencies of Brahmanism do not allow their writings to find place in any syllabus. But it must be remembered that dignity and pride of literature does not lie in its inclusion in any syllabus. Kabir and Raidasa did belong to Dalit class but these poets showed no concern to get their writings prescribed in any formal system in order to raise their prestige in the eyes of society. They never called their literary work as Dalit literature. It is an impenetrable truth that writings of Kabir and Raidasa are more acceptable, more comprehensive and timeless than the verses even of Ramcharitmanas. A *doha* verse of Ramcharitmanas—

Dhol, Ganwar, Sudra, Pasu, Nari.....

does not find favour among all but verses of Kabir like—

Tu Baman Bamni Jaya
To Aan Bah Kahe Nahin Aaya

and a socialistic verse of Rai Dasa—

Aisa Chahun Raj Mein, Jahan Mile Sabhi Ko Ann,
Chhoto Baro Sub Sum Bassein, Raidas Rahe Prasann".

are accepted by one and all. Every section of the society will appreciate these verses and the meaning they depict.

When the very word Dalit was not prevalent in Hindi literature and there was no Dalit writer worth the name, Hazari Prashad Dwivedi, a critic, included the poem entitled 'Complaint of an Untouchable', composed by Heera Dom, in the magazine *Saraswati*. It was a revolutionary step. This poem was in Bhojpuri. The truth is that a good creation has inherent quality and grandeur to get itself evaluated. A litterateur creates his creation and desires to let it remain a form of literature only.

Litterateur Tej Singh says that non-Dalit research scholars, finding Dalit literature being discussed in Hindi realms, have started writing critical reviews along with their research work in the name of Dalit awareness. Such research papers and critical reviews are produced mostly to create misunderstanding and false notions about Dalit literature.

Literature should not be associated with varna-based nomenclature. If this trend is not checked literature would assume different names — literature produced by Dalits would be Dalit literature, that produced by women would be women's literature, that produced by Kayasthas would be Kayastha literature and so on. Will it not amount to mockery of our varna-opposing efforts and varna-opposing mentality?

Partisan attitude prevalent in Hindi literature must be done away with. Need of the hour is liberal and impartial attitude in the fields of review and criticism so that no literary figure belonging to any class or gender feels ignored and shunned. Literature must be free from the narrow contours of nepotism. Reasonable control and check must be exerted on the expression of personal feelings in the larger interests of society. The so-called Dalit litterateurs must inculcate initiative and a self-propelling force in them. Otherwise, it would encourage varna disparity in literature and such literature would not only harm the social structure but even present a wrong picture of Indian social and literary progress before the world community. Need of the hour is to bring about cultural awareness and spiritual sobriety and esteem in literature.

Part V

The Role of Human Development Workers

Forty

Sanatana Concept of Social Work

Bhartendu Prakash

True social work is undertaken by one who gives to society what he has. One who does 'social work' for livelihood is not a social worker:

— Editor

Service is a unique characteristic of Indian culture. It can transport us to the realms of bliss. That is why, our scriptures say — Service, thy name is supreme religion. Service is to perform duty righteously. Duty is religion. On this belief stands the superstructure of our society. No religion can excel in grandeur the religion of service. This ideal of service has inculcated in Indian society a lofty idea that mankind is one human family. The world is one community. Protection of all creatures is our creed and this creed has harmonised us with nature. Social service with devotion and religious fervour is the message propagated by the *Rigveda*. Upanishads go a step further. They say, God is the master of all things. Receive things with a feeling of renunciation and not with greed.

Ancient and Modern Social Service

Every man is subjected to three debts, says our ancient Indian philosophy. They are debt of the parents, of god and nature, and of the teacher and religious instructor. The sacred duty of man is to repay these debts. Faithful, righteous and sincere performance of duties helps man repay the three debts. Materialistic approach is not the driving force behind the performance of duties. In their hearts, all members of the society nurture this notion that they are doing their duties for their own salvation. This maintains a healthy balance in society. There is no distinction between selfless service and performance of duties. Spiritual urge is behind social service. This was the picture of social service in ancient India.

Today, a number of non-government organisations have been brought into being with a view to perform social service. They are aided by government and foreign agencies. They are registered and are governed by written rules and regulations. Aims and objectives of such organisations are specific. Professionals are establishing such organisations and they are proving means of employment for the professionals. Many personal interests and equations work behind the foundation of these organisations. Materialistic attitude is all-pervasive and this has disfigured the very face of these organisations. They have become personal and private properties of individuals or group of individuals. Today, they are the best means to satisfy personal, social, economic and political ends. They are popularly known as NGOs. They include trusts established by industrialists and international clubs and associations backed and run by particular classes of society. These organisations have spread their wings to cover almost all aspects of human life. Religious fervour is scantly visible. Everything has been commercialised. Nobody looks at social service from a spiritual angle. Thus, there is absence of any feeling of duty.

Basic Elements of Sanatana Dharma

The thing which holds us or retains us is *dharma*. It prevents us from going down. Sanatana Dharma has no beginning and no end. It is all pervasive and eternal. It imparts worldly and other worldly well-being. "I am in all and all are in me"— it is based on this principle. Natural traits and qualities establish the dharma of different objects. *Dharma* cannot be narrow, cramped, restricted and circumscribed. Attributes of Dharma are steadiness of mind, forgiveness, endurance, non-indulgence in stealing, purity, subjugation of senses, discerning intellect, learning, knowledge, truth, evenness or wrathlessness.

Dharma propagates happiness and prosperity for all. Sanatana culture is God-oriented. This culture has displayed the possibility of attaining the highest goal, *moksha* by apprehending the knowledge of God. Materialism brings worldly comforts while spiritualism brings otherworldly comforts. Followers of spiritualism by getting rid of materialism could reach the higher rungs of the ladder of progress.

Values impart importance to things. All departments of life depend on values for their very existence. A small erosion and decline in these values render these things sapless and they fail to contribute anything to society.

Organisations for social service should not be a heterogenous amalgamation of different varnas. Their purity guarantees cooperation from their respective varnas. Social workers would earn their livelihood accordingly. It will not be difficult for the social workers to command necessary cooperation for social upliftment if they lead a simple life and earn their livelihood independently. The best arrangement is where the concerned community bears the expenses incurred on its well-being itself. For this social workers and organisations should keep in mind the following:

1. People should be aware of proposed undertakings and their possible results.
2. Coordination with the general public is essential and social workers can win the hearts of people thereby.
3. Workers should be transparent in their speech and deeds.
4. Social workers should be bound to work for a longer period of time with faith and patience to win the confidence of the concerned community.
5. Social workers must review the work done and without concealing their shortcomings should try to improve upon them.
6. Social workers should be morally sound.
7. Without employing any coercive or commanding method, social workers should help the community in the analysis of its own views.

Without people's contribution, social work of any organisation can come to a standstill. But this contribution should be in the shape of donation. Feeling of well-being of the world is inherent in donation. God owns everything. To distribute one's belongings is *dharma*. To give and take alms (offerings) is religious. Offering is worst when it is taken for the satisfaction of one's own stomach. Begging results in pity for the beggar. Sanatana concept takes man from individuality to collectivity, from subjectivity to objectivity. The stress on the ideal *sarve bhavantu sukhinah* has made Sanatana Dharma religion of the world — the Universal Religion.

Forty One

Livelihood of the Social Worker

Bharat Gandhi

Society should take care of the minimal needs of the social worker.

—Editor

The question of using money for promoting social work is a controversial one. A major portion of the money spent by the social workers filters to the weaker and smaller sections of society. Comparatively speaking, the more the money in the hands of the social worker, the more the benefit to society.

Those who want to give social service the shape of a profession argue that financial incentives are a powerful and effective weapon. Money encourages one to work enthusiastically. It can inspire a man to do hard labour. Why should not this weapon be used in social work? Many persons would like to take up social work as a carreer if it is found that a social worker has the opportunity to lead a prosperous life. This would also help the society get rid of incapable social workers. The logic is that if for the healing of the body five long years are to be spent in studies, then why leave the vast society at the mercy of so-called incapable social workers.

The fact is that social work has failed to find a place of respect in the formal economic system. In some remote corner of the subconscious the idea resides that social work is worthless. It can be interesting if it becomes a source of livelihood.

However, social work is not worthless. Actually, society must shoulder the responsibility to provide each and every person with food. This work has to be performed by someone. These are social workers. Persons who are inclined towards social service and who have an inborn quality and capacity to do must not have to leave social work and join some government institute to earn their livelihood. The society should take the responsibility of providing such social workers with food, shelter and clothing so that they engage themselves in works according to their own interests and '*samskaras*.' This arrangement would also solve the problem of unemployment to a greater extent.

Some questions and answers regarding the functions and duties of social workers are as follows:

Q. What prompts social work?

A. Some people get this urge genetically or from their previous life. At an appropriate age they feel this urge and as a man rushes to quench his thirst, in the same way, the social worker rushes towards like-minded people and co-workers. Some people, after some accident and incidents in life, get enthusiastic and anxious and are inspired to do social work. The first reason is hereditary and the second is environmental.

Q. Why should man work for society?

A. For two reasons. Firstly, some people enjoy social service. Secondly, the contribution of the social activists is a necessity for others.

Q. What are the measures of social transformation and evaluation according to Sanatana outlook?

A. The aim of social change is to meet the needs of the people. So strategies are made and activities carried out in proportion to the needs and ways of fulfilling them

Q. What similarity do we find in Gandhian constructive workers, Leninist Marxist party revolutionaries and Brahmanas of the *Manu Smriti*?

A. Many similarities can be seen. Social helix of DNA of all these people is dominant and they have a larger sense of pride than normal.

Q. Any dissimilarity?

A. The intellect of the Gandhian and Brahmana is focused within the past of the time scale because of inborn reasons while those of Marxist is focused within the future of the time scale. It is just as if one is male and the other is female by birth.

Q. What were their means of livelihood?

A. Society was not prosperous during the period of the *Manu Smriti*. It was left to the rationality of men to either fill the Brahman's belly or starve him. The mental attitude of most of the Gandhian workers is fixed in the period of the *Manu Smriti*. They want to make the then prevalent values the ideals of today. Their livelihood was intact because of their ancestral property or because of extra income of the rich. Livelihood of Leninist/Marxist revolutionary was due to like-minded prosperous people or because of the reward, bounty or gratuity for state service rendered.

Q. How could these people earn their livelihood while opposing the state?

A. People who liked them, whether parents or friends, arranged their livelihood.

Q. Should economic means to help the social worker be indigenous or foreign?

A. This would be settled by the nature of work. If the effect of the work is limited to the boundaries of the nation it is but natural that means should be indigenous. If this effect is good and beneficial to the foreigners also they should bear its expenses. It is not bad for economic progress if indigenous social workers bring foreign exchange to this country.

Q. What is the hidden purpose and meaning of foreign aid to NGO?

A. It is wrong to say that it is some foreign conspiracy. Foreign aid to abet terrorism and anarchy is wrong. It must be opposed tooth and nail. To consider the aid and assistance given by a foreigner to the handicapped — which the natives cannot extend — to be a deep conspiracy is nothing short of mental cynicism.

Q. Is review of Indian tradition essential in the context of nurturing NGOs financially?

A. Undoubtedly very essential.

Forty Two

Social Worker and Society

Satya Prakash 'Bharat'

The social worker and society have to work with each other. Social worker cannot be supported by the State.

— Editor

In the Sanatana conception, a person who is inspired by his own inner urge, goaded by the feelings of love and sympathy and by the call of duty and does work for the sake of others is called a social worker. These works could be done individually or in a group. Building of a canopy, assembly hall and inn, laying of roads, tree planting, guest feeding, supply of water in summer and even education and healing were different forms of social work. Such society was considered to be developed where its members did not lack the basic needs of life. Even commerce and trade was linked with social service. Purpose of trade was not to fill the coffers but to serve society without harming own interests. Feelings ruled supreme in trade. To put one's surplus means for the betterment and rise of others was the conception of social service.

But today social service has degenerated into a means of earning livelihood and amass riches. It has become a tool not only for earning money but also for indulgences. The needy get nothing. The men who are to be served go empty-handed and while social workers gulp down all the benefits. So the social worker has become a stigma on society. Is there any difference between a social worker and a government servant? Today even government undertakes works related to schools, hospitals, wells, roads and entertainment and so does a social worker. Earlier there was a distinct difference between the two. The government servant doing the jobs enjoined on him by the government used to get paid for the service done. His job was simply to get the work done by other persons but a social worker used to spend his spare time in helping the society. The social worker was simple. He worked according to his urge and inner values.

A creative social worker doing creative work would not weigh it with money. If a social worker gives preference to money he lowers his status. There would be no difference between his life and the life of an ordinary man. In my view only that man should plunge in the field of social service who does not weigh his work with money and who has full faith in society. A person who works for money is not a social worker but a servant.

Man of a possessive nature cannot be the ideal of society and humanity. The social worker was well-awakened and sensible. His duty was to raise his voice against injustice, irrationality and *adharma*. Today, social work is being done in abundance but social workers are silent like Bhishma against injustice, corruption and immorality. In the ancient period the social worker was fearless and unattached; he had guts to speak the truth and society had unflinching faith in him. But today a social worker is slave of money. He does social work for luxuries and comforts. He is an intimate partner of the prevailing social system and has no relation with and faith in society. He runs unconsciously but methodically like a machine.

Forty Three

Social Worker and the State

Roshan Lal

True social change will come from persons who hare not depended for their own livelihood on the existing system. The purity of their thought will itself galvanise the people into good behaviour.

—Editor

The Sanatana Indian conception of social development, is altogether different from the present NGO conception. It will be ridiculous to compare them. The ancient Indian conception was thought-oriented whereas social service in the present context is service-oriented. Ancient Indian society may not have had professional social workers, but there were many meeting places in the form of pilgrimages, *ashramas* of the sages and enriched centres of learning for the learned who had the capacity to dedicate themselves fully for social well-being. In those centres serious discussion regarding condition of society, its problems and their solutions were held freely and fearlessly. They used to discuss the merits and demerits, relevance and irrelevance of the established social set-up. This discussion and thinking was comprehensive and unprejudiced and was free from all kinds of fear, pressures and selfish motives. This thinking definitely served the society by bringing about changes in the established set-up.

Most of these thinkers were not worried about their livelihood and personal responsibilities. They did not fear the state's coercive power. They desired no state protection. They had unstinted and unflinching love for and attachment to society. They presented their views and suggestions to the state without fearing the wrath of the ruler.

The work culture of present day NGOs is quite different. Being dependent on some rich people or commercial houses and organisations or government for their survival, they chalk out their plans and schemes according to the line of actions and guidance of their patrons. It is natural that these plans and schemes would conform to the structure and parameters of the established set-up. Neither rich and prosperous tycoons nor the state authority has desire to bring about fundamental change in the established system. The primary aim of the work undertaken by them is not to allow public anger against the established system beyond a certain limit. They play the role of safety valves to save the system from a possible explosion. No primary change is contemplated. These NGOs are just like the dispensaries which exist and work by the sheer strength of money donated by pharmaceutical companies and where the people who are victims to the side-effects of the medicines supplied by these companies get treated.

Social Work in Sanatana Tradition

Adi Guru Shankaracharya resorted to open support of the scriptures to destroy controversies and to establish monotheism. He compelled scholars having different views to fall in line with him. He neither took the help of the government nor did he use any coercive power to establish his views. He challenged prevalent beliefs on the strength of principles and right thinking and presenting pure and true beliefs as alternatives. He clarified and settled their doubts once for all.

I want to draw your attention towards the ancient tradition of Maha Kumbha which Indian society still has deep faith in. The purpose to establish this tradition was to hammer out an excellent path for appropriate changes in the established system. People who were fearless and ready to negate their own identity, who were well versed with the condition of the society in which they lived and who had a discerning intellect had open discussion in such gatherings which were organised in different parts of the country. They presented their observations before the society. They suggested changes or alternatives for betterment of the social system. Pages of history are sprinkled with such gatherings where learned men pondered over various problems and presented remedies.

Many scholars of the present day have come up with new ideas for social well-being but these are not acceptable. Disagreement shows that they are defective. The society is not to blame for this state of affairs. Thinkers themselves should sift the defects in their thinking and try to improve upon their idea. Well-considered and scholarly views would certainly put forward alternatives for a better social set-up.

Index

Abhyudaya (material prospect), 113
Abhyudaya - nihsreyasa
doctrine of, 158
Absolute Truth, 188
Abstinence / renunciation, 22
Acharmimansa, 67
Acquisition oriented society, 36
Action
motives of, 31
types of, 32
Aesthetics
Swami Vivekananda on, 187
Ahimsa (concept), 53
American society scenario, 200
Anthropocentric viewpoint
strong/naive, 134
Aparigraha, 90, 105
Aranya Devata (Tagore), 178
Aristotle
on thinking capabilities, 201
Artha, 48-49, 51, 84, 205
Arthashastra, 143
Aryan/Dasas fight with Dasyus, 278
Aryan-Sudra matrimony, 279
Aryans
advent of, 273-74
non-Aryan battles, 274
and Varna System -
origin, 274
social conditions, 278
Asana, 91, 129
Asceticism, 20
Ashrama System (four), 18-20
Astanga Yoga, 89, 130
stages of, 89-90
Asteya (concept), 53
Axiomatic Theory of Social Choice, Sen, 185

Basic human values principles, 58
Banaprasthya, 205
Beauty and truth
Vivekananda on, 188
Body form of soul, 173
Brahmacharya / Brahmachari, 42, 90
Brahmins
duty, 281
origin, 266, 278
status post Vedic period, 281
British period
-caste system in, 262

Canonical Analysis Structure (Poverty) Matrix, 219-20
findings, 221
implications, 222
linkages, 222
state-wise analysis, 223
Andhra NFHS Data, 224
Bihar NFHS Data, 225
MP NFHS Data, 226
Rajasthan NFHS Data, 227
UP NFHS Data, 228

West Bengal NFHS Data, 229
Goa, Kerala, Tamil Nadu, 230
Goa-Structure matrix, 231
Kerala-Structure matrix, 232
Tamil Nadu-Structure matrix, 233
Caste word usage, 26
Caste concept
emergence, 259
changes (period-wise), 259-263
Caste Associations Suggestions / directions, 283-84
Casteism
ill effects of, 276
impact, 276
Charvaka
philosophy, 65
Rig Vedic materialism, 71
Character Building, 216
Christianity
view of man and nature/ universe, 202
Civic Code (core value of), 142
Circle of moral considerability, 135
Common framework/values, 142
Complete Works of Swami Vivekananda, 87, 92
Consumption
and happiness, 18, 35
and environment inter-relationships, 116
Planning, 211
Control of Opinion, 194
Conflict Age, 196
Conflicts, tension and Human Development, 95
Control of Senses, 43
Cooperatives Amaratya Sen on, 182
Daily Life Governance
Puranas, 251
Dalit
position of, 26
word, 286
Dalit Literature
writing of,
meaning of, 285
Dalit writers
anguish, 286-87
and epic, 287
Daya/Dava
concepts of, 53
Debts of man (ancient scriptures), 291
Declaration on the Right to Development, 174
Degeneration of Politics (India), 207
Desecrates, Review of mental progress and survival, 201
Detachment and tolerance, 44
Desires (*vasana*), 17-18
Desires (Categories), 25
Desirable actions, 32
Development
and purusharthas, 57
of an individual, 106-107
term, 157
in social sciences, 157
concept of, 160
Developed Countries (Consumerism in), 124
Developed Human Beings, 139
Dharma
doing of, 23-24, 57
on *Kama/artha*, 52
meaning, 24-25
on material pleasures 50, 52
texts, 48
constituents of 53-54, 84
and truth, 250

Dharma Sastra period and Varna, 261
Dharmashastras and material comforts, 51
Dharana, 91, 129
(Geeta on), 143
Dhyana, 91, 129
Duty performance, 291

Earth Summit Agenda-1992, 76
Economic development
consequences of, 22
ill effects, 250
Ecological balance
Tagore on, 178
Ecological World View, 80
Ecological problems, 136
Economic liberalisation (India) - consequences, 208
Economic prosperity and wealth relation, 171
Eco-ethical human living, 177, 179
Gandhian, 208
Eco-system negative impact, 75
Education
aim of, 58
needs of man, 173
Employment importance of
-Gandhi, 209
Enjoyment (Upanishads on), 31
and renunciation, 31
Environment
and human development, 95, 115
protection (Puranas), 252
man's relationships with, 136
Issues-India, 125
Environmental Conference Summits, 125
Epics and Dalit writers, 287
Evolution of human beings, 133
Existence - Cognition
Bliss, 188
Exploitation of Resources
View on, 203

Factor Analysis
Model of Human Development Index, 238-241
Use of
-reasons, 241
Fertilizers Use
Gandhi on, 210
Food habits (Kurma Purana), 251
Food for Body / mind, 89

Gandhi
on resources usage, 35
on human development, 84, 100
Gandhian principles
truth/non-violence, 209
Gandhian economics, 210
Galileo's conflicting views, 201
Geographical Conditions and Socio-economic development, 249
Gita
on desires, 33-34
on renunciation, 32
on social work, 62
Global Civic Ethics, 142
Goals (human), 48
Goal (human development), 57
Good/Bad deeds, 88
Good governance
in Mahabharata, 146
elements of, 146
Grahasthya, 205
Growth and Development approach, 160
Gram Swaraj (Gandhi), 211
Grihasth conduct of, 250
Gyanmimansa, 66

Happiness
- and consumption, 35
- concept of, 17-18

Hindi Literature Partisan attitude, 288
Hindu doctrine of labour, 70
Hitopadesha, 143
Holistic development, 98
Human Conduct Directives (Ancient texts), 250
Humanity (concept), 134
Human Development, 21, 26
- approach, 94, 139
- Sanatan view, 99, 154
- Gandhian, 100-101
- Buddha on, 154
- concepts, determinants, 153
- Modern perspective, 173
- UNDP definition, 185
- UNDP Report - 1991, 161-62
- Report, 174
- of others, 27

Human Development in India
- history of, 83

Human Deprivation, 183
- causes (Sen on), 183

Human Development Index, 22, 100
- objection to approach, 23
- criteria, 25
- definition, 55
- dimensions of, 163
- UNDP's, 163, 235
- India and World countries-1993, 165
- Parameters - steps, 166

modern/ancient Indian approach, 167
Human efforts/labour, 84
Human Resource Development
- objectives ancient system, 158

Human/sub-human beings, 135
Human Quality Improvement formulae (Vivekananda), 114
Human Welfare (Smritis), 252

Ideal individual Taittiriya Upanishad, 168
- *Hitopadesha*, 143

Immortal existence (Sanatana), 41
Income/expenditure concept Indian/Sanatana, 99
Indexing of development, 155
Indian
- culture, 142
- tradition of Human Development, 84
- caste system, 269

Indian Viewpoint of Human Development, 96, 98, 105
- basic concepts, 98
- western view comparison, 105

Irrigation Gandhion, 210
Isavasyopanishada on enjoyment, 31, 34

Jati System (creation), 27

Kal (time)
- Atharvaveda on, 97

Kal-shakti, 98
Kama, 48-49, 84-85, 167, 205
Karma
- term, theory, 144
- public officials, 144-45
- *Dharma*, 269

Kathopanishad on Yoga, 128
Kautilya
- on happy life, 48
- on restraint, 84
- on welfare, 143

King (conduct of) Mahabharata, 146-48

King/Brahmin Status Comparison
    post-Vedic period, 280
Krishna, Lord duties, assigning to Varnas, 270
Kurma Purana on conduct of man, 251-52

Labours of Life, 65
Later Vedic Period and Varna System, 279
Law of nature
    Vivekananda, 92
    and man, 98
Lester Brown on
    sustainable society, 76
    materialism, 79
Literature/language appreciation Vivekananda, 191

Madhya Pradesh District-wise HDI, 236-37
    values, 243
Mahabharata
    on good governance, 146-47
    on *purushartha*, 146-47
    on Varna, 257
Mahbub-ul-Haq
    HDI approach, 163
Manu Smriti
    on Varnas, 25
Man's Evolution
    Eastern view, 110
    Western view, 109
    World view, 110
Marriage Rules in Varna System, 275
Marxian approach to society, 93
Market economy
    vices of, 212
Maslow's
    basic need types, 47, 109
    need fulfilment approach, 56
Materialism, 19
    in Rigveda, 68
    doctrine, 68
    Charvaka/Rig Veda, 72
    types, 69
Material pleasures and dharma, 51
Mechanistic to Spiritual Elevation, 113
Medieval Period Varna in, 261
Middle Income Class in India
    -emergence of, 206
Modernisation theory, 93
Modern Period Caste-Varna in, 262
Modern education
    aim, 215-16
Moksha, 20, 48, 57, 68, 84, 143, 173
Money Economy Expansion, 206
Monetary factor in Social Work, 295
Multinationals and Consumerism, 38

Nature
    worship, 69
    and self, 110, 177
National Family and Health Survey, 217
Nationalistic Spirit development of, 253
Need hierarchy (Maslow), 109-10
New Order (feature), 203
Newton's Laws of motion, 202
New Indices of Development, 200
NGOs
    as social workers, 27
    in social service, 292
    work culture in, 302
Niyama (in Astanga Yoga), 90, 129
    philosophy, 105

Objective of Life
ancient Indian approach, 167
stages of life, 205
Occupational Freedom, 26
Organisation for Social Service (nature), 293

Paintings/art appreciation-Vivekananda, 190
Panchayati Raj System, 211
Panchjanah/Panchkristya, 277
Parameters of development, 201
Patanjali on Yoga, 128
Politics of Casteism, 271
Post-Vedic Period
Caste/varnas in, 260
varna variation, 280
Poverty-fertility
infant mortality relationships, 217-18
Poverty Index Computing, 218
State level, 218
Individual level, 218
Present Varna / Caste Scenario, 282
Pratyahara, 91, 129
Pranayama, 91, 129
Process/Processors (Raja Yoga), 88
Public Officials
and spirituality, 145
dharma/karma of, 144-45
Punishment (concept of), 143-44
Purity (value of), 43
Purushartha, 20, 48, 84, 167
Purusharthas and development, 57
Purusha Sukta verses on castes/varna, 266
Purusha-tantra, 168
Quality of Life Belief, 35

Rajasika relinquishment, 33
Rajayoga (Patanjali's), 88
Ramcharitmanas and Dalit writers, 287
Religion and Science, 81
Rigveda,
and Materialism, 65
and Varnas, 266
Religion
characteristics, 42
defining, 195
Relinquishment, 32
Renunciation of actions, 32
Renunciation
and Human Development, 21
in Geeta, 32
Vivekananda on, 77
Tagore on, 197
Roger on growth process, 56
Rural Panchayat System
Tagore, 180

Salvation of Soul, 84
Samadhi, 129
Sambaya Niti, 179
Sanatana
approach to development, 156
values, 41-42, 45
dharma - usage, importance, 61-62
view on human development, 99
concept, 299, 302
-degeneration of, 299
Dharma, 292
Sarika, 286
Santosh, 90
Sanyasa, 31, 205
Satyam, 90
Sattvika relinquishment, 33
Sarvodaya / antyodaya (Gandhi), 209

Science
and faith, 202
and religion, 20, 81-82
Scientific discoveries, 202
Self-Actualization
-Maslow's, 56
Selfish interests, 44
Self Control, 32, 216
Self Realization goal, 139
SEMI-PACE Indicators (H.D), 186
Sen Amaratya, 177
on dangers of globalisation, 38
Social Change, 64
Social Choice & H.D, 185
Social Development
Sanatana concept, 301
Social environment (view on), 105
Social Work, 291
as profession, 28
in ancient India, 301
purpose, 62
inspiration for, 63
Social Workers, 27, 291
livelihood, 28, 295
functions/duties, 296-97
Soucha, 90
Soul existence and Rig Veda, 71
Spiritualism, 19
Spiritual education, 23
development-measures, 175
Spirituality, 142
in governance, 148
Stages of Life, 205
State of Mind elevation (Indian Scriptures), 113
Stockholm World Conference on Human Environment, 129
Sudra
origin, 274
repentence of, 274
Vishnu Purana on, 275
Status, 279
Sustainable Human Development, 186
Sustainable growth (development of)
ancient view, 157
future outlook, 169
Sustainable Development and Consumerism, 116-18
Sustainability levels, 118

Tagore, Rabindranath
on goodness of man, 39
on eco-ethical human living, 177
on sustainable development, 179
Tagore, and Amaratya Sen (comparison), 181
Tapasya, 90
Tatvamimansa, 66
Television (impact), 195
Technological innovation, 135
Tendencies of human beings, 94
Tiruvalluvar
on good administration, 143
on punishment, 144
The Political Economy of Hunger, 182
Tilak, Lokmanya on Social Work, 62
Time (Kal) and Human Development, 97
Trivarya
nature of, 49-50
Truth, 42
and non-violence, 209
Truth - Good - Beautiful
concept (Vivekananda), 188
Trusteeship concept (Gandhi), 100

Unconscious desires, 18-19
removal objective, 24
UNDP Human Development Index, 140, 163-64, 235-36

United Nations Human Development Report (1997), HDI, 218
Universe Principle of (Vivekananda), 87
Universal Brotherhood/Welfare, 43, 142
Unlimited Material Progress, 75
Utilitarianism, 116, 185

Values
 importance of, 106, 154, 293
Value - Personality Development, 154
Vanaprastha and Social Work, 28
Varimax technique of Factor Analysis Model of HDI Variable-wise details, 244
Varna/Jati
 as social system for HD, 25
 determination, 25, 273
 evolution of, 26, 62
Varna, 269
 word, origin, 255-56, 265, 269
Varna System
 and power, 258
 duties/rights, 275
 in Vedas, 266
 Manusmriti, 270
 re-establishing, 272
 merits/demerits, 257
Varnashrama Concept, 271, 277
Vatsyayana on conflicting activities, 49
Vedic Period and Caste System, 260
Vedas, 65
 knowledge of, 69
 meaning, importance, 41
Vedic Materialism, 73
Vedantic world view, 80
Vivekananda, Swami
 on desire and consumption, 36, 78-79, 92
 on renunciation, 77
 on principles of universe, 87
 outlook of, 189
 on aesthetics, 187
 on Human Quality Improvement, 114
Virat Purusha/Swarupa, 62

WECD (World Commission on Environment and Development) UN, 76
Weberian School's
 approach to society, 94
Western concept of Human Development, 95, 105, 199
Western Consumers Psychology, 36
Wisdom/Knowledge increase in, 106
Working
 importance of, 23
Yajur Veda on Universal Brotherhood, 44
Yajnavalkya on *dharma*, 53
Yajna performance, 68-69
Yama/Niyama, 130
Yama in (Astanga Yoga), 89, 129
 philosophy, 105
Yantra Sarvasva, 70
Yoga
 word usage, 127-28
 tradition, historical evidence, 127
Yoga Sadhana
 steps, 129
 aims, 130
Yoga - Ksema doctrine, 159
Yuktananda Swami
 - human values, 58